Governing China in the 21st Century

Series Editor

Yijia Jing, Institute for Global Public Policy, Fudan University, Shanghai, China

Since 1978, China's political and social systems have transformed significantly to accommodate the world's largest population and second largest economy. These changes have grown more complex and challenging as China deals with modernization, globalization, and informatization. The unique path of sociopolitical development of China hardly fits within any existing frame of reference. The number of scientific explorations of China's political and social development, as well as contributions to international literature from Chinese scholars living and researching in Mainland China, has been growing fast. This series publishes research by Chinese and international scholars on China's politics, diplomacy, public affairs, and social and economic issues for the international academic community.

Grace Yuehan Wang

Dragon Innovation: Shenzhen

Lessons for the West and Global South Countries from China's Leading Innovation Cluster

palgrave
macmillan

Grace Yuehan Wang
Media and Communications
London School of Economics
London, UK

ISSN 2730-6968 ISSN 2730-6976 (electronic)
Governing China in the 21st Century
ISBN 978-981-95-9636-2 ISBN 978-981-95-9637-9 (eBook)
https://doi.org/10.1007/978-981-95-9637-9

This Palgrave Macmillan imprint is published by the registered company Springer Nature Singapore Pte Ltd.
The registered company address is: 152 Beach Road, #21-01/04 Gateway East, Singapore 189721, Singapore

For my parents,
and those who generously shared their time and supported me.

For anyone,
who has faith in the beauty of humanity,
who believes in the value of hard work.

Competing Interests The author has no competing interests to declare that are relevant to the content of this manuscript.

Contents

List of Figures

List of Tables

CHAPTER 1

China Innovation Myth

Shenzhen Technology Fame

I was a little girl in kindergarten when I first heard of the Chinese city, Shenzhen. My grandfather who traveled back from his business trip to Shenzhen and Hong Kong, gifted me an exquisite music box. I asked him if he went abroad, as I never saw anything that exotic. "Not a foreign country but special places in China." His words planted the curious seeds in me, though I had absolutely no idea what "special" meant at that time.

When I was conducting interviews during my fieldwork in Shenzhen in 2017, my interviewees inquired about this research frequently. I told them that it is about Shenzhen's technological innovations and the comparisons with Silicon Valley in the United States. The most common response was: You must know a lot about Silicon Valley and the secret recipes for making Silicon Valley a successful technology center. People's enthusiasm and determination in making a Silicon Valley in China is beyond imagination. "Innovation is the driving force," is a catchphrase among people in Shenzhen. Although Shenzhen – Hong Kong– Guangzhou was ranked as the No. 2 global innovation cluster in 2017, ahead of Silicon Valley, which ranked the fifth,[1] most people in Shenzhen, or in China at large, still believe undoubtedly that China is lagging behind the United States in great deal. "We need to play catch up and work diligently," is a popular sentiment.

G. Y. Wang, *Dragon Innovation: Shenzhen*, Governing China in the 21st Century, https://doi.org/10.1007/978-981-95-9637-9_1

In 2025, when I am completing my book in China, a UK native who worked as a consultant before the pursuit of her doctoral study in global health and economics, paid herself a China trip to Shenzhen and Shanghai in the summer of 2025, an arrangement organized by the Chinese Language and Culture for Business London.[2] "Some people on the China trip have corporate sponsorship, but I paid everything out of my own pocket," she told me. I was amazed at her enthusiasm and determination for this voluntary tour to Shenzhen and Shanghai. "Pretty much every piece of news about China tech is negative from the news media outlet I have consumed. I thought maybe China is far ahead of the world in tech and business innovation." She started to learn Chinese four years ago and is certain that she is going to use Mandarin Chinese in her future. "If China tech were weak, Chinese technology companies should not have been under attack and attracted so much attention all the time, right?" Her curiosity and future plan for her career led her to China for the first time in 2025.

This young UK professional's desire to understand and to build a connection with China is amplified by the U.S.–China trade war and technological competition. In 2018, U.S. trade tension with China marched into a technological war over future national supremacy and global power. Chinese technology companies have become one of the major targets. Chinese netizens jokingly described the technological war between China and the United States, as a war between the United States and Yue Hai street in Nanshan district in Shenzhen (*深圳市南山区粤海街道*), where leading Chinese technology companies such as Tencent, Huawei, DJI, BYD, Han's Laser, Mindray started their corporate ventures. For many Chinese firms that were faced with the sudden ban on high-end technological components, they started to stockpile U.S. computer and electronics products, in case of the "silicon curtain" from the United States.[3] Since 2016, U.S. exports to China in semiconductors and other electronics components have risen unstoppably within the category of computer and electronics products exports. One of the major contributors to the surge of semiconductors imports in the last few years is Huawei Corporation. Its rapid development and adoption of 5G networking equipment, cloud computing, artificial intelligence, as well as its high-end smart phones, require Huawei to store efficient, high-performance chips. Huawei, the largest telecommunications manufacturer in the world, was thrust into the spotlight of the U.S.–China trade tension despite its limited market share in the United States. All of the sudden, reporters from all over the world flocked to interview mysterious Huawei CEO, Ren Zhengfei, in order to reveal the secrets: How could an unknown Chinese company rise to the number one telecommunications manufacturer in the world, an industry the United States used to lead globally? Ren Zhengfei, Huawei's CEO, welcomed those domestic and international journalists for interviews, to Huawei's headquarter. "I am thanking them for promoting us," Ren said in an interview with CBS journalist Bianna Golodrgya that the claims spread by influential U.S. politicians that Huawei's 5G is threatening U.S. security has helped promote Huawei brand internationally. Otherwise, not so many people on the world stage would pay a visit to Huawei and Shenzhen.[4] U.S. journalist Bianna Golodrgya commented that Mr. Ren was being sarcastic for his appreciation. China's AI vibrancy ranking drops from the world No. 1 in 2017 to No. 2 since the start of 2018, a global AI vibrancy ranking conducted by human-centered artificial intelligence center at Stanford University.[5] "Silicon Curtain," by all means, is having an impact on China's semiconductor and high-tech industries. Shenzhen, is where the story begins.

Shenzhen is home to headquarter of Huawei, the world's largest telecommunications manufacturer; ZTE corporation, a Chinese multinational telecommunications equipment and systems company; Tencent, the most valuable internet giant in China; DJI (Da Jiang), the cutting-edge drone manufacturer; Ping An Insurance and Technology Group, the first private insurance enterprise in Chinese Mainland; BYD, the global electric vehicle leader. Shenzhen's booming high-tech sector has earned the city a significant place in the technological world across the globe. "Go to Shenzhen," "You are a Shenzhener once you are here" are city slogans to attract global technical talent, entrepreneurs, and venture capitalists who embrace their dreams to become the next global tech superstar. "Shenzhen is the Hollywood of hardware products,"[6] says Eric Pan Hao, founder of Seeed Studio, an IoT hardware enabler which sells electronics hardware components to the international markets through online website. He thinks Shenzhen has everything in hardware components. HAX, the hardware manufacturing startup incubator & accelerator, which is part of the top venture capital firm SOSV in Silicon Valley, founded HAX Shenzhen in 2012. It was the only hardware manufacturing incubator under SOSV's international hardware startup ecosystem in 2012, outside of Silicon Valley. What makes Shenzhen attractive to tech entrepreneurs all over the world? How could a Chinese fishing village with no prestigious research universities ace the innovation race in China and in the world? What enables a notorious copycat assembly to upgrade its innovation ecosystem? What are Shenzhen's innovation advantages and weaknesses compared to other established technology centers that are facing serious economic slowdown? The questions in the list go on and on. With all the inquiries and puzzles in my head, I took on the journey to research Shenzhen's transformation from a special economic zone to a global innovation cluster.

Why Does Shenzhen Matter?

It is impossible to fully understand China's technological performance and capacity without comprehending Shenzhen, the city that made it possible for Chinese entrepreneurs like Huawei's Ren Zhengfei and Tencent's Pony Ma Huateng, to establish private enterprises, including technology ones in China back in 1987. Since the official launch of China's Open and Reform policy, China's economy has gone through a tremendous rise, overtaking Japan in 2010 to have become the second largest economy in the world.[7] Along with the rise of China's economy is its technological achievements and its innovation capacity. According to the Innovation Index released in 2018,[8] based on international patent filings and scientific publishing activity, a ranking produced by INSEAD, the World Intellectual Property Organization and the Cornell SC Johnson College of Business, China ranked at No. 17 in the top 20 most innovative countries in the world while the United States ranked No. 6. This marked the first time that China, as an economy, entered top 20 in the Global Innovation Index. As China's technological capacity continuing to rise, many people, both inside and outside of the country, start to label China as the "Silicon Dragon" and strenuously try to find out its Silicon Valley. Zhong Guan Cun in Beijing, famous for its renowned research universities in China, is often considered as a top candidate. The city Hangzhou, with the global recognized native-born e-commerce giant Alibaba, and the birthplace of DeepSeek, has attracted increasing popularity and global attention in recent years. Among all the guesses and speculations, Shenzhen, the special economic zone located in Pearl River Delta, Guangdong province in the South of China, emerged as the Silicon Valley of Hardware. The growing number of patent applications from Shenzhen is an indicator as scholars like Schmookler (1962) use patent applications as a measurement of innovation. In that vein, the World Intellectual Property Organization released that in 2019, China topped the United States for the first time in the last forty years, becoming the No. 1 source of international patent applications, with the number of patent applications of 58,990 and a growth rate 10.5% (the U.S. 57,840 with a growth rate 2.8%) (see Table 1.1). Huawei, has remained the top one corporate intellectual patent filer since 2017, with 4411 published PCT applications in 2019, despite the international geopolitical impact on Huawei technologies worldwide. Guangdong Oppo Mobile Telecommunications of China, in short Oppo, headquartered in Shenzhen, ranked the fourth global corporate filer, with a number of 1927 applications. Ping An Insurance and Technology Group from Shenzhen secured the No. 8 spot with a number of patents applications 1691 (see Table 1.2).[9] In total, three Chinese companies headquartered in Shenzhen and one Chinese company from Beijing, BOE Technology Group, are in the Top Ten Corporate Filers for International Applications filed under the Patent Cooperation Treaty (PCT) in 2019. In the 2024 Global Innovation Index, Shenzhen–Hong Kong–Guangzhou cluster ranks No. 2 globally, followed by Beijing (China), Seoul (Republic of Korea) and Shanghai–Suzhou (China), ranking 3rd, 4th and 5th, respectively. San Jose–San Francisco cluster (United States of America) decreases from No. 5 in 2019 to No. 6 in 2024. In terms of top 10 PCT applicants in 2024, Huawei remains to top the global list with a number of 6600 PCTs, while Contemporary Amperex (CATL), BOE technology and Xiaomi Mobile Software are the other three Chinese firms entering the top 10 global PCT applicants list.[10]

In both 2024 and 2025, the top 100 Science & Technology clusters remain to be predominantly located in three regions as previous years did: North America, Europe, and Asia, China topping the rank while the United States following closely (see Table 1.3). In 2025, the methodology change of the innovation index has made Shenzhen–Hong Kong–Guangzhou (the Greater Bay Area) top the global innovation cluster ranking for the first time, surpassing Tokyo-Yokohama, as Shenzhen cluster performs stronger VC deals. San Jose–San Franciso cluster rises up to No. 3 in 2025 from No. 6 in 2024 also because of the measurement of VC deals (Table 1.4). As shown in Table 1.4, Shenzhen–Hong Kong–Guangzhou and Beijing cluster in China indicate relatively healthy and balanced STI indicators overall, compared to San Jose–San Fransico in the United States. China's leading global innovation cluster centering around Shenzhen is not only a showcase of China's innovation capability. More importantly, it indicates China's unique innovation path.

Table 1.1 Top ten countries for international applications filed under the Patent Cooperation Treaty (PCT) in 2019 (*Note* World Intellectual Property Organization, Infographics 2019. https://www.wipo.int/export/sites/www/ipstats/en/docs/infographic_pct_2019.pdf)

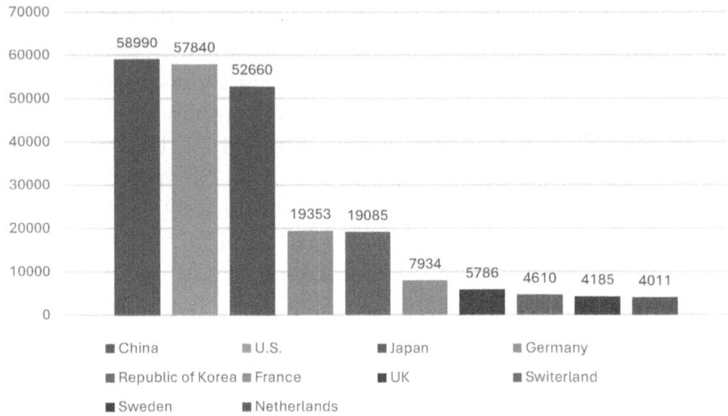

Table 1.2 Top corporate filers for international applications filed under the Patent Cooperation Treaty (PCT) in 2019 (*Note* World Intellectual Property Organization, Infographics, 2019. https://www.wipo.int/export/sites/www/ipstats/en/docs/infographic_pct_2019.pdf)

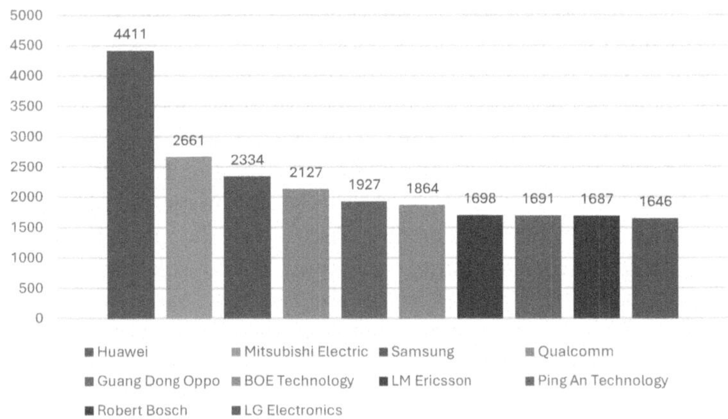

Table 1.3 Global economies with three or more top 100 S&T clusters, 2025

Economy name	*Top 100 clusters*
China	24 (two fewer than 2024)
United States	22 (two more than 2024)
Germany	7
India	4
United Kingdom	4
Republic of Korea	3
Japan	3
Canada	3
Australia	2
France	2

Note GII Top 100 S&T Clusters
Retrieved from: https://www.wipo.int/documents/d/global-innovation-index/docs-en-2025-gii-2025-clusters-top100-ranking.pdf

Table 1.4 Top five global innovation clusters 2025

Rank	*Cluster name*	*Global share of publications (%)*	*Global share of PCT filings (%)*	*Global share of VC deals (%)*
1	ShenzhenHong KongGuangzhou	2.4	9.0	2.9
2	Tokyo–Yokohama	1.4	10.3	2.2
3	San Jose–San Francisco	0.7	3.9	6.9
4	Beijing	4.0	3.8	2.9
5	Seoul	1.7	5.4	3.1

Note GII Top 100 S&T Clusters
Retrieved from: https://www.wipo.int/documents/d/global-innovation-index/docs-en-2025-gii-2025-clusters-top100-ranking.pdf

China Innovation Myth

China's innovation becomes outstanding in various areas in recent years with regard to global R&D companies, VC deals, publication quantity and quality. In areas such as R&D expenditures, China is now No. 1 in the world, with volumes that overshadow most high-income economies. In 2023, China's growth in R&D at the rate of 8.7% continues to surpass that of the OECD, the United States (1.7%) and the European Union (1.6%).[11] It is critical to note that the analysis of making China's technological hub, Shenzhen and the growing Greater Bay Area, is not to determine or to compare which national innovation experience is superior. Instead, it is an empirical analysis to reveal the diverse, multidimensional, and multicultural aspects of human reality. Francis Gurry, the fourth director general of the World Intellectual Property Organization from 2008 to 2020, credited China's innovation success down to a "very deliberate strategy on the part of Chinese leadership to advance innovation and to make the country a country whose economy operates at a higher level of value."[12] Gurry further noted that Chinese model does use state subsidies to a greater extent than its western counterparts do. China's innovation represents a completely different experience from the West that is working.[13] In fact, Gurry's comments spoke to the popular understandings of China's innovation model due to its "non-democratic" state in the western sense. But, it is insufficient to credit China's innovation success to state subsidies.

The story of Shenzhen, from an agricultural fishing village to China's first special economic zone, the ground-breaking pioneer in China's economic reform, and then being upgraded and transformed into its new destiny: A leading global technology hub, has unpuzzled the trajectory of a successful innovation ecosystem and cluster in the global south. More importantly, Shenzhen innovation experience shows that the long-term celebrated Silicon Valley model is not the only innovation prototype available. Imitating Silicon Valley or western innovation experiences may not work for countries in the global south, where poverty alleviation is unresolved. In fact, Shenzhen enjoys unique cultures, institutions, and governance to grow itself into a global innovation center. Shenzhen's innovation success challenges the widely known "China innovation success," which credits everything to the Chinese state and stated-led approach. This book, built on my experience growing up in China and nearly ten years research and observation, unpacks the myth of China's development and innovation path, through the lens of Shenzhen. China's innovation experiences present lessons for the global south and the world to follow as they seek to advance their economies and aim to realize national technological innovations in the new era of artificial intelligence. To learn from China's innovation lessons, as a start, it is essential to eradicate existing misunderstandings, both positive and negative ones, which include Chinese culture, its governance structures, public–private partnership, its institutions as well as regional economic development with

Chinese features. The following section presents ubiquitous China innovation myth and key content of every chapter that is embedded in each myth.

Myth One

Chinese society has long been viewed as an ethnic homogeneity, with Han as the ethnic majority. China's education system is notorious for its rote learning, which emphasizes on memory and the conformity of the authority. Abundant academic research and media articles try to untangle the reasons why China innovates or why China can't innovate, but most of them have been built on the conventional and stereotypical understanding of Chinese culture, a government dominated top-down system that lacks risk-taking spirits and creativity.

"Chapter 4, City Culture—Experimental and Entrepreneurial DNA," stems from personal stories when I first heard of the phrase, Xia Hai (下海), which refers to people's exploration of wealth creation business opportunities on their own in China. Shenzhen, as a typical migrant city, imitates Silicon Valley's entrepreneurial culture. But most importantly, it is the "Shenzhen Dream," a term I coined in Chapter 4, that ignites the hope for possibility and prosperity among Shenzhen's early migrants, people from across China. Vivid stories with Chinese politicians and entrepreneurs who relocated to Shenzhen demonstrate the significance of institutional innovations in China's Open and Reform. Conversations with early migrants reflect how the collective Shenzhen Dream interacts with individual ambitions, and how these symbiotic dynamics turn out to work successfully in Shenzhen. Documents of self-made female businesswomen who grow from factory girls to Hurun or Forbes ranked business elites, pose the question to the understanding of Chinese society and global innovation at large: What comes first? A special innovative soil that nurtures experiments or a group of people who long for adventures to cultivate unique fertile ground?

Shenzhen's experimental and entrepreneurial DNA penetrates in various aspects of this city. A key innovative cultural characteristic, magnified and widely known to the world through Shenzhen's tech companies, is the confidence in its self-capacity to make, to innovate and to create. "Chapter 6, The Entrepreneurial Ecosystem in Shenzhen," describes how Shenzhen has earned itself the title of Silicon Valley of Hardware, how maker culture flourishes in Shenzhen, and how Shenzhen connects the global maker community with its local industries. "Chapter 7, Shenzhen Grassroots Participatory Innovation: Let the People Make" documents Shenzhen's electronics manufacturing upgrading as well as the significance of process innovation. Knockoff and copycat products are not unique to Shenzhen and to China. Industries in the global south countries are often geared toward low-cost and labor-intensive sectors because of international division of labor and global geopolitics. What has enabled Shenzhen to realize its industrial upgrade to become a global tech powerhouse that not only generates advanced technology products but also contributes to the global supply chains? "I do not like the brand Apple, because I do not like monopoly," the comment made by a grassroots entrepreneur at Hua Qiang Bei electronics market reflects the rebellious spirit among tech entrepreneurs in Shenzhen (see Chapter 7). This spirit does not differ from the hacker-oriented innovation culture in the West. The belief, "Yes I can," seems to be fundamental in cultivating any successful innovation cluster. The encouragement of talented and ambitious individuals supports competition and innovation in societies. Forje (2009) argues that colonial histories in many developing countries have created a legacy in which adventurous, risk-taking and entrepreneurial instincts are suppressed. If so, how can developing countries rebuild their social cultures and boost their confidence, and what can they learn from Shenzhen?

Myth Two

Shenzhen is the first Chinese city which eradicated food coupons, a symbol of China's planned economy (see Chapter 2, The Genesis of Shenzhen). The neglect of Shenzhen, until the recent U.S.–China tech rivalry, reveals incomplete understanding of China's development and innovation path since its Open and Reform in 1979. Studies of western technology centers and innovation often downplay the role of state in building and developing innovation clusters. "Chapter 3, China, the New Development," classifies Shenzhen development into four stages and documents Shenzhen urban planning and development with deliberate efforts. To fully understand Shenzhen's economic miracle and its innovation path, no one can deny the role of the state: "Ji Zhong Li Liang Ban Da Shi" (集中力量办大事) which means the utilization of concentrated power and resources to focus on what matters the most.

Shenzhen is a state planned development product. This argument was grounded in history. As the first special economic zone in China, Shenzhen's economic development is impossible without the supportive groups of leaders from central government in Beijing. According to Vogel (2011), local government officials used to invite leaders from Beijing to spend winter in warm sub-tropical Shenzhen. In this way, Shenzhen city government officials gradually built up a support group in Beijing's core power center who showed unhesitant support for the consistency of Open and Reform policy. State involvement and government support are not unique to China, though. It even exists in Silicon Valley, where has long been viewed as a not anticipated, not planned success. Cowhey and Aronson (2017) highlighted appropriate government policies as one of the five national innovation system elements. Appropriate policies may include research and development support to enterprises, or policies associated with foreign trade and investment. According to O' Mara (2005), the federal and state government funding in the United States during the Cold War promoted technological advancement in the form of university research and labs. Saxenian (2014) stated that California state government invested in the infrastructure and tried to develop public services, such as transportation, housing, healthcare, and higher education. As a special economic zone, Shenzhen enjoys a lot of autonomies and the benefits of special policies which contribute to its economic and technological development. In 1979, when Shenzhen was set as the country's first special economic zone, China belonged to a low-income national economy. China used Shenzhen to realize national pilot business reforms. Huawei, Ping An, and Tencent, along with other private enterprises are results of that experimental economic reform. This shows that Beijing central government and political system in China is not rigid. It opens the door for "special treatment" when needed, and it demonstrates the development potential of a city with flexible and special policy in China. The importance of national pilot programs, in areas of economic and social welfare reforms, is frequently noted by policymakers and development practitioners in the global south countries such as Indonesia (see Chapter 5, Local Governance: Bureaucratic Entrepreneurs). National pilot programs, for instance, in the form of special economic zones, are indispensable in countries with massive land areas and complex governance systems. Shenzhen, as a national pilot program, has pioneered in sustainable development in China long before Chinese EV has dominated the global market. Supported by the Chinese central government and the local state, Shenzhen is the first Chinese city to promote ELV adoption. It released the *Shenzhen New Energy Vehicle Promotion and Application Work Plan (2021–2025)* in 2021.[14]

Myth Three

The U.S.–China technological competition has seriously challenged U.S. global technological leadership since World War II. To maintain its technological supremacy, particularly in strategic areas such as artificial intelligence and quantum computing, many people rush to examine China's innovation ecosystems and conclude that the centralized model offers China strategic advantages (Wessner & Sharma, 2025). In contrast, this book reveals that despite China's centralized political system, Shenzhen's economic and technological success demonstrates the significant role of adventurous and risk-taking local government officials, namely "bureaucratic entrepreneurs" (Hsing, 1998) in this context, plays in generating and implementing special policies with the autonomies obtained from Beijing.

Shenzhen was one of the few special economic zones in the 1980s, including Zhuhai, Xiamen, and Shantou. However, none of the other three cities has received phenomenal success like Shenzhen did. Contrary to widely spread conventional wisdom that Shenzhen's rise and success is credited to its physical proximity to Hong Kong, I argue that Shenzhen's geographical vicinity to Hong Kong was only the necessary but not sufficient condition to its developmental achievements. Moreover, if Shenzhen's technological success solely stems from its geographical proximity to Hong Kong, like the conventional wisdom claims, then why Hong Kong failed to become a leading tech center? The importance of entrepreneurial politicians in creating economic growth and environments for innovation to grow is noted in Thompson's work: "That is, political innovators may be – must be – spawned to complement the economic ones generated in the private sector" (Thompson, 1965, p. 47). Shenzhen local government officials act as "bureaucratic entrepreneurs" (Hsing, 1998) to actively seek for foreign direct investment and react to international industrial needs with great flexibilities. Shenzhen's integration into the global economy at the infant stage of its development enables it to take part in global manufacturing, financial, and knowledge networks. According to Hsing:

> Almost 80% of the Chinese who have migrated overseas came from Guangdong, and the next largest number from Fujian. Many began earning their living abroad through one of the "three knives" (cooking, hair cutting, or construction) but rose to become one of the "three highs" (intellectuals, owners, or white-collar employees). Many of the overseas Chinese maintained family ties with the region. When China opened the door to foreign investors in the late 1970s, a series of special policies was made to give Guangdong and Fujian the flexibility to take advantage of its spatial and sociocultural proximity to the overseas Chinese in East Asia. (Hsing, 1998, p. 22)

This indicates the close ties people in Shenzhen, or in Guangdong have with overseas Chinese and their capitals which benefit the city or region's step into foreign capital. Shenzhen local government officials' aggressive and outgoing working attitudes largely guarantee Shenzhen's timely and fast responses to international environment and economic trend. "Chapter 5, Local Governance: Bureaucratic Entrepreneurs" depicts how Shenzhen bureaucratic entrepreneurs act as city matchmakers and platform politicians. That is why Shenzhen stood out from other special economic zones and cities in China. The underestimate of "bureaucratic entrepreneurs" type of Chinese government officials will neglect the role of local government as well as a type of public–private partnership that turns out to work in Shenzhen, with the possibility to work in other cities or countries (Fig. 1.1).

Myth Four

It is widely known that China's innovation clusters are catalyzed by strategic intent to back up a predetermined strategy designed and cultivated by the government. The Chinese government plays a critical role in shaping the startup ecosystems through policies and regulations. This book, however, tracing back to Shenzhen's electronics and innovation driven urban development strategies in the 80s, demonstrates the exploratory nature of Shenzhen industrial and innovation path under the umbrella of economic planning. The synergic connecting power of a successful innovation ecosystem and cluster can be realized and magnified through manpower and deliberate initiatives.

Shenzhen has become a critical node in the electronics industries because of its local government support and civic participation, thanks to pioneering regulations such as *Notice of Shenzhen Municipal People's*

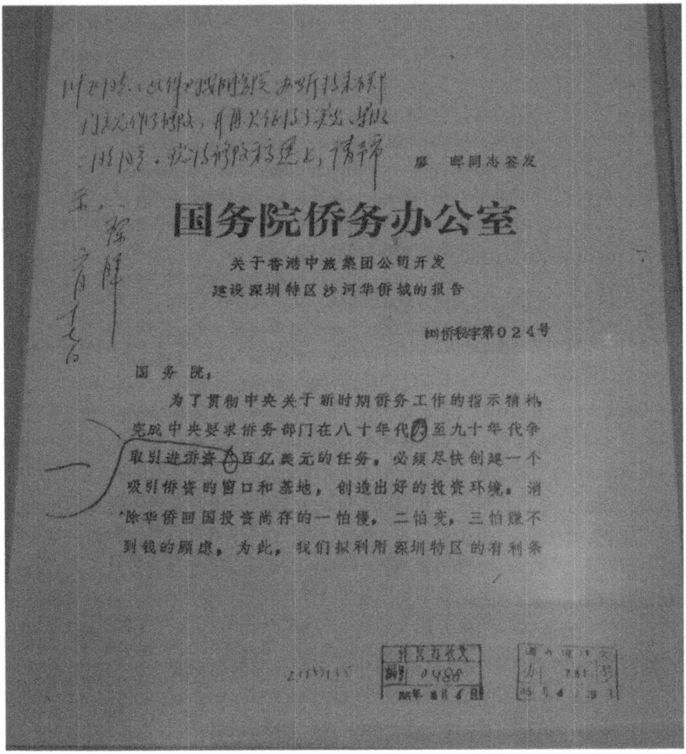

廖 晖同志签发

国务院侨务办公室

关于香港中旅集团公司开发
建设深圳特区沙河华侨城的报告

侨秘字第024号

国务院：

为了贯彻中央关于新时期侨务工作的指示精神，完成中央要求侨务部门在八十年代乃至九十年代争取引进侨资五百亿美元的任务，必须尽快创建一个吸引侨资的窗口和基地，创造出好的投资环境，消除华侨回国投资尚存的一怕慢，二怕变，三怕赚不到钱的顾虑，为此，我们拟利用深圳特区的有利条

Fig. 1.1 1988 Overseas Chinese Affairs Office of the State Council—Attract overseas Chinese investment in Shenzhen (*Note* Photo taken by the author at Shenzhen Museum)

Government on Issuing Several Regulations on Further Supporting the Development of High-Tech Industries[15] (see Chapter 5, Local Governance: Bureaucratic Entrepreneurs). Chapter 5 reveals the entrepreneurial roles local politicians played in attracting investment, building Shenzhen—based trade and technology platforms, as well as designing and implementing local industrial strategies by connecting Shenzhen's geographical and strategic advantages with the international market. As noted in "Chapter 7, Shenzhen Grassroots Participatory Innovation: Let the People Make," when Taiwan manufacturing industries started to shift their production networks to the Chinese Mainland, some cities in

Guangdong, such as Dongguan, accommodated garment factories from Taiwan, but Shenzhen deliberately attracted electronics focused factories to align with its city development strategies. When internet industries and talents concentrated in Beijing in the early 90s, Shenzhen local government officials tried their best to have successfully persuaded the central government to host China's first Hi-Tech Fair in Shenzhen, which enabled local tech entrepreneurs such as Tencent's Pony Ma, to secure fundings from venture capital firms. In-person interviews with Tencent's CEO and its management team documented how Tencent obtained life-saving money through venture capitalism, a concept the founding team was even unaware of back then (see Chapter 5). Though Chinese technology entrepreneurs are no stranger to venture capitalism nowadays, back then, Chinese entrepreneurs such as the founding members at Tencent had to learn what venture capitalism was. In 2000, the city government issued regulations on venture capital investment in Shenzhen's high-tech industries during the second Hi-Tech Fair, China's first official government regulation on capital investment.[16] This book presents examples in different chapters to explain the exploratory nature of Shenzhen development and reveals how "crossing the river while feeling the stone" helps build an effective public–private partnership that supports Shenzhen's regional innovation.

Myth Five

This book reveals that firm-level R&D investment is one of the key contributors that enables Shenzhen to leapfrog from a fishing village to have become the headquarter of leading Chinese technology companies. More importantly, findings in this book refute the popular belief that all China's innovation ecosystems rely heavily on government funding. In fact, China's innovation clusters, for instance, the famous ones that centered around Shenzhen, Shanghai and Beijing, demonstrate distinct regional innovation characteristics, especially in terms of R&D expenses. Tables 1.5, 1.6, 1.7 indicate government R&D and corporate R&D spending from 2016 to 2020 in Beijing, Shanghai, and Shenzhen. Those municipal statistics clearly challenge the existing views on China's innovation clusters. It is obvious that corporate R&D investment in both Shanghai and Shenzhen exceeds government R&D funding in great deal, while government R&D in Beijing consistently surpasses corporate fundings in research and development. This book, by examining Shenzhen innovation ecosystem and comparing it with other famous technological cities in China, shows that innovation success in China is not "one recipe for all." Shenzhen's trajectory, from China's first special economic zone that has been pioneering in economic and business reforms to an innovation hub where has incubated world-renowned technology firms, sheds light on the understanding of fostering innovation clusters in both developing and developed countries in the age of artificial intelligence. "Chapter 7, Shenzhen Grassroots Participatory Innovation: Let the Make People" and "Chapter 8, Shenzhen R&D Ecosystem" investigate how corporate R&D has supported Shenzhen's innovation ecosystem by building a complete supply chain as well as by investing in applied research to fuel enterprise development. Moreover, does corporate R&D investment refer merely to financial expenditure? My conversations with Huawei employees at their European style campus demonstrate the significance of employees' loyalty during difficult turmoil, which cannot be simply explained by critics such as "corporate propaganda" or "nationalism" (see Chapter 9, Human Capital and National Competitiveness).

Table 1.5 Beijing Government R&D vs Corporate R&D from 2016–2020. Unit: 10,000 (*Note* Beijing Statistics Bureau. https://nj.tjj.beijing.gov.cn/nj/main/2020-tjnj/zk/e/indexch.htm)

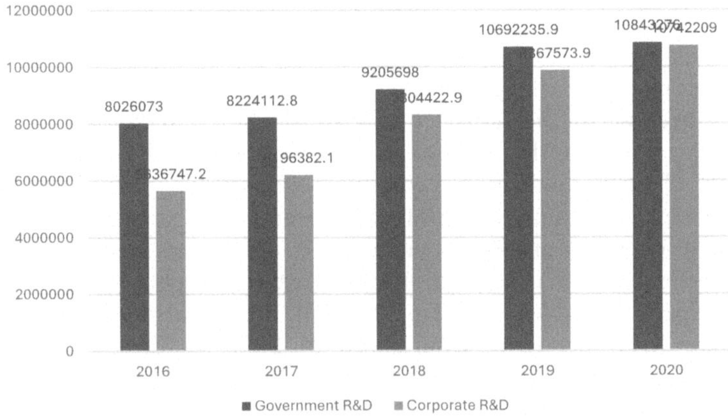

Table 1.6 Shanghai Government R&D vs Corporate R&D from 2016–2020. Unit: One Hundred Million (*Note* Shanghai Statistics Bureau. https://tjj.sh.gov.cn/tjnj/20210303/2abf188275224739bd5bce9bf128aca8.html)

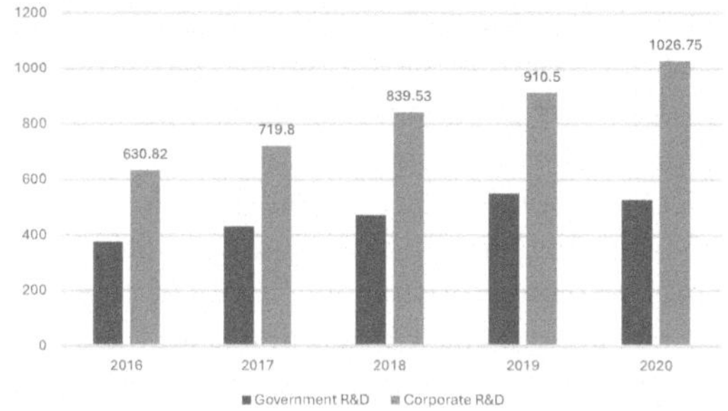

Table 1.7 Shenzhen Government R&D vs Corporate R&D from 2016–2020. Unit: 10,000 (*Note* Shenzhen Statistics Bureau. https://tjj.sz.gov.cn/zwgk/zfxxgkml/tjsj/tjnj/content/post_8386382.html)

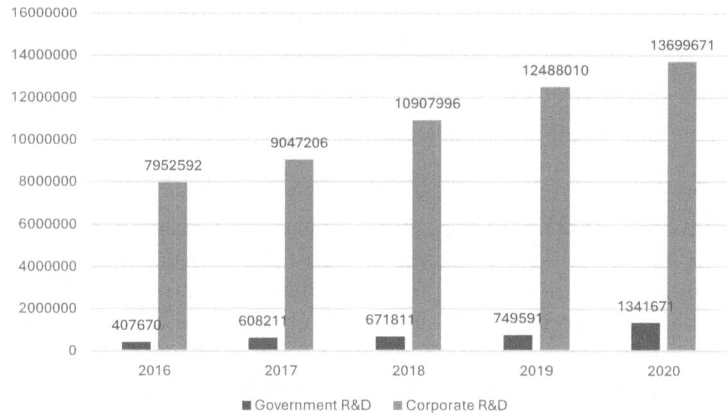

Myth Six

Corporate investment in R&D in Shenzhen, as shown in Table 1.7, is the critical contributor that enables leading Chinese technology companies to incubate and grow in Shenzhen. This phenomenon challenges traditional understandings of the role of universities in innovation success, since Shenzhen did not enjoy prestigious research universities, particularly in its early times (see Chapter 8, Shenzhen R&D Ecosystem and Chapter 9, Human Capital and National Competitiveness). Shenzhen's economic and innovation experience presents countries in the global south that are struggling with their education systems and research capacities with alternative ways of approaching development and innovation. How can developing countries or regions develop local innovation clusters when leading research universities are absent?

There are two critical opinions regarding the role of university research and the development of high-technology industry. Saxenian (1985, 1994) notes the reciprocally strong relationship between top notched research universities in the bay area in the United States and the success of Silicon Valley. Their relationship is built on long-term collaborations in terms of sharing research, venture capital investment on alumni's startups, and training to local workers offered by such universities (Saxenian, 1994). However, Oakey (1985) posits this point of view, and argues that relationship between universities and local high-technology industry may not be that important:

> It is often assumed that because local firms with technical needs, and universities with relevant expertise are juxtaposed, then interaction occurs. But detailed evidence on the extent of links between high-technology scientific instruments firms and universities in Britain has indicated that contacts were infrequent. (Oakey, 1985, p. 101)

Rosenberg (2002) expresses similar views that relationship between university research and the success of tech firms is overestimated. "Most tech companies are not developing fundamental IP but applying generic or existing technology… they are not likely to draw heavily on fundamental research or hire the most qualified PhDs, if they need PhDs at all" (Rosenberg, 2002, p. 16). Scholarly conclusions on the role of universities and technological innovation vary due to their analytical context differences.

The analysis of Shenzhen innovation cluster is significant because there was no widely acknowledged and well-known research university in Shenzhen since its establishment as the first special economic zone. "Chapter 8, Shenzhen R&D Ecosystem" and "Chapter 9, Human Capital and National Competitiveness," examine well-developed vocational education systems and virtual universities in the early 90s to make up for the absence of top-ranked physical universities in Shenzhen. Meanwhile, applied innovation and entrepreneurship institutes established in the early 90s reveal Shenzhen's strong regional innovation characteristics. This book reveals a close similarity between Shenzhen and Taiwan in their respective development of industry - research partnerships in the high-tech industries. Research Institute of Tsinghua University in Shenzhen (in short, RITS; 深圳清华大学研究院), co-established in 1996 by Shenzhen city government and Tsinghua University, on one hand, fulfils the mission of promoting economic development in Shenzhen; on the other hand, it facilitates Tsinghua University's scientific achievements and technology transfer. Shenzhen's close ties with leading research universities in other cities and provinces undoubtedly show the importance of knowledge networks. Labor, knowledge workers or talent, are not separate from knowledge reservoirs, like universities and research institutions. For countries in the global south, they do not have to wait for the establishment of research universities for local innovation to blossom. Getting connected with the right nodes matters. The book displays how Shenzhen has established and expanded its domestic and global knowledge and research networks.

Myth Seven

This book reveals that technology enterprises are the driving forces of the patent increase in Shenzhen region, which further contribute to local and regional technological innovation greatly. Table 1.8 shows that, Shenzhen–Hong Kong ranked No. 3 in China in terms of patents filed from 1991–1995, while it rose to top 1 from 2011–2015, thanks to the thrive of local enterprises. Corporate research within enterprises is as equally critical as university research though enterprises are often seen as profit-driven entities. "Chapter 6, The Entrepreneurial Ecosystem in Shenzhen" investigates how a mature supply chain earns Shenzhen the title of "Silicon Valley of Hardware" and how hardware supply chains interact with local enterprises. "Chapter 8, Shenzhen R&D Ecosystem," details how Huawei, Tencent and Ping An cultivate and develop their organizational innovation. For instance, Tencent's famous WeChat mini program is a product of successful intraorganizational innovation. BGI Genomics's long-term investment in scientific publishing has earned itself a global leader in its field which attracts global scientists to publish their scientific contributions to the company's flagship academic journal, GigaScience

Table 1.8 Global innovation hotspot concentration, patents, and selected countries

Country	*Patents 1991–1995*	*%*	*Patents 2011–2015*	*%*
China	Beijing Shanghai Shenzhen – Hong Kong	36.5	Shenzhen – Hong Kong Beijing Shanghai	52.2
Germany	Frankfurt Cologne–Dusseldorf Stuttgart	37.4	Frankfurt Stuttgart Cologne–Dusseldorf	29.4
France	Pairs Lyon Grenoble	47.1	Pairs Grenoble Lyon	42.8
United Kingdom	London Manchester Cambridge	30.0	London Cambridge Oxford	35.0
India	Bengaluru Mumbai Delhi	41.9	Bengaluru Hyderabad Delhi	46.2
Japan	Tokyo Osaka Nagoya	80.5	Tokyo Osaka Nagoya	83.4
United States	New York City San Jose–San Francisco Boston	19.4	San Jose–San Francisco New York City Boston	23.4

Note 2019 World Intellectual Property Report, the chapter of Global Networks of Innovation Hotspots, p. 41

(see Chapter 8, Shenzhen R&D Ecosystem). Shenzhen innovation experience provides entrepreneurs and tech firms in both developing and developed countries with lessons on the utilization of corporate capacity to foster local innovation clusters. Local enterprises are more than patent filers. They are innovative nodes with unique corporate features which can link local industries with a broader regional or global economy.

Myth Eight

Though China has been leading the global innovation race as a global south country, it has its own challenges for building nation-wide healthy entrepreneurial culture and continues to support private enterprises. Some of the issues have not been discussed much both in China and on the world stage, as social and cultural evolutions and struggles are sometimes neglected in economy & technology dominant conversations. In "Chapter 6, The Entrepreneurial Ecosystem in Shenzhen," the comparison between startup incubators & accelerators in Shenzhen and Silicon Valley indicates the lack of supportive mentorship to budding Chinese entrepreneurs from an ecosystem perspective. As documented in the analysis, established Silicon Valley investors and successful entrepreneurs often do startup mentorship pro bono because they like to keep themselves sharp and updated with fresh ideas and new developments in related industries. The lack of mentorship in Shenzhen depicts a serious Chinese innovation drawback, which requires societal efforts in a long run. How to reignite an encouraging entrepreneurial culture should not merely be a government-led initiative. Social participation shall be awarded. Fostering an encouraging and supportive social culture is consistent with suggestions put forward on formulating China's Fifteenth Five-Year Plan for National Economic and Social Development on October 23rd, 2025. In the official document, it states that China needs to foster an open and competitive innovation ecosystem with global competitiveness. It is necessary to support innovation and entrepreneurship among young scientific and technological talents.[17]

Myth Nine

China's technological breakthroughs as well as the number of billionaires residing in Chinese metropolitan cities such as Beijing, Shanghai and Shenzhen have undoubtedly present the outside world an image of a wealthy nation. People in western countries, who travel to China for businesses and academic exchanges, expressed that China is now a developed country and it needs to admit that during my interactions with them. Is China a developed country? According to the World Bank, China is an upper-middle-income country (see Chapter 3, China, the New Development). It eradicated extreme poverty in 2020, according to the World Bank's Upper-Middle-Income Country (UMIC) poverty line in 2021. China's Open and Reform in 1978 has lifted millions of people out of poverty and created economic miracles which enable some adventurers to become wealthy individuals. Economic opportunities also make some Chinese cities and regions affluent where continue to attract international investment. Individual realizations as well as economic leapfrog reflect Deng Xiaoping's words when the Chinese leadership decided to set special economic zones: Let some people get rich first (see Chapter 2, The Genesis of Shenzhen). But China's development approach reached its limits and has led to economic imbalances, for instance, regional economic disparity. Therefore, in recent years, how to enhance China's regional development coordination has become a key national topic. In "Chapter 5, Local Governance: Bureaucratic Entrepreneurs," I coined a term "Shenzhen–Inland collaboration model" to describe how inland cities in China provided raw materials to Shenzhen for processing and export, as well as how Shenzhen local government officials actively recruited talents from regions such as Xi'an, Wuhan and Hunan when the Open and Reform began. Now, Shenzhen has become a leading global technological powerhouse, as the one "who gets rich first," thus, Shenzhen starts to partner with the less developed regions to support their economic and technological development. A noticeable example is the "special economic zone + old revolutionary base area collaboration model", "特区 + 老区模式.[18]" My interviews with Shenzhen headquartered AI company that is building their factory in Jiangxi province, one of the old revolutionary base areas, is an example of the "special economic zone + old revolutionary base area collaboration model," a continuance of the "Shenzhen–Inland collaboration model" (see Chapter 10, New Innovation Hubs are Possible).

Optimizing and promoting coordinated regional development is one of the key topics in China's Fifteenth Five-Year Plan for National Economic and Social Development. Reducing regional development disparity is considered as an important move in advancing China's high-quality development in its next stage. In 2024, residents' disposable income per capita in Shenzhen was 81,123 RMB while it was 36,007 RMB in Jiangxi province.[19] Income and consumption inequality, infrastructural imbalances, the gap in educational resources and technological innovation, demonstrate economic and social disparity across regions in China. It is not accurate to name China as a developed country just based on the technological power and economy in its highly developed coastal regions. Therefore, to correctly comprehend China's development approach and innovation path to offer other global south countries and the world constructive lessons, it is necessary to examine its unique historical, political and social context (see Chapter 2, The Genesis of Shenzhen and Chapter 3, China, The New Development).

Global Innovation in a Changing World

From the first time I knew about Shenzhen in kindergarten, my fieldwork in Shenzhen and the Greater Bay Area, to the finalization of the book, the world has undergone tremendous changes with rapid and profound technological transformations and geopolitical shifts. These changes create both challenges and opportunities for countries, particularly the ones in the global south: the restructuring of global supply chains, unprecedented climate change and energy transition, disruptions in international trade, and more importantly, the new round of technological disruption brought by artificial intelligence. Additionally, rising xenophobia and anti-immigrant policies in some global north nations are beginning to slow brain drain from some regions, which presents an opportunity for talent source countries to focus on effective domestic policies to make it appealing for skilled talents to stay. The significance of establishing innovation clusters and ecosystems has never been greater. In addition to China and India, as shown in 2025 Global Innovation Cluster Index, six middle-income countries from the global south enter the top 100 innovation cluster list (see Table 1.9). The desire to build local innovation clusters and the devotion to advancing local and regional technological development is more than statistical numbers. Young African entrepreneurs I interacted with during my work in Africa showed me their cautious optimism in building an innovation driven African continent. Brain circulation from the U.S. to Indonesia, Malaysia and other ASEAN countries in recent years start to focus on building indigenous technological products that serve their respective countries and markets. With all the optimistic development, however, many countries in the global south still face political struggles, corruption, weak governance, and lack of sustainable financing to build STI infrastructures and innovation ecosystems. The development of artificial intelligence, on one hand, offers global south countries opportunities in the technological arena; on the other hand, the complexity of the global economy has also made it difficult for individual countries to develop their innovation ecosystems to compete with multinational technology giants in general. This reality, as argued by Leloğlu (2024), propelled some countries to turn to South-South Cooperation to pull resources, share knowledge and build development alliances rather than rely on traditional international organizations led by the global north. "The futuristic city in China," a university professor who is a South African native screamed when she heard that I

Table 1.9 Middle income countries that have clusters in top 100, 2025

Rank	*Cluster name*	*Country*
49th	Brazil	São Paulo
58th	Istanbul	Turkey
63rd	Tehran	Islamic Republic of Iran
79th	Mexico City	Mexico
83rd	Cairo	Egypt
86th	Kuala Lumpur	Malaysia

Note GII Top 100 S&T Clusters
Retrieved from: https://www.wipo.int/documents/d/global-innovation-index/docs-en-2025-gii-2025-clusters-top100-ranking.pdf

am writing a book on Shenzhen, a friendship city of Cape Town since 2015.

China's economic leapfrog and innovation success has undoubtedly instilled confidence in citizens of many global south countries that their nations are capable of poverty alleviation and technological innovation breakthroughs. Though Shenzhen has been positioned as "the open window to the world" since the Open and Reform, most foreigners, in my experiences, immediately think of Beijing or Shanghai when they talk about China or their traveling or work to China. If Shenzhen is China's open window to the world, why don't people think of Shenzhen first? Why don't people get to understand China's first special economic zone to investigate what exactly "special" about this city that has become the No.1 innovation cluster domestically and internationally? What can cities in Africa and Asia that aspire to become "Silicon Cape" "Silicon Savannah" or the Silicon Valley of Asia learn from Shenzhen? How does Shenzhen innovation differ from cultures, institutions and patterns that mapped out for western technology centers? If you are curious to figure them out, you are reading the right book in front of you.

Notes

1. *The Top 100 Science and Technology Clusters*, written by Kyle Bergquist and Carsten Fink, released by the World Intellectual Property Organization in 2020.
2. According to the official introduction, The Chinese Language and Culture for Business London (CLCB) is a part-time executive

program for leaders and managers with a global vision and a particular interest in doing business in China. It is run by the Confucius Institute for Business London (CIBL) at the London School of Economics and Political Science, jointly with Tsinghua University in Beijing.

3. Article originally retrieved from the Bloomberg Technology: https://www.bloomberg.com/news/articles/2019-12-03/china-stockpiles-foreign-tech-as-silicon-curtain-descends.
4. Interview is retrieved from: https://www.youtube.com/watch?v=HipQxNCVoBA
5. HAI center global AI vibrancy tool can be accessed at: https://hai.stanford.edu/ai-index/global-vibrancy-tool
6. Information is retrieved from: https://www.sohu.com/a/289496567_809801
7. Article published on The Guardian in February 2011: China overtakes Japan as world's second-largest economy. Retrieved from: https://www.theguardian.com/business/2011/feb/14/china-second-largest-economy
8. Report is retrieved from: https://www.wipo.int/edocs/pubdocs/en/wipo_pub_gii_2018.pdf.
9. Patent information from World Property Intellectual Organization. Report published in 2020: https://www.wipo.int/pressroom/en/articles/2020/article_0005.html
10. Information is retrieved from: https://www.wipo.int/web-publications/pct-yearly-review-executive-summary-2025/en/pct-yearly-review-2025-executive-summary.html.
11. Information is retrieved from: https://www.france24.com/en/20200407-in-first-china-moves-ahead-of-us-as-world-s-top-patent-filer
12. Information is retrieved from: https://www.france24.com/en/20200407-in-first-china-moves-ahead-of-us-as-world-s-top-patent-filer
13. Article published on Reuters in April 2020: In a first, China knocks U.S. from top spot in global patent race. Retrieved from: https://www.reuters.com/article/us-usa-china-patents-idUSKBN21P1P9
14. Information is retrieved from: https://daoinsights.com/opinions/pioneering-sustainability-shenzhen-is-more-than-chinas-silicon-valley/

15. Shenzhen City Government issued the first version of the document in 1998, translated into Chinese: 《关于进一步扶持高新技术产业发展的若干规定》Document can be retrieved from: https://www.sz.gov.cn/zfgb/1998/gb135/content/post_10115835.html.
16. Information is retrieved from: http://www.chtf.com/liaojiegaojiaohui/lijiehuigu/chtf2/
17. 中共中央关于制定国民经济和社会发展第十五个五年规划的建议. Information is retrieved from: https://www.gov.cn/zhengce/202510/content_7046052.htm.
18. Shenzhen and Jiangxi province collaboration. Information is retrieved from: https://gzw.sz.gov.cn/gkmlpt/content/8/8205/post_8205353.html#1904
19. Information is retrieved from: https://m12333.cn/policy/presf.html and https://m12333.cn/policy/pkbir.html.

CHAPTER 2

The Genesis of Shenzhen

I am the son of the people. I deeply love my country.
—Deng Xiaoping[1]

Visions of a New China, Deng Xiaoping has opened the Middle Kingdom's doors to the world. This is a magnificent feat that is unique in human history.
—1979 Time Magazine

Era of Change

On a day in 2024, I was browsing online on my Taobao App which automatically recommends a customer's favorites based on my previous browsing history or big data analytics, as part of the shopping algorithm. One item caught my eye though I did not search for similar things. It was a Chinese food coupon, (粮票) from a store named antique collections. I clicked that webpage and went into that online store that is filled with food coupons from different provinces of China with various numerical values. As someone who was born after China's Open and Reform in 1978, fifteen years before the official termination of food stamps in China in 1993, my vague memory as a kid holding a grain ration booklet (粮本) waiting outside a food supply store started to pop into my head. Both food coupon and grain ration booklet symbolize planned economy in

G. Y. Wang, *Dragon Innovation: Shenzhen*, Governing China in the 21st Century, https://doi.org/10.1007/978-981-95-9637-9_2

China. The food coupon from this Taobao antique collection store draws a complete contrast between the prosperous e-commerce and millions of domestic made and imported commodities in China with the past old days when Chinese households had to rely on government planned food ration to feed a family. Shenzhen, a special economic zone, is the first Chinese city which eradicated food coupons. Starting from April 1st, 1993, in accordance with the State Council's *"Notice on Accelerating the Reform of the Grain Circulation System"* (《关于加快粮食流通体制改革的通知》), food coupons were started to be canceled, and the supply of food commodities began to operate in a market-oriented system. Until 1994, food coupons were completely terminated all over China which marks the end of an era.

My personal memory indicates that I was growing up toward the very end of China's planned economy in a historical transformation. In 1991, the Soviet Union collapsed. Before that, in the 1980s, neo-liberal economic thinking gave the impression that economic planning, used dominatingly by the Soviet Union, was a theory and a practice of the past. Kafouros wrote:

> Capitalism, the dominant paradigm then, and the sole paradigm now, was once again hailed as the superior, or at least the only realistic way to handle every socio-economic aspect of this planet's continuance. This loss of economic organization discussion occurred as the administrative methods for running an economy, with foremost among them being economic planning, were inseparably linked to the collapse of the various People's Republics. In essence, they were held responsible for it leaving the theories of economic planning to fall into complete oblivion. (Kafouros, 2009, pp. 527–528)

Capitalism's triumph over economic planning did not happen overnight. People in the Soviet Union during the 1970s saw little material progress and their education infrastructure was in poor condition (Spulber, 1969). Though China aligned with the Soviet Union in the communist political orientations, the lack of material wealth and progress in the Soviet Union's late development stage undermined the idea that China should maintain its highly centralized, state controlled economic system with no market opportunities. China's quest for its own developmental path, its Open and Reform policy in 1978, emerged at a critical time. My own comprehension about China's historical choice becomes much more perspicuous as I started to interact with many people who were born and grew up in the so-called global south, namely developing countries that are still struggling to alleviate their own citizens out of poverty. Some of those countries, were actually more economically advanced than China was in the 70s. "We should learn from China, if not replicate," many of them said so. How should developing countries assess the current global geopolitics to navigate international cooperation in the form of foreign investment and technology transfer? How will a country's specific geographical features and political structure influence its economic governance? This chapter provides a concise background of the Open and Reform policy's international and domestic contexts which lead to the official implementation of special economic zones, emphasizing the argument that China's development choice is a result of its own national characteristics and the historical international environment. Given China's massive geographical territory, establishing special economic zones for experiments before distributing possible successful development lessons to other cities and provinces has worked in China. This chapter serves two key purposes in this book. By laying out the backgrounds for setting up special economic zones as a beginning of China's economic development, it highlights the argument that it is too simplified to understand China as a whole, in terms of its economic policy and technological innovation strategies. China's regional economic development and innovation is built on the successes or failures of experiments and attempts in special economic zones such as Shenzhen. Shenzhen, as China's first special economic zone, is still playing its pioneering role in leading China's economic reform, private economy and technological development (see Chapter 5, Local Governance: Bureaucratic Entrepreneurs). Deng Xiaoping's groundbreaking closing ceremony speech at The Third Plenary Session of the Eleventh Central Committee in 1978 demonstrates the significance of governance, state capacity and institutions in directing China's economy and industrialization, a fact that is often overlooked and much criticized by some observers.

Open and Reform Policy Background: International Context

Before the Open and Reform policy established in 1978, China endured a ten-year Cultural Revolution from 1966 to 1976. For many Chinese, this was a catastrophic decade. Mao Zedong, often called, the great leader, who led the Chinese people's fight for the new China, planned the Cultural Revolution, launched it, and had more control over it than anyone else (Evans, 1993). As written by Fraser, following the victory of 1949, Mao Zedong continued to promote "a class struggle [that was] by no means over. The class struggle between the proletariat and the bourgeoisie will continue to be long and tortuous and at times will even become very acute" (Fraser, 1967, pp. 17–18). Mao argued that it was critical to fight the bourgeoisie, to strengthen the proletarian national governance, which is part of the "continuous revolution" (Niu, 1996). Mao's vision of a good society was one in which all people resembled each other in outlook, level of education and standard of living. He also had a strong distaste for individualism and held a grudge against the educated classes of the old China which can be reflected from his writings: "Our point of departure is to serve the people whole-heartedly and never for a moment divorce ourselves from the masses, to proceed in all cases from the interests of the people and not from one's self interests or from the interests of a small group" (Mao, 1965, p. 1096). By the start of 1965, Mao became angry that the Communist Party's central apparatus, which was under the control of Deng Xiaoping and Liu Shaoqi, had taken charge of the policy-making decisions. Mao saw Deng as "an independent kingdom" (Evans, 1993).

Ten years of Cultural Revolution dragged China into a decade of political struggle which stifled China's economic, cultural, and educational advancement. Deng Xiaoping was unfortunate to be one of the victims in this political cultural revolution as he showed himself to be a "petty intellectual" whose ideas were not aligned with Mao's thinking in how and who should lead the country forward at that time. Deng was called "the number two capitalist-roader" in the Red Guard press during the revolution and went to exile. Deng suffered until in 1972 when Mao agreed to bring him back to Beijing from his exile and praised Deng as a rare talent who fought vigorously against the Soviet revisionism (Evans, 1993). Furthermore, Mao proposed that Deng rejoin the military commission and suggested to the commission that Deng should be appointed chief of staff of the armed forces. This did not happen, but later Deng was promoted to the politburo and to the commission which meant no one could match his positions both in the military and the government. Deng believed that his time away from daily politics in Beijing during the Cultural Revolution enabled him to think and envision long-term national development goals for China (Vogel, 2011).

Deng Xiaoping regained power at the end of the Cultural Revolution and was assigned the first important task in his new role to address the United Nations General Assembly as the Chinese representative in 1974. This was Deng's first overseas visit since his travels and studies to France in 1925 and Moscow in 1926. Deng's previous overseas education and travel experiences seemed to pave a road for his international reengagement. His cowboy picture in Texas later suggested that he had a masterful skill of engaging with western politicians and businesspeople to present them with a new China that was ready to embrace different social and cultural values. At the Special Session of the United Nations General Assembly, the first special session ever to specifically discuss the significance of opposing imperialist exploitation and the need to transform international economic relations, Deng's speech propounded Mao's theory. He classified the world into three parts: the two superpowers (the United States and the Soviet Union); the second world (developed countries besides two superpowers); and the third world (developing countries in Asia, Africa, Latin America and some other regions). China was part of the third world.

As the Chinese representative, Deng's discussion of cooperation for international development addressed the significance of political and economic independence for developing countries at a historical time when the United States and the Soviet Union maintained military bases everywhere, stationed ponderous forces abroad and exploited the raw materials and natural resources in the developing countries. Deng stressed that:

> We maintain that the safeguarding of political independence is the first prerequisite for a third world country to develop its economy. In achieving political independence, the people of a country have only taken the first step, and they must proceed to consolidate this independence, for there still exist remnant forces of colonialism at home and there is still the danger of subversion and aggression by imperialism and hegemonism. The consolidation of political independence is necessarily a process of repeated struggles. In the final analysis, political independence and economic independence are inseparable. Without political independence, it is impossible to achieve economic independence; without economic independence, a country's independence is incomplete and insecure.
>
> The developing countries have great potential for developing their economy independently. As long as a country makes unremitting efforts in the light of its own specific features and conditions, advances along

> the road of independence and self-reliance, it is fully possible for it to attain gradually a high level of development never reached by previous generations in the modernization of its industry and agriculture.[2]

Deng stressed the significance of maintaining political independence in the midst of two superpowers' cold war by calling support and solidarity of other developing countries. It is unclear if Deng or the Chinese central leadership already had the initial vision of the Open and Reform policy, in the form of market-oriented state capitalism when Deng addressed the importance of achieving a high-level development that matches with China's own specific characteristics and conditions at the Special Session of the United Nations General Assembly. In Deng's speech, he further emphasized the importance of keeping natural resources in a nation's own control despite the need for foreign capital at the initial stage of economic development among developing countries:

> In many developing countries, the production of raw materials accounts for a considerable proportion of the national economy. If they can take in their own hands the production, use, sale, storage and transport of raw materials and sell them at reasonable prices on the basis of equitable trade relations in exchange for a greater amount of goods needed for the growth of their industrial and agricultural production, they will then be able to resolve step by step the difficulties they are facing and pave the way for an early emergence from poverty and backwardness. (from footnote 2)

Deng addressed China's position as a third world socialist country. His speech implicitly demonstrated his vision of China's national goals and its development: As a country with tremendous natural resources and raw materials, China needed to maintain its political independence without external interference to trade with foreign countries on fair prices to gradually alleviate the country out of poverty. Deng's speech drew a large audience in China and internationally. His visit to New York made him known internationally and let him see the modern western world for the first time in decades. Yet, there is no accounting of how he felt about his New York visit (Evans, 1993): Did he see the economic gap between the United States, a superpower and his home country? Did the gap further determine him on the poverty alleviation of the Chinese people? Did he think of capitalism as a possible mechanism for China's economic development?

Two months after the *Treaty of Peace and Friendship between Japan and the People's Republic of China*[3] was signed in August 1978, Deng visited Japan as the Vice Premier of the People's Republic of China. His international reputation was climbing. The negotiations about this agreement started in 1974 and were strongly opposed by the Soviet Union whose national economy was in crisis and was burdened by extravagant military spending. By 1978, the Soviet Union and China were enemies as part of the continuous Sino-Soviet split driven by ideological divisions, different economic visions among two Communist states, and attitudes towards the West (Radchenko, 2010). In the same year, Deng Xiaoping was named as the Man of Year by *Time Magazine* before his official visit to meet with the U.S. President Jimmy Carter in January 1979. Deng was welcomed during his visit to the White House. Since Deng's reinstatement in 1974, he made many foreign visits. His United Nations speech along with his international tours to the United States,[4] Japan, Singapore, and elsewhere paved the way for China's economic development and helped China lay the groundwork for its economic reform and advancement at the international stage through diplomatic efforts. The signal is clear: China is a country that seeks for peaceful and friendly international environment and cooperation to eradicate domestic poverty, advance its national economy and realize its industrialization.

> The policy of taking economic construction as the key link must never be changed; the Open and Reform policy must never be altered. The party's basic line must not be shaken for 100 years. We must properly draw the lesson from the former Soviet Union and handle well the relationships between the party center and localities. We must uphold the leadership of the CCP.[5] The CCP's status as the ruling party must never be challenged.
>
> —Deng Xiaoping

Open and Reform Policy Background: National Context

The Third Plenary Session of the Eleventh Central Committee in 1978 was a major turning point in modern China. Before the closing ceremony speech given on December 18, 1978, Deng Xiaoping was visiting Singapore, one of the four "Asian tigers" (or Asian dragons in Mandarin 亚洲四小龙) in November 1978. Among the four Asian tigers, Singapore realized its national independence in 1963, and Hong Kong, at that time, was still a British colony. South Korea and Chinese Taiwan, remained within American economic system and military orbit (O'Donnell et al., 2017). While Deng was in Singapore, a high-level delegation led by Vice Premier Gu Mu visited France, Germany, Switzerland in Western Europe. Gu Mu returned with the message that foreign countries, including those capitalist ones, were interested in investing and helping to modernize China's industrial production (Cheng, 2011). Gu Mu's report had a tremendous influence on government discussions, particularly on the possibility of reforming China's economic system (Vogel, 2011). Can China use western economic logic to its advantages without compromising its political independence and principles? According to Castells (1996), the "Singapore Model" was popular among Chinese Communist Party leaders because the idea of fully developing economically and technologically without losing state control appeals strongly to the Chinese Communist Party. Deng's visit in Singapore enabled him to see for himself a country with no natural resources that has developed economic prosperity through foreign direct investment, technology transfer, and deliberate attraction of global talents. As soon as Deng returned to Beijing, he drafted his closing ceremony speech for The Third Plenary Session of the Eleventh Central Committee in December in consultation with other senior party leaders. In his widely circulated speech *Emancipate the mind, Seek truth from facts, Unite and look forward,* [6] (*解放思想, 实事求是, 团结一致向前看*) Deng emphasized the importance of economic decentralization with Chinese characteristics which sent out a clear economic development message:

> I want to focus on the issue of promoting economic democracy. At present, the power of our economic management system is too concentrated, and the power should be boldly decentralized and distributed in a systematic and planned way. Otherwise, it is not conducive to fully stimulate the enthusiasm and motivation of the state, locality, enterprises, and individual workers. It is also not conducive to modern economic management and labor productivity. Local governments, enterprises and production teams should be given more autonomy in operation in provinces, cities, and autonomous regions. There are so many provinces, cities, and autonomous regions in our country. A medium province is equivalent to the size of a large country in Europe. It is necessary to have unified understanding, unified policies, unified plans, unified command, and unified actions while giving out more autonomy in economic planning, finance, and foreign trade management.

In Deng's national speech, he emphasized the significance of granting certain cities or regions local autonomies to develop national economy. Economic decentralization with Chinese characteristics means that a city, a province, or a particular industry can experiment before a unified national economic or industrial plan comes out. If the experiment is successful, then other cities, provinces or industries can gradually replicate and spread the successful experiences. This guidance is exactly what enabled Shenzhen, China's first special economic zone, to release China's first private enterprise regulation as well as the first national document that encourages technical talents to facilitate product commercialization by establishing technology enterprises (see Chapter 5, Local Governance: Bureaucratic Entrepreneurs). Further, Deng's comparison of a medium sized Chinese province with a European country, as an extended interpretation of the economic decentralization, focuses on the significance of local government: If effective local governance could be implemented, each medium-sized province in China would have the potential to develop according to their geographical characteristics and regional competitiveness. Importantly, unlike Mao Zedong's egalitarian ideology that required the equality of opportunities and the same living standards in society, Deng encouraged people in certain regions to earn more income and to live wealthier lives earned through their ingenuity and industrious work. He encouraged people to work diligently towards a prosperous personal and national life:

> In terms of economic policy, I think we must allow some regions, some enterprises, and some workers as well as peasants to earn more income and to live better lives due to their industrious work. If some people's lives are improved, it will inevitably produce positive influence as developmental role models which can further drive and motivate people from other regions and enterprises to learn from them. In this way, the entire Chinese national economy will continue to develop in a wave-like manner, and the people of all ethnic groups and of all regions in the country will be able to get richer relatively faster.

Encouraging some people to get rich first through their hard work as well as motivating some regions to develop fast, in essence, is a form of incentives and competition. In fact, the exact governing philosophy still operates in China nowadays. For instance, the many mini-Silicon Valleys and the blossom of robotics and artificial intelligence centers across China is a result of regional and industrial competitions in the field of technological innovation. Healthy competitions can generate regional collaboration which will continue to contribute to China's national development and innovation. The "special economic zone + old revolutionary base area collaboration model" exactly matches the essential spirit of Deng's speech then (see Chapter 1, China Innovation Myth).

Back in 1978, the Third Plenary Session of the Eleventh Central Committee established a new strategic route centered on economic development and construction in modern China. The strategy moved away from class struggle and political turmoil during the Cultural Revolution from 1966–1976. Deng's messages encouraged party leaders and fellow members to think freely and to encourage constructive criticism among party members. Deng set a national tone to get rid of the ideas and ideologies of the Cultural Revolution. His messages on managing the economy following the advanced foreign and scientific methods demonstrated his openness in learning from the outside, even from "capitalism economies" whose ideologies and political systems differ from China's. At that time of his speech in 1978, Deng's economic measures were not meant to build China into a global innovation hub or to transform China into a global economic powerhouse though China became the world's second largest economy after 2010.[7] Instead, his objective was to bring Chinese people out of poverty after decades of domestic and international political turmoil in what was once known as the Middle Kingdom (Du, 2020). His emphasis on the central government's decentralization in granting local governments and organizations more autonomy laid a solid foundation for the Open and Reform policy and the establishment of special economic zones in Guangdong and Fujian provinces. These historical policy conditions for Shenzhen's economic and industrial rise are essential. Next section details how the idea, special economic zone, comes into fruition, as an experiment of economic decentralization stated in Deng's closing ceremony speech for The Third Plenary Session of the Eleventh Central Committee in 1978.

Cross the river while feeling the stone.[8]

—Anonymous

Regardless of black cats or white cats, as long as it can catch mice, it is a good cat.

—Deng Xiaoping

Special Economic Zone

In November 1978, during the Central Committee Working Conference in Beijing, the second secretary of the Guangdong Provincial Party Committee, Xi Zhongxun (China's President Xi Jinping's father), proposed that the central government should allow Guangdong province to set up an office in the Hong Kong Special Administrative Region to establish direct contact with factory manufacturers from Hong Kong and Macao. Given their physical proximity and historical relationships, Xi Zhongxun suggested that the central government could effectively grant Guangdong province the autonomy to deal with any economic business such as processing of incoming materials, compensation trade, exports, and imports to increase local economic efficiency.[9] Deng's closing speech at the Third Plenary Session of the Eleventh Central Committee in December 1978 undoubtedly gave delegates from Guangdong province more confidence to exercise its provincial and geographical advantages. Guangdong delegates wanted to begin pioneering experiments with economic development and reconstruction which was built on its geographical proximity to Hong Kong and Macao, in addition to Guangdong province's overseas Chinese diaspora networks. Furthermore, the Guangdong delegation petitioned Deng Xiaoping and other senior leaders in Beijing during April and May 1979 in the hope of obtaining "special lands" in Guangdong province to establish industrial export ports and trade cooperation zones where foreign investors and businesspeople could invest to build factories and to manufacture exported products to sell in the international markets. The proposal that Xi Zhongxun presented to Beijing authorities in April 1979, pushed the boundaries of acceptability, hoping to attract foreign direct investment and develop private enterprises (Du, 2020). Private enterprises did not exist in any Chinese city in 1979. As written in previous section, the lessons learnt from the "Four Asian Tigers" especially during Deng's visit to Singapore in late 1978, betting their economic success on attracting foreign capital investment and technology transfer, convinced the Communist Party leaders that this was the route China should follow. There was a debate on whether to name the "special lands" as "export processing zones" since this was the term Taiwan used at that time in its Kaohsiung Export Processing Zone.[10] Deng offered his support unhesitatingly by suggesting it be called a special economic zone. "It is better to call it special economic zone. The central government does not have any money. We can give you some [special] policies. You guys go do whatever you can do to kill a bloody road [to develop the country and to boost the economy]."[11] In fact, special economic zone is adapted from the term "special zone" which has an implicit patriotic tone as it was previously employed to designate districts for special administrative and military purposes, like Shan Gan Ning Special Zone (陕甘宁保卫区) in northwestern China during China's anti-Japanese War from 1931 to 1945. The term "special economic zone" corresponded with central leadership's guidance that economic zones operate under unified national political system. Deng's confirmation and support strengthened and encouraged Guangdong local government officials to take advantage of their indigenous economic, cultural, physical and natural resources under favorable international situations to make the first step in China's economic reconstruction (Fig. 2.1).

One of the special economic zones established then is the city of Shenzhen. As Fig. 2.2 shows, on July 19, 1979, the central government in Beijing officially issued the Central Committee Document No. 50, granting both Guangdong and Fujian provinces "*Special Policy, Flexible Measures*" to explore setting up special economic zones. August 26th, 1980, is set as Shenzhen's birthday as China's first special economic zone according to the official document. Long viewed as an empty fishing village, Shenzhen's predecessor was Bao'an county, officially listed as a county during the Eastern Jin dynasty (A.D. 317–420) in ancient China. It is necessary to note that Shenzhen was not an empty fishing village (though it has been viewed as "empty") before it was designated as China's first special economic zone. Its origin can date back to as early as four or five thousand years ago. In 214 BC, the emperor of the Qin dynasty, Qin Shihuang (秦始皇) unified China and set up three counties in Ling Nan (岭南) area: Nan Hai, Gui Lin, and Xiang Jun county. Shenzhen belonged to Nan Hai county at that time. The earliest known *Bao'an Annual* document about Bao'an county dates from the Jin dyansty (265–420 AD). In Eastern Jin dynasty, about 331 AD, the imperial court

Fig. 2.1 Symbolic statue of Shenzhen pioneering bull (*Note* The picture represents the spirit of Shenzhen: Pioneering and kill a bloody road. Photo taken by the author at Shenzhen Museum)

established Dong Guan county in South China, with jurisdiction over six counties, covering Bao'an county which included the geographical locations of today's Dongguan, Shenzhen, Zhuhai, and Hong Kong.[12] The *Bao'an Annual* document is the first document from the imperial time that identifies the site that later become Shenzhen as the region's political and administrative center (Du, 2020). Bao'an county's name was changed to Xin'an county during the Ming dynasty, as the name Xin'an (新安), "New Safety" was originated from the phrase "Reform the Old and Construct the New, Turn Danger into Safety."[13] This historical record interestingly indicates that Shenzhen area was expected to be a reforming and pioneering place even back to ancient Chinese dynasty from the interpretation of the name Xin'an. Nan Tou Gu Cheng[14] in Shenzhen established about 1394 AD in the Ming dynasty, was the political center of the greater Shenzhen, Hong Kong and Macoo area before the late

Qing dynasty. Nan Tou Gu Cheng was active with grocery stores, shops, administrative halls, shrines, markets, and schools. The Maritime Defense Hall, dating from the early sixteenth century, was rebuilt into the Dong Guan headquarters hall in 1679. In 1801, the building was reconverted and used as Feng Gang Academy to provide education and scholarship by the direct command of the Qing imperial court.[15] The economic prosperity and education initiative was short lived due to foreign invasion, though. In 1842, after the First Opium War, the Qing dynasty signed an unequal treaty with the Great Britian, namely the *Nanjing Treaty*, and Hong Kong island in Xin'an county was occupied by the British. In 1860, after the Second Opium War, the Qing dynasty signed another unequal treaty with the United Kingdom, the *Beijing Treaty*, which the United Kingdom further forced the Qing dynasty to give Kowloon Penisula in Xin'an county to the British. In addition, the Qing government and the United Kingdom signed the *Special Regulations on the Extension of Hong Kong Boundary Sites* which leased the New Territories in Xin'an county to the Great Britain for 99 years. By then, one third of the Xin'an county was ceded to the United Kingdom, which is today's Hong Kong before its 1997 return to the People's Republic of China. Shenzhen, also a part of Xin'an county, remained part of Chinese Mainland's territory. Shenzhen's history with Hong Kong, dating back to ancient dynasties, demonstrates that opening Shenzhen as a special economic zone has its historical reasons. Shenzhen was tied to Hong Kong since the Ming and Qing dynasties by physical adjacency, transportation, and trade. Hong Kong's thrive as a British colony showed that Chinese coastal cities can benefit economically from their locational advantages for trade and export-oriented economy. Shenzhen's history with Hong Kong also suggests that their people were connected and shared similar cultural and social roots dating back to the ancient times. This might explain why the other special economic zones established during the same time period, particularly Zhuhai, did not prosper as much as Shenzhen did though Zhuhai is close to Macao Special Administrative Region. Cultural similarities, societal roots, and familial ties may facilitate economic transactions and capital investment between Shenzhen and Hong Kong under special policies. The evolution between Hong Kong and Shenzhen, the changing dynamics of these two cities, as well as the Greater Bay Area initiative, will be discussed in different chapters of this book.

Fig. 2.2 Original document of 1979 central government's official approval on granting special economic policies to both Guangdong and Fujian province (*Note* Photo taken by the author at Shenzhen Museum)

Looking back at Chinese history, it is clear that political power changed over the past thousand years, but power and wealth have always accumulated and concentrated in the northern part of China, with the only exception being Nanjing, a city in the south of Yangtze river, which served as the capital of Six Dynasties.[16] People in the South and Southwest were usually characterized as rural and uncivilized during ancient times. Note that during the late Qing dynasty, Great Britain had an international trade deficit with the Qing dynasty. To change its unfavorable situation, the British sent an expedition from Europe to Guangdong province in southern China and started the First Opium War to demonstrate its power. This particular history shows that the utilization of cities in the South of China as an open window of new China's economic development is entrepreneurial and innovative.[17] This is an active and self-voluntary opening up. The Chinese central government actively opened those coastal cities to participate in international trade and global economy. Jonathan Bach (2017) wrote in the chapter *Shenzhen: From Exception to Rule* in the book *Learning from Shenzhen* that China's experiment with special economic zones came at a time when international companies increasingly spread manufacturing processes in a complicated division of labor in terms of design, labor, production, assembly and transport all over the world. Shenzhen, a former fishing village and China's first special economic zone, has been leading in opening the national and regional economy and building a friendly business and trade environment.

"We take many UK delegates to Shenzhen and the Greater Bay Area for visits when they came to China," a senior level manager who works at a non-profit organization that promotes China-UK business and cultural relations said to me. Their organization, headquartered in Beijing, has hosted many high-level UK delegates and took them to visit Shenzhen's tech companies, science parks and labs in the Greater Bay Area since the new UK administration took office in 2024. Those visits make me wonder if the nature of those high-profile foreign visits to Shenzhen is similar to that of Chinese visits to major cities in the United States, the Western Europe and Japan in the 70s, as documented in this chapter under international context. "No, no, no," my interviewee further explained, "most of the UK delegates came to Shenzhen to learn about its economic development and technological innovation, to make sure 'seeing is believing.' In fact, they did not know how advanced Shenzhen or China is in the global technological arena. But when Chinese delegates visited the industrialized economies before 1978, the Chinese knew we were far behind, and we wanted to learn from the developed countries." The ignorance of Shenzhen's economic success along with their curiosity about its technological leapfrog is also confirmed by another informant. "In 2019, I hosted a UK delegate to Shenzhen. Among that group of people, only one of them heard of Shenzhen." Not surprisingly, to some foreigners, the escalated U.S.–China trade war since 2018 makes Shenzhen, as well as many tech companies in Shenzhen well-known, which expedites their visits to this leading global technological hub in China. This phenomenon was briefly described in Chapter 1, China Innovation Myth. People want to figure out why: Why has a third world country evolved into a tech powerhouse that is capable of competing with the United States? What role do Chinese state and local institutions play in "economic decentralization" as Deng addressed in his speech for The Third Plenary Session of the Eleventh Central Committee in 1978? How can a city Shenzhen,

Fig. 2.3 Shenzhen county people's government (*Note* Photo taken by the author at Shenzhen Museum. On October 19th, 1949, Shenzhen people's government was founded)

next to Hong Kong, develop its technological capacity, that overshadows Hong Kong, a once British colony and an international financial center? "Chapter 3, China: The New Development" first explores those inquiries from the perspective of Shenzhen urban economic planning since its nascency (Fig. 2.3).

Notes

1. On February 14, 1981, Deng Xiaoping wrote a preface for the 《Selected Works of Deng Xiaoping》entitled "I am a Son of the Chinese People". Deng Xiaoping wrote: "I am honored to be a citizen of the world as a Chinese. I am a son of the Chinese people, and I deeply love my country and my people." Information is retrieved from: http://rd.reformdata.org/xinwen/2021/show-2435.html
2. Speech by Chairman Deng Xiaoping, the delegation of the People's Republic of China, at the Special Session of the United Nations

General Assembly on April 10, 1974. The speech is published by Foreign Languages Press and translated into English by Christian Liebl. The online version is available at Deng Xiaoping Internet Archive (Marxist.org).

3. From 1975, China and Japan started negotiations for the conclusion of a treaty of peace and friendship, and in August 1978, the Foreign Ministers of the two countries met in Beijing to sign the Treaty of Peace and Friendship Between the People's Republic of China and Japan. The Treaty stipulates: The Contracting Parties shall develop durable relations of peace and friendship between the two countries on the basis of the Five Principles of Peaceful Co-Existence; The Contracting Parties affirm that in their mutual relations, all disputes shall be settled by peaceful means without resorting to the use or threat of force; The Contracting Parties shall endeavor to further develop their economic and cultural cooperation and to promote exchanges between the people of the two countries. The two parties declare in the Treaty that neither of them should seek hegemony in the Asia–Pacific region or in any other regions and that each was opposed to efforts by any other country or group of countries to establish such hegemony. The Treaty also stipulates in explicit terms that "the present Treaty shall not affect the position of either Contracting Party regarding its relations with their countries". Excerpt online from Diplomatic History, Ministry of Foreign Affairs of the People's Republic of China.
4. The Sino-Soviet split (1956–1966) put the two communist countries, the People's Republic of China and the Union of Soviet Socialist Republics at odds. For the United States, the breakdown of relations between the Soviet Union and China was a diplomatic opportunity. By the early 1970s, the United States began to initiate diplomatic contacts with China though relations between the two nations had been severed in 1949 following the successful communist revolution in China. In 1972, President Richard Nixon surprised the world by announcing that he would visit China.
5. CCP stands for Chinese Communist Party.
6. Speech by Deng Xiaoping at the closing ceremony of the Work Conference of the CCP Central Committee on December 13, 1978. The original Chinese translation of his speech is named: 解放思想, 实事求是, 团结一致向前看。The original report in Mandarin

Chinese can be found at: http://www.reformdata.org/1978/1213/2172.shtml.

7. According to the article published by Jonathan Eckart in 2016 on World Economic Forum, since 2010, China has become the world's largest exporter and second-largest importer of merchandise goods, as well as the fifth largest exporter and third largest importer of commercial services.
8. Cross the river while feeling the stone, in translation, 摸着石头过河, has been a popular slogan till now in directing China's economic development.
9. Information is retrieved from: http://dangshi.people.com.cn/n/2015/1011/c85037-27684510.html
10. In 1966, Taiwan established its first export processing zone, Kaohsiung Export Processing Zone. Taiwan and Chinese Mainland had neither business contact nor other communications until 1987.
11. Documented in Memoirs of Gu Mu, in Mandarin Chinese, 《谷牧回忆录》, published in 2009. "杀出一条血路", in translation, "to kill a bloody road" was a popular slogan when economic development just started in China in the early 80s.
12. Information can be retrieved from Shenzhen Basics: http://www.sz.gov.cn/en_szgov/aboutsz/profile/content/post_1357629.html
13. This piece of information was obtained while I paid a visit to the exhibition at the Shenzhen Museum. It was seen as an important strategic town on coastal defense.
14. Nan Tou Gu Cheng, in Chinese character: 南头古城, located in Nanshan district in the current administrative district in Shenzhen, still remains as a tourism site nowadays.
15. Li Lu and Jie Cui, "Bainian Laoxiao Nantou Zhongxue Tanyuan" (origins of the hundred-year-old Nantou Secondary School), Nanfang Daily, January 13, 2011.
16. Eastern Jin dynasty (东晋) is established by the last of the Western Jin (西晋). It governs a limited area lying to the South of Yangtze River, this dynasty was recorded as a single dynasty in Chinese history. Six Dynasties 六朝, is a collective term of six dynasties in a certain period of ancient China.
17. New China, compared to Old China, refers to the People's Republic of China founded in 1949.

CHAPTER 3

China, the New Development: *Shenzhen, Plan with a Global Vision*

Time is money. Efficiency is life.

—Yuan Geng[1]

From China's First Special Economic Zone to a Technopole

Shenzhen is a state planned development product. In 1980, the People's Liberation Army went to Shenzhen and started city infrastructure construction from scratch. There are two major scholarly voices regarding Shenzhen's economic success: One praises the model success as the logical result of coherent policies and plans, while the other one argues that Shenzhen's success emerged out of a period of unlawful experimentation which allowed for a series of exceptions to Shenzhen model's own policies (O'Donnell et al., 2017). Both these two perspectives fail to comprehensively conclude factors contributing to Shenzhen's economic success and technological development. What role does industrial policy play in national development? How could this particular special economic zone evolve into a prominent global innovation hub while many worldwide special economic zones struggle to leapfrog economically, let alone transforming into global technological centers? Economist and Nobel laureate Friedrich Hayek argued that incentives and information are two critical

G. Y. Wang, *Dragon Innovation: Shenzhen*, Governing China in the 21st Century, https://doi.org/10.1007/978-981-95-9637-9_3

factors in industrial policy. Even when incentives were not a problem, central economic planning (i.e., socialism) would fail largely because the planners cannot have the information to plan an economy well. If Hayek's argument were universally true, Shenzhen's planning and industrial upgrading must have been attributed to pure luck, which is, of course, not correct.

Some analysts argued that since the very beginning when Shenzhen was set as the first special economic zone, Shenzhen functioned as a model city for the rest of China and as a demonstration for the world to see China's economic reform commitment. This view is not exactly wrong, though Shenzhen's experimental success was not guaranteed initially. "Cross the river while feeling the stone" is not a retrospective slogan. As the first special economic zone in China, Shenzhen's economic experiment is impossible without the supportive groups of leaders from central government in Beijing (see Chapter 2 for details on Open and Reform international and domestic contexts). Shenzhen local government's deliberate and adaptable industrial city planning has been matching international market trends as well as Shenzhen's changing developmental needs (see Chapter 5: Local Governance: Bureaucratic Entrepreneurs). Shenzhen is one of the few special economic zones in the 1980s in China, including Zhuhai, Xiamen, and Shantou. Its developmental objectives in the 1980s as a special economic zone in low-income Chinese national economy were to, according to the 2019 World Investment Report (see Table 3.1 for details): (1) stimulate industrial development and diversification; (2) offset weaknesses in the investment environment; (3) focus on economic growth, employment, and export earnings; (4) implement experimental business reforms. None of the other three cities (i.e., Zhuhai, Xiamen, and Shantou) has received phenomenal economic success and technological innovation breakthroughs like Shenzhen did. To understand Shenzhen's technological success and the making of China's leading technology hub, it is essential to keep in mind that Shenzhen was not a planned technopole, but a special economic zone that grows into an innovation-oriented city. Shenzhen's transformation from a special economic zone to a technological hub is an evolving journey. The missions and goals of special economic zones alter with its national income economy. In the past forty years, China has grown into an upper-middle income economy (defined by the World Bank),[2] thus, Shenzhen's role as a special economic zone changes accordingly. Two main updated goals include: (1) focusing on improving innovation abilities; (2) attracting and enhancing high-tech industries. To fully understand Shenzhen's economy and innovation path, no one can deny the role of the state: "Ji Zhong Li Liang Ban Da Shi" (集中力量办大事) which means the utilization of concentrated power and resources to focus on what matters the most. As mentioned in "Chapter 1, China Innovation Myth," Shenzhen's development trajectory demonstrates the exploratory nature of Shenzhen industrial and innovation path under the umbrella of economic planning.

This chapter lays out an introductory understanding of Shenzhen's development stages since its establishment as China's first special economic zone in 1979 and puts its emphasis on the role of industrial policy and planning that sets a foundation for the rise of high-tech industry in Shenzhen and its peripheral areas. Shenzhen's economic and technological success reveals the importance of forward-thinking and adaptable judgement in industrial planning as well as the significant role local government, namely Shenzhen city and district government in this context, plays in generating and implementing special policies with the support of central leadership in Beijing. Shenzhen local government officials have been playing a key role in pioneering institutional innovations in private economy and high-tech development and regulatory reforms in China (see Chapter 5). In fact, as shown in Table 3.1, Shenzhen's economic and industrial developmental path, in general, parallels with those objectives set for special economic zones in different levels of national economy. Though Shenzhen and the Greater Bay Area have already emerged as a leading innovation hub in China, with its increasingly influential capabilities in Asia, it is meaningful to comprehend Shenzhen's development and its technological innovation from the perspective of a developmental trajectory, rather than an analysis of an existing innovation ecosystem. Critics of Shenzhen's growth and success abound. In contrary to the acclaim for deliberate government planning and state capacity at both the national and local levels, many argue that "Shenzhen success" stemmed from a period of unlawful experiments which enables the combination of the logic of socialism and the logic of capital in a myth making (O'Donnell, et al., 2017). In spite of western critics, such as "playing capitalism with communist pieces" as David Stark (2009) put it, the need to comprehend China's developmental model is prevalent among policymakers in the developing countries. "Europe or the United States developed their economies and industrial societies over hundreds of years ago," a financial analyst and a policy observer in South

Table 3.1 Special economic zone development ladder

	Zone policy objectives	*Common types of special economic zones*
High-income economy	• Provide an efficient platform for complex cross-border supply chains • Focus on avoiding distortions in the economy	• Logistics hubs free zones only (not industrial free zones) • Innovation and new industrial revolution objectives pursued through science parks without separate regulatory framework, or though incentives not linked to zones
Upper-middle-income economy	• Support transition to services economy • Attract new high-tech industries • Focus on upgrading innovation capabilities	• Technology-based zones (eg., R&D, high-tech, biotech) • Specialized zones aimed at high value-added industries or value chain segments • Services zones (eg., financial services)
Middle-income economy	• Support industrial upgrading • Promote GVC integration and upgrading • Focus on technology dissemination and spillovers	• Specialized zones focused on GVC-intense industries (eg., automotive, electronics) • Services zones (eg., business process outsourcing, call centers)
Low-income economy	• Stimulate industrial development and diversification • Offset weaknesses in investment climate • Implement or pilot business reforms in a limited area • Concentrate investment in infrastructure in a limited area • Focus on direct employment and export benefits	• Multi-activity zones • Resource-based zones aimed at attracting processing industries

Note Source is from 2019 World Investment Report, Chapter Three, p. 141

Africa said to me during a personal exchange. "We need to learn some recent developmental lessons and China provides us (i.e., South Africa) with its relevantly fresh experiences." Therefore, the lessons and implications from a developmental angle are more far-reaching than merely an analysis of a cluster of innovation and secret recipes for creating profitable startups. Most importantly, it is more likely for developing countries and regions in the global south that are still low-income national economies to learn from Shenzhen's lessons and China's experiences to advance their economies while developing their technological capacity simultaneously.

Plan With a Global Vision

Throughout history, there were dispersed attempts by several countries to attract foreign investment with a different set of rules to allow them to take advantage of cheap labor, lower or no taxes as well as exemption from regulations. For instance, Puerto Rico, was promoted in 1948 as a special economic zone for U.S. companies to produce and manufacture there with tax and duty exemptions. Starting in the 1960s, countries such as India, Mauritius, the Philippines and Kenya started to create export processing zones but with limited economic impact. It is the "Asian Tigers" (i.e., Singapore, Chinese Hong Kong, South Korea and Chinese Taiwan) which contributed their rise to export-led growth that had a tremendous impact in the developing world. Thus, when Shenzhen came into existence in 1979 as a special economic zone, it quickly became a part of rapidly expanding global system where companies increasingly distributed and expanded their production process across the globe.

This section details the progression of Shenzhen development in four stages: (1) 1979–1992; (2)1993–2002; (3) 2003–2014; (4) 2014 to present. I divide the developmental stages mainly based on milestone plannings in terms of Shenzhen's regional status, internationalization as well as its industrial influence and its power of connectivity in the broader South of China. The categorization of Shenzhen developmental stages varies according to specific purposes by different authors and analysts. The setup of Shekou Industrial Zone with a close physical proximity to Hong Kong during Stage One (a special export processing zone within Shenzhen), the strategy to position Shenzhen as an international city during Stage Two, the vision for Shenzhen to develop together with Hong Kong as a key regional innovation hub during Stage Three, Shenzhen's link with Taiwan as well as early overseas Chinese diaspora's connection with

Guangdong province, reflect the motto in Shenzhen special economic zone's experimentation: Cross the river while feeling the stone, a slogan being carried on till now. Timely correction toward both national and local economic developmental needs matters in the implementation and execution of effective planning and industrial strategy.

Stage One: Start Off

During the first stage, from 1979 to 1992, Shenzhen worked on its urban city infrastructure to lay a solid foundation for its future city development. Vivid memories were described by both domestic workers and international visitors to Shenzhen during this period in my interviews with them (see Chapter 4, City Culture: Experimental and Entrepreneurial DNA). High demand for urban design talents enriches some labors, while leaving some outsiders wondering about the reasons for massive city infrastructure construction. At this stage, central government's vision for Shenzhen special economic zone was to become an industrial and agricultural export base while attracting tourists from Hong Kong and Macau to Chinese Mainland (Sun, 1991). Agricultural industries refer to farming, forestry, fishery, and animal husbandry.[3] Agriculture played a significant role in Shenzhen's initial economic development stage which, to some extent, refutes the popular view that Shenzhen was an empty fishing village with nothing. In fact, the name Shenzhen itself, means "deep water channels" in Chinese, derived from one of the townships in Bao'an county.[4] A large esturine bay is framed by the coasts of Shenzhen, Dongguan, Zhongshan, Zhuhai, Hong Kong and Macau, between the Pearl River and the South China Sea. Those rivers provide a natural transportation system for shipping and trade throughout the region. Shenzhen's reputation as a "fishing village" is associated with its proximity to the Pearl River's natural resources. At the far end of the Pearl River estuarine system, the salt wetlands are home to shrimp, fish, and migratory birds. Table 3.2 shows the gross product in Shenzhen during its first development stage in 1979, 1980, 1985, and 1990. Revenue of the primary industry in 1979 and 1980 accounted for a higher percentage than the percentage of the secondary industry (see Table 3.3), indicating that Shenzhen had a foundation in agriculture. But gross domestic product from the primary industry continued to decrease while the percentage of that from the second industry, including industry and construction, maintained their growth, with construction achieving its peak in early 80s.

Table 3.2 1979–1990 Shenzhen development stage one gross product (10,000 Yuan)

Year	*Shenzhen gross product*	*Primary industry*	*Secondary industry*	*Tertiary industry*
1979	19,638	7273	4017	8348
1980	27,012	7803	7036	12,173
1985	390,222	26,111	163,586	200,525
1990	1,716,665	70,220	769,319	877,126

Note Information gathered from Shenzhen Statistics Bureau https://tjj.sz.gov.cn/zwgk/zfxxgkml/tjsj/tjnj/content/post_3086000.html

Table 3.3 Percentage of Shenzhen gross product in primary, secondary, and tertiary industry (Unit: %)

Year	*Shenzhen gross product percentage*	*Primary industry*	*Secondary industry*	*Tertiary industry*
1979	100.0	37.0	20.5	42.5
1980	100.0	28.9	26.0	45.1
1985	100.0	6.7	41.9	51.4
1990	100.0	4.1	44.8	51.1

Note Information organized from Shenzhen Statistic Bureau

Secondary industry such as mining, manufacturing, electric power, gas and water production, and construction started to grow exponentially according to the Shenzhen city government's industrial development plan. Table 3.3 shows that secondary industry's percentage in Shenzhen's Gross Product grew from 20.5% in 1979 to 44.8% in 1990, counting almost half of the city's gross product in the early 90s. Table 3.4 confirms my interviewees' authentic experiences that in the first stage of Shenzhen's development, urban construction contributed tremendously to its domestic gross, particularly in the year 1981, 1982, and 1983, in the respective amount of 15.5%, 26.5% and 25.5% (see Chapter 4, City Culture: Experimental and Entrepreneurial). In 1980, Wu Nansheng, the then new mayor of Shenzhen, along with his team, published a new city development plan, *The General Planning of Shenzhen Special Economic Zone* (《深圳市城市建设总体规划》[5]). This planning stressed the importance of Shenzhen's industrialization, emphasized the importance of building an export-oriented economy in Shenzhen, as well as the need to attract foreign direct investment. In 1982, Shenzhen government revised its 1980 planning vision and proposed that Shenzhen should develop an electronics-based industry and produce electronics products mainly for international markets in its proposal submitted to Guangdong provincial and Beijing central government, *Shenzhen Social and Economic Development Planning Outline* (in Chinese: 深圳经济特区社会经济发展规划大纲). Meanwhile, Shenzhen should maintain its economic expansion and continue its development in industries such as tourism and agriculture. In fact, according to Shenzhen Statistics record, since 1992, at the end of the first Shenzhen development stage divided in this chapter, the percentage of Shenzhen primary industry gross domestic product had been decreasing, from 1992's 3.3% to 2009's 0.1%. On the contrary, the percentage of industry (included in the second industry) has increased from 1992s 37.1% to 2009s 43.8% (Fig. 3.1).[6]

Shekou Industrial Zone, the export industrial zone in the then rural Bao'an county symbolized the beginning of Shenzhen's industrial development in an export-oriented economic direction. China Merchants Group (招商局), a central state-owned enterprise[7] based in Hong Kong, led by Yuan Geng, a native of Guangdong and the Vice Chairman of the China Merchants Group in 1978, took the lead in building and developing Shekou Industrial Zone. The China Merchants Group was established in 1872 during the Qing dynasty as the China Merchants Steam Navigation Company by a prominent imperial court officer Li Hongzhang to engage in modern international shipping following the

Table 3.4 Percentage of Shenzhen gross product in secondary industry (Unit: %)

Year	*Secondary industry*	*Industry*	*Construction*
1979	20.5	11.8	8.7
1980	26.0	13.8	12.2
1981	32.3	16.8	15.5
1982	38.1	11.6	26.5
1983	42.6	17.1	25.5
1984	45.5	22.1	23.4
1985	41.9	26.2	15.7
1990	44.8	37.6	7.2

Note Information organized from Shenzhen Statistic Bureau

深圳經濟特區
社會經濟發展規劃大綱

一九八二年十一月三十日

Fig. 3.1 Shenzhen social and economic development planning (*Note* Photo taken by the author at Guangdong History Museum)

First Opium War. Later, it developed international shipping routes to Japan and Southeast Asia, thus becoming a substantial shipping and regional trade company. It was reorganized as the national China Merchants Group under Guo Min Party (the Nationalist Party) during China's civil war. After the civil war, its headquarters moved to Hong Kong, a colony of the Great Britain before 1997. With support and approval from the central government, Shekou Industrial Zone was designated as a special zone within Shenzhen special economic zone. Shekou, located in Nan Tou Gu Cheng, was the best location given its natural resources of water, its electricity supply, an existing regional economy, its proximity to Hong Kong as well as its historical reputation as the most developed area in Bao'an county. At the initial founding of Shekou Industrial Zone, Yuan Geng coined a slogan, which later became a famous catchphrase all over China: "Time is money; Efficiency is life."

This mantra was originally stated as "Time is money. Efficiency is life. Customers are emperors. Security is law." Yuan removed the last two sentences because people were afraid to consider customers as emperors in the communist party controlled planned economy since the party, not customers, should be at the top. The concern and fear over a slogan, to some extent, reflected party leaders' tentative visions for Shenzhen and their careful ideological attempts even in the economic arena.[8] "Cross the river while feeling the stone": Is there a red line in Shenzhen's development and modernization? How much autonomy did local government officials have? An urgent question faced by those pioneering political leaders was how to attract foreign investment and generate revenues to build the local economy since they only obtained "special policies" rather than funding from the central government in Beijing. How to attract foreign investment and build business connections for international trade became challenges for Shenzhen city government officials.

As the first special economic zone, Shenzhen's key objective was to develop into a successful national pilot program to generate useful experiences for the rest of China in building a successful national economy. Li Hao, the Shenzhen Mayor and Party Secretary in 1986, summarized the city's ten economic exploratory ideas and successful experiments since 1978 during the first developmental stage in the *Shenzhen Special Economic Zone Advancement towards An Outward-oriented Economy*.[9] Due to limited local industrial resources in Shenzhen, local government officials actively sought collaborations with cities and provinces from inland China to procure industrial production raw materials such as cotton. For instance, the Nan Fang Cotton Mills obtained their raw materials from inland cities, conducted refined manufacturing works in Shenzhen, and then exported those products overseas. This "Shenzhen – Inland collaboration model" helped many inland regions find a market for their natural resources, and also enabled Shenzhen to focus on manufacturing and exports as Shenzhen began to explore its export-oriented economy. The model also strengthened state-led economic development during China's economic modernization: As a special economic zone, Shenzhen enjoyed "special policies" allowing it to seek necessary raw materials to advance its industrial development. Other Chinese cities and provinces supported Shenzhen's development while also seeking for trade and business opportunities through this open window. The model coined in this book covers many aspects of Shenzhen's cooperations with inland Chinese cities, ranging from industrial raw materials to scientific

Table 3.5 Shenzhen gross output value of industry over levels from 1979–1992 (10,000 Yuan)

Year	*Total*	*Light industry*[10]	*Heavy industry*
1979	6061	5240	821
1980	8444	7077	1367
1981	24,282	22,762	1520
1982	36,212	31,832	4380
1983	72,041	57,561	14,480
1984	166,803	132,369	34,434
1985	241,213	188,659	52,554
1986	330,454	256,545	73,909
1987	547,722	423,150	124,572
1988	993,775	760,294	233,481
1989	1,440,533	1,044,386	396,147
1990	2,104,696	1,570,896	533,800
1991	3,077,749	2,156,668	921,081
1992	4,198,920	2,824,688	1,374,232

Note Information retrieved from 2010 Shenzhen Statistical Book

research collaborations (see Chapter 5: Local Governance: Bureaucratic Entrepreneurs). Table 3.5 displays Shenzhen industrial evolution from a weak foundation, 5240 RMB output value in the light industry in 1979, grows to 2,824,688 RMB in 1992. Actually, the growth trajectory from 1979 to 1992 indicates that Shenzhen, at its initial development stage, focused on "three supplies and one compensation" (三来一补) industrial model: Shenzhen factories and enterprises processed supplied raw materials, assembled components according to supplied samples, usually provided by foreign enterprises including the ones founded by Hong Kong and Macao businesspeople.

Stage Two: Open Window as An International City

In the second stage from 1993–2003, Shenzhen local government revised its city development objectives to adapt to the municipal developmental needs as well as the external business environment. In 1995, the Municipal Party Committee proposed to transform Shenzhen into an international city with socialist characteristics, as a showcase of China's economic modernization. Shenzhen debuted as an open window to the international markets (Sun, 1991). Shenzhen local government embraced the electronics-based, innovation-led industries after deliberate planning and examining international market trends. In fact, the emphasis on development of science and technology was supported by Deng Xiaoping, during his southern tour to Shenzhen in 1992.

From 1978 to 2003, during Shenzhen's first and second development stages, economic planning plays a critical role in guiding and directing Shenzhen's development direction. Table 3.6 demonstrates that during Shenzhen's second development stage, export-driven growth continued and the annual average growth rate was unprecedented. Thus far, it is safe to conclude that Shenzhen has followed its urban economic planning in its first two stages and has realized its export-oriented economy with certain municipal financial returns. It is said that "three supplies and one compensation" (三来一补) trade model has earned Shenzhen its first pot of gold. Shenzhen's development exploration reflects central leadership's spirit and China's historical circumstances: "The central government does not have any money. We can give you some [special] policies. You guys go do whatever you can do to kill a bloody road [to develop the country and to boost the economy]" (see Chapter 2, The Genesis of Shenzhen).[11] Since 1995, Shenzhen has comprehensively revised its previous urban planning in the 80s, which has been approved by the State Council. The revised plan redefined and updated the city's functions, development goals, and proposed to build Shenzhen into a high-tech industrial base, an electronics-based manufacturing city targeting international markets. This decision was largely influenced by Taiwan's success in developing its electronics industries starting in the 1970s. In 1973–1975, American and Japanese industrial production fell significantly due to the oil crisis from the Middle East, which led to the first post-war global financial crisis. This financial crisis alerted Li Guoding,[12] known as "Economic Master in Taiwan" and "Taiwan High-technology Master." Li realized that Taiwan, an island with no natural resources, needed to develop and maintain its economic competitiveness and advantages, decrease its dependence on the external resources and avoid restrictions and control from other political forces. In 1977, Li toured Silicon Valley to learn about the U.S. electronics and semiconductor industries. He saw the potential of electronics industries and believed Taiwan should follow that path since it did not require many natural resources and relied instead on human capital and knowledge. Since 1980, Taiwan has vigorously promoted industrial transformation and upgrading, focusing on supporting high-tech industries such as information electronics and precision equipment. The Hsingchu Science Park, established in 1980, is now the major high-tech and science development technopole center in Taiwan. Among all Taiwanese high-tech initiatives, the Foxconn Technology Group was ascendant. It specializes in R&D and the manufacturing of computers, communications, and consumer electronics. In 1988 Foxconn opened its first Foxconn electronics manufacturing factory in Shenzhen, which laid the foundation for electronics manufacturing in Shenzhen at a later stage. Taiwan's electronics manufacturing connections with Shenzhen, and its impact on Shenzhen's high-tech development will be further analyzed in the "Chapter 7, Shenzhen Grassroots Participatory Innovation: Let the People Make."

By far, economic growth and development in Shenzhen is largely credited to the plans of the Chinese central government and Shenzhen city government, along with the special policies in special economic zone. It also benefited from close connections that Guangdong province has with its overseas Chinese. According to Hsing (1998), the coastal south, such as Guangdong and Fujian provinces, has closer connections with the overseas Chinese than the rest of China. At that time, nearly 80% of the Chinese who had migrated overseas came from Guangdong and most of them maintained family ties with the region. The emigrants to the United States and elsewhere started their new lives as low levels service workers like cooks, masseurs, and dish washers, but they and their children quickly rose to become intellectuals, business owners, white-collar employees or entrepreneurs. When the Open and Reform policy was implemented in late 1970, people in Guangdong province took advantage of their spatial and sociocultural proximity to the overseas Chinese, especially in Southeast Asia. They attracted the overseas Chinese capital back to its province

Table 3.6 Shenzhen exports and imports from 1995–2003 (USD 10,000)

Year	*Total imports and exports*	*Exports*	*Imports*
1995	3,876,960	2,052,736	1,824,224
1996	3,905,342	2,120,781	1,784,561
1997	4,500,921	2,561,844	1,939,077
1998	4,527,417	2,639,611	1,887,806
1999	5,042,750	2,820,811	2,221,939
2000	6,393,982	3,456,333	2,937,649
2001	6,861,055	3,747,955	3,113,100
2002	8,723,148	4,655,704	4,067,444
2003	11,739,941	6,296,201	5,443,733

Note Information organized from Shenzhen Statistic Bureau

(Hsing, 1998). In addition, Hong Kong entrepreneurs helped connect Guangdong with the world market. In particular, Hong Kong's advanced and efficient telecommunications systems provided Guangdong with easy access to the outside world (Hsing, 1998). People in Shenzhen were able to catch up with the development trends through Hong Kong. The outward-oriented economy in Guangdong province was also accelerated by Hong Kong's information networks, marketing, and financial channels (Kwok & So, 1995). Shenzhen benefited from the foreign investment networks and the timely business and trade information. "Jie Chuan Chu Hai" (借船出海), borrowing others' ships to sail the sea, was used to describe the cooperative relationship between Shenzhen and other cities in Guangdong and Hong Kong during this historical period. Table 3.7 shows the sources of foreign direct investment in Shenzhen in the second development stage and Table 3.8 shows the registration status of foreign-invested enterprises by selective major regions in China at the end of year 1998 and 1999. Table 3.9 indicates the total value of foreign investment in six major provinces: Guangdong, Jiangsu, Fujian, Shanghai, Beijing, and Zhejiang. Among these provinces, Guangdong province was at the top in both 1998 and 1999 in terms of the number of registered foreign invested enterprises and the total foreign investment among major coastal and central cities and regions, with a tremendous gap compared to the second ranked Jiangsu province.

Table 3.7 Foreign investment and signed contracts with foreign capital in Shenzhen

Note Information organized from Shenzhen Statistic Bureau

Table 3.8 Year of 1998 and 1999 number of registered foreign-investment enterprises

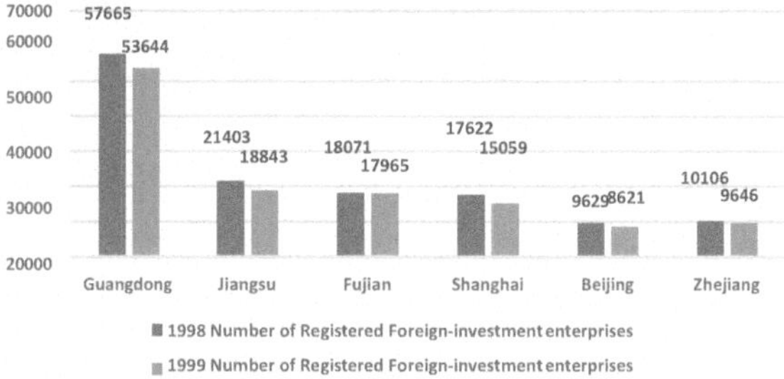

Note Information is organized from China's Ministry of Commerce

Table 3.9 Year of 1998 and 1999 foreign investment value in six major provinces (USD 10,000)

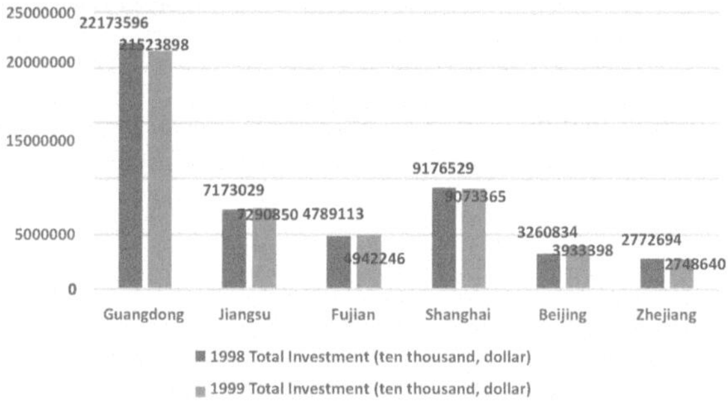

Note Information is organized from: https://www.stats.gov.cn/yearbook/1999/q20c.htm

In 2003, the value of the four major high-tech products in Guangdong province was 644.109 billion RMB, accounting for 94.65% of the province's high-tech product output value. Of this, 60.95% was in electronics information technology, 4.26% in biotechnology, 12.71% in new materials technology and 16.73% in optical-mechatronics technology. The output value of electronics information technology continued to rank the first, which added to the status of the information technology industry.[13] In 2003, Guangdong province ranked the nation's first in terms of high-tech products export. Six cities in the province, namely Guangzhou, Shenzhen, Zhongshan, Huizhou, Fushan and Zhuhai were regarded as National High-tech Industrial Development Zone, of which

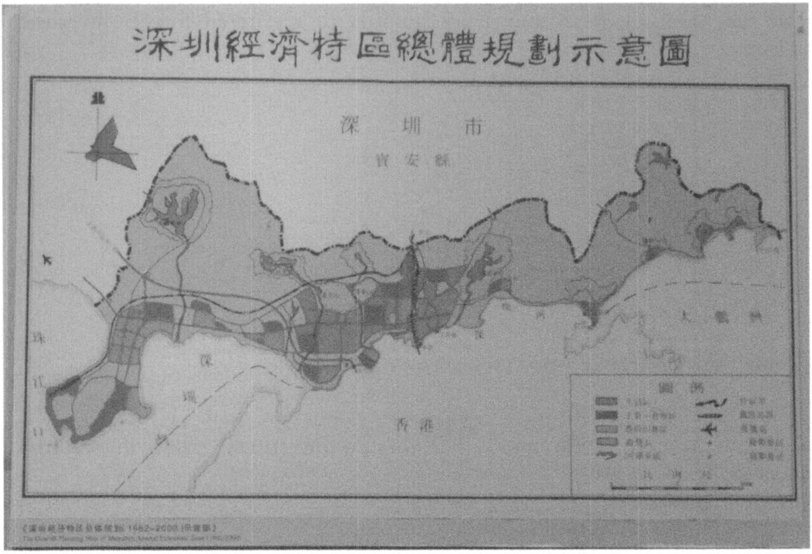

Fig. 3.2 The overall planning map of Shenzhen special economic zone 1982–2000 (*Note* Photo taken by the author at Shenzhen Museum)

Shenzhen toped in total industrial value output with 248.279 billion RMB (Fig. 3.2).

Stage Three: Informational Development and High-Tech Industry

The third development stage started in 2003. Shenzhen Urban Planning Bureau along with the China Urban Planning and Design Institute developed *Shenzhen 2030 Urban Development Strategy* (《深圳*2030* 城市发展策略》) and officially published it in 2007. This strategic and visionary document highlighted Shenzhen's role in technological development and innovations in China. This planning strategy positioned Shenzhen to be the "independent innovation model city," "a national high-tech industrial base," "regional trade center," and "an international city that develops together with Hong Kong." To develop Shenzhen into an international metropolitan city, numerous new transportation and infrastructure projects were constructed following the *Shenzhen 2030 Urban Development Strategy*. On June 1st, 2007, ten years after Hong Kong's return to Chinese Mainland, the Shenzhen Bay Bridge opened to traffic which shortens the time to drive from Hong Kong to Shenzhen. "I do not dare to take my kids out during weekends because shopping malls and restaurants are so crowded, as there are more and more Hong Kongers coming to Shenzhen to spend their weekends," a Shenzhen resident who used to work in Hong Kong vividly depicted the Hong Kong–Shenzhen effect. In addition, Shenzhen developed closer relations with Hong Kong via physical infrastructures and also built several freeways to Guangzhou, Xiamen, and other cities in the Pearl River Delta area to increase its regional connectivity as a nodal city. All the regional development projects happened before the official implementation of the Greater Bay Area initiative in 2019 (detailed below in Stage Four) which clearly demonstrated Shenzhen's regional influence as well as the potential to develop the Greater Bay Area centering around a leading innovation city. Table 3.10 indicates Shenzhen's R&D expenditure in 2005, in comparison to another eight cities in Guangdong province, that are included in the Greater Bay Area initiative. Shenzhen's R&D expenditure and city government's financial funding in science and technology tops in Guangdong province, more than twice that of Guangzhou'. Shenzhen's city commitment to developing its innovation-oriented economy has been consistent.

Table 3.10 R&D expenses and local government's funding on science and technology in major cities in Guangdong in 2005

	Research and development expenditure (100 million yuan)	*GDP percentage %*	*Local government financial funding in science and technology (ten thousand yuan)*
Guangzhou	47.29	0.91	189,887
Shenzhen	124.51	2.51	326,043
Zhuhai	7.19	1.13	20,384
Foshan	30.61	1.28	48,052
Dongguan	8.29	0.38	35,918
Zhongshan	12.04	1.37	22,757
Jiangmen	2.39	0.30	13,743
Huizhou	1.71	0.21	7155
Zhaoqing	1.32	0.29	8634

Note 2005 Statistical Bulletin of Guangdong Province's Science and Technology Funding: http://stats.gd.gov.cn/tjgb/content/post_1430093.html

Shenzhen's electronics and technology industries as well as its export-oriented economy helped with its shift from labor-intensive to innovation-oriented industries, which later became the major growth drivers. Shenzhen's industrial structure came to be dominated by computer, communications, electronics equipment manufacturing, and other high-tech manufacturing industries. The industrial structure extends to the high end of the value chain. Advanced manufacturing and high-tech manufacturing have gradually become the main driving force for the growth of Shenzhen's economy. In 2017, Shenzhen's advanced manufacturing and high-tech manufacturing industries accounted for 69.5% and 64.9% of the added value of the high-tech industrial enterprises. Industrial upgrading is accompanied by increasing numbers of branded high-tech Shenzhen companies. For instance, Da Jiang (DJI), the cutting-edge drone company, ranked 35th by *Fast Company* (2018) in the list of "World's Most Innovative Companies of 2018." Huawei, Tencent and BYD were all created and have grown into leading technology enterprises in Shenzhen mainly because pioneering institutional documents and regulations for private enterprises in technology industries were established during Stage Two, from 1993–2003. (see Chapter 5, Local Governance: Bureaucratic Entrepreneurs) Table 3.11 shows high value industries that emerged in Shenzhen since 2009. Table 3.12 indicates that since 2004, the value of high-tech exports in Shenzhen surpassed that of the imports, and it was gradually increasing which demonstrated that Shenzhen has simultaneously achieved its export-oriented economy as well as its city status as a national high-tech industrial base as planned. Most importantly, R&D expenditure (i.e. the expenditure of enterprises, research institutes and higher education institutions) in Shenzhen during Stage Three has been steadily increasing. Table 3.13 shows the ratio of R&D expenditure to Shenzhen's GDP percentage from 2009 to 2015 with a comparison with R&D expenditure to USA's GDP percentage during the same periods. The figures indicate that, the United States's R&D expenses to its GDP were steady, with an average ratio of 2.7% in almost ten years, while Shenzhen's increased from 3.41% in 2009 to 4.18% in 2015. Though the U.S. GDP was calculated based on dollar value while Shenzhen's was on RMB, the ratio demonstrated the efforts Shenzhen spent on R&D in its local economy.

During the third stage, Shenzhen's innovation competence skyrockets thanks to its large amount of municipal expenditure on R&D. Meanwhile, Shenzhen and its surrounding cities in the Pearl River Delta start

Table 3.11 Added value of emerging industries in Shenzhen from 2009 to 2017

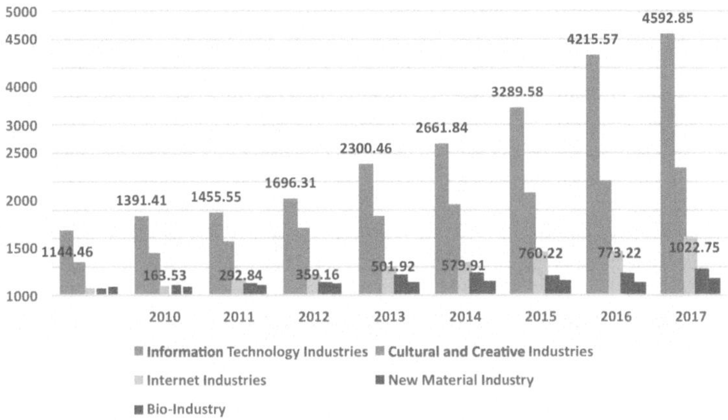

Note Information organized from Shenzhen Statistics Bureau, 2018

Table 3.12 Total imports and exports of Shenzhen high-tech industry from 2003 to 2012 (USD 10,000)

Year	*Total imports and exports of high technology industry*	*Imports*	*Exports*
2003	5,158,146	2,643,846	2,514,300
2004	6,928,262	3,422,565	3,505,697
2005	8,868,653	4,159,435	4,709,218
2006	11,536,580	5,401,421	6,135,159
2007	13,463,800	6,209,300	7,254,500
2008	14,099,495	6,162,273	7,937,222
2009	15,345,520	6,843,409	8,502,111
2010	19,770,075	8,897,407	10,872,668
2011	22,416,000	9,936,000	12,480,000
2012	25,206,532	11,084,532	14,122,000

Note Data from 2013 Shenzhen Statistical Yearbook, Chapter 15 Science and Technology

to display some initial signs of the emergence of a nascent technopole. In *Technopoles of the World: The making of twenty-first century industrial complexes*, Castells and Hall (1994) examined different types of technopoles across the globe. The first kind was considered as the "true

Table 3.13 R&D expenditure of GDP, Shenzhen vs USA from 2009 to 2015 (percentage in GDP in local currency)

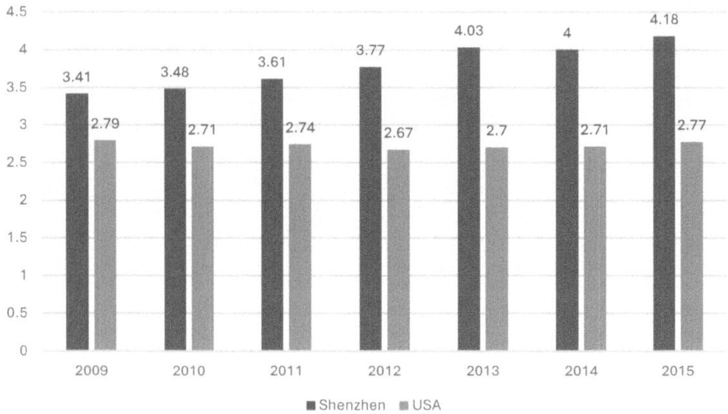

Note Shenzhen R&D data is retrieved from 2016 Shenzhen Statistical Yearbook, Chapter 15. USA R&D data is retrieved from the World Bank Group data: https://data.worldbank.org/indicator/GB.XPD.RSDV.GD.ZS?locations=US

command centers of the new industrial space" (Castells & Hall, 1994, p. 10) which links R&D and manufacturing, such as Silicon Valley. The other similar kind to the first type is those that developed out of old industrial regions, like Boston Route 128, which went through reindustrialization and a process of transformation. The second type was categorized as science cities such as Japan's Tsukuba and Korea's Taedok which focus on scientific research with no direct link to manufacturing. These first two types have links to universities. By contrast, the third type of technopole is built to promote industrial growth, to increase economic productivity, and to generate jobs through the way of attracting high-technology manufacturing firms to a certain place. This certain space enjoys some privileges due to the carefully planned high-technology and business area, as a result of government initiatives (Castells & Hall, 1994). The major goal of the third kind of technopole is to promote economic growth, for instance, Hsinchu in Taiwan, Sophia-Antipolis in France, and Cambridge in England. Shenzhen's developmental trajectory is similar to the third type of technopole, which speaks to the key argument in this chapter that it is critical to understand Shenzhen from its origin as a special economic zone rather than an existing technopole.

The third kind of technopole, closely links industrialization and economic development. Porter (2000) uses the word "clusters" to illustrate locations as a challenge to the conventional way in thinking how companies configure, how institutions operate to generate regional competitive success, and how governments should promote national economic development. As Porter put it:

> Clusters are geographic concentrations of interconnected companies and institutions in a particular field. Clusters encompass an array of linked industries and other entities important to competition. They include, for example, suppliers of specialized inputs such as components, machinery, and services, and providers of specialized infrastructure. Clusters also often extend downstream to channels and customers and laterally to manufacturers of complementary products and to companies in industries related by skills, technologies, or common inputs. (Porter, 2000, p. 15)

The relationship between clusters and innovation demonstrates the fact that "innovation itself" is a geographic process" (Feldman & Florida, 1994, p. 18). By saying innovation is geographic, it means that innovation is organized around geography with local or regional enterprises, organizations, R&D centers, networks of institutions, concentrated knowledge workers and talents, along with capital flow and investment in technologies (Feldman & Florida, 1994). The official launch of the Greater Bay Area initiative in 2019 marks the region's economic capacity, industrial capability and innovative competitiveness: an integration of manufacturing, R&D, and financial services (Fig. 3.3).

Stage Four: Regional Integration—The Greater Bay Area

The Greater Bay Area initiative updates Shenzhen and its surrounding cities' development progress. Geographically, the Greater Bay Area includes nine cities in Guangdong province (Guangzhou, Shenzhen, Zhuhai, Foshan, Huizhou, Dongguan, Zhongshan, Zhaoqing and Jiangmen) and two special administrative regions, Hong Kong and Macao. As described in Stage Three, physical transportations and infrastructures were built to connect cities in Guangdong, Hong Kong and Macao. On February 18th, 2019, the "*Outline Development Plan for the Guangdong – Hong Kong – Macao Greater Bay Area*" (《粤港澳大湾区发展规划纲要》) was officially released. This document provides

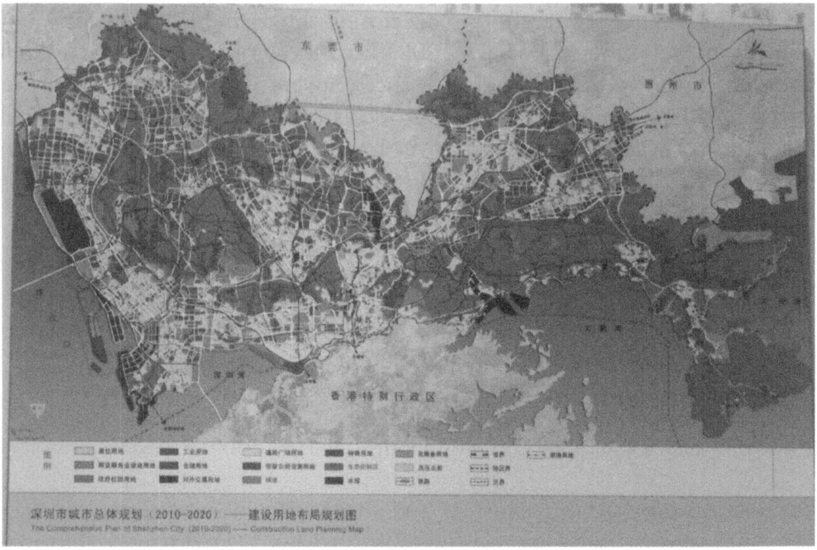

Fig. 3.3 The comprehensive plan of Shenzhen city (2010–2020) (*Note* Photo taken by the author at Shenzhen Museum)

a comprehensive plan for the strategic positioning, development goals, and spatial layout of the Guangdong-Hong Kong-Macao Greater Bay Area, an urban mega-region in the South of China in the Asia–pacific region. In fact, urban mega-regions play a significant role in the global economy (Florida & Ayres, 2008). Castells (1996) noted the significance of megacities as the transformation of urban forms across the globe:

> Mega-cities are the nodes of the global economy, concentrating the directional, productive, and managerial upper functions all over the planet: the control of the media; the real politics of power; and the symbolic capacity to create and diffuse messages. Not all of them (for example, Dacca or Lagos) are dominant centers of the global economy, but they do connect to this global system huge segments of the human population. They also function as magnets for their hinterlands; that is, the whole country or regional area where they are located. Mega-cities cannot be seen only in terms of their size, but as a function of their gravitational power toward major regions of the world. (Castells, 1996, p. 434)

Shenzhen has accumulated its gravitational power and influence especially during its second and third development stages by prioritizing its economy on innovation-oriented high-tech industries. Its strategic geographical location enables its reach to the hinterlands in Chinese Mainland, Hong Kong and Southeast Asia. Shenzhen's political influence on the international stage, has also been amplified due to the U.S.–China tech competition and trade war since 2018. In the *Outline for the Greater Bay Area Initiative*, it emphasizes on city's leading and driving role for collaborations based on physical proximity within the Greater Bay Area, for instance, between Hong Kong-Shenzhen, Guangzhou-Foshan, and Macau-Zhuhai. Each nodal city in the Greater Bay Area is designated a specific role according to its existing competitive advantages, its gravitational power to the peripheral regions and its development potentials with the region. Table 3.14 indicates four major cities' role for regional planning. Clearly, the Greater Bay Area (Shenzhen, Guangzhou, Hong Kong and Macao) is undoubtedly planned to evolve into a world-level innovation-oriented cluster, with four major cities in the Greater Bay Area being positioned to elevate their respective international status.

A key objective for the Greater Bay Area, documented in the "*Outline Development Plan for the Guangdong – Hong Kong – Macao Greater Bay Area*" (《粤港澳大湾区发展规划纲要》[14]) is to optimize its regional innovation environment. To do so, three specific goals are proposed: (1) deepen the reform of regional innovation system; (2) facilitate scientific and technological product commercialization; (3) strengthen the protection and utilization of intellectual property rights. Though the Greater Bay Area is often compared to Silicon Valley, Tokyo Bay Area, and New York Metropolitan Area in China, the formation of each region as well as their functions in respective national economies differ in great deal. Only the Greater Bay Area among the four is the result of government planning to keep up with its regional and national development needs. According to the 2016 & 2024 Shenzhen Statistical Yearbooks, there were no PCT International Patent Applications in Shenzhen from 1999 to 2003. Table 3.15 shows the number of PCT from 2004 to 2019 in Shenzhen alone. Invention patents and PCT skyrocketed since 2004 which not only shows the number of high-tech enterprises in Shenzhen has increased but also indicates that more and more technology enterprises realize the importance of intellectual property and the need for internationalization of their organizational entities and their products. Thus, to achieve continuous high-quality development in science and technology,

Table 3.14 Shenzhen, Guangzhou, Hong Kong, Macao development planning under the Greater Bay Area initiative

	Positioning in the Greater Bay Area
Shenzhen	• Play the leading role as a special economic zone, a national economic center and a leading innovation hub • Accelerate the development as a modern international city and become a world-influential innovation city
Guangzhou	• Lead as a capital city and gateway in Guangdong province • Strengthen its function as an international trade center and a comprehensive transportation hub • Enhance its role as a provincial science, education and cultural center • Build an international metropolis
Hong Kong	• Enhance Hong Kong's status as an international financial, shipping, trade center and an international aviation hub • Strengthen its position of global offshore RMB business hub, its function as an international asset and risk management center • Promote the development of industries, such as finance, trade, logistics, professional services, towards high-end and high-value-added directions • Develop innovation and technology sector, cultivate emerging industries • Build an international legal and dispute resolution service center in the Asia–Pacific region • Create a more competitive international metropolis
Macao	• Build a world-class tourism and leisure center • Build a service platform for China-Portuguese-speaking Countries Business Cooperation to promote economic diversification • Create a cooperation base that promotes multicultural exchanges

Note Information is gathered from Mandarin Chinese document: 《粤港澳大湾区发展规划纲要》, *Outline Development Plan for the Guangdong–Hong Kong–Macao Greater Bay Area:* https://www.gov.cn/zhengce/2019-02/18/content_5366593.htm#1

it is critical to upgrade Shenzhen's service industries such as finance and law, in which Hong Kong is positioned to play a crucial role within the Greater Bay Area.

Qianhai Shenzhen-Hong Kong Modern Service Industry Cooperation Zone (前海深港现代服务业合作区) is a designated demonstration area for strengthening cooperation between Hong Kong and Shenzhen. It is a special zone within Shenzhen special economic zone, which initially was implemented in 2010. When I visited Qian Hai in 2019, many startup founders from Hong Kong registered their businesses there, because they got startup funding from Shenzhen local government. Funding and

Table 3.15 Shenzhen patents filing from 2004 to 2019

Year	*Number of patents certified*	*Invention patents*	*PCT Number of PCT International patent applications*
2004	7737	864	331
2005	8983	917	789
2006	11,494	1361	1661
2007	15,552	2257	2170
2008	18,805	5409	2709
2009	25,894	8132	3800
2010	34,951	9615	5584
2011	39,363	11,826	7933
2012	48,662	13,068	8024
2013	49,756	10,987	10,049
2014	53,687	12,040	11,639
2015	72,150[15]	16,957	13,308
2016	75,043	17,666	19,648
2017	94,250	18,926	20,457
2018	140,202	21,309	18,081
2019	166,609	26,051	17,459

Note Data is retrieved from 2016 Shenzhen Statistical Yearbook, Chapter 15 Science and Technology

supportive startup policies attract young ambitious Hong Kong founders to Qianhai, whereas many of them had difficulties navigating cultural and business differences. Some participated in workshops organized by Shenzhen entrepreneur associations to understand policies and regulations. In the book *Learning from Shenzhen* (O'Donnell et al., 2017), authors noted that Chinese central government has been planning the integration of Shenzhen and Hong Kong into one metropolitan area with the increasingly narrowed economic gaps between the two cities. In their words, Hong Kongers perceive Shenzheners as vulgar cousins not because of their impoverishment and poor financial status, as was the case in the 1980s. Rather, some Hong Kongers gradually developed contempt towards their Shenzhen brothers because of the latter's flaunty materialism. As Eric Orlander, the editor-in-chief of the China—Global South Project noted: The change of Hong Kongers' attitude towards Shenzheners parallels some white Americans' perceptions of affluent Mexicans or Mexican Americans (see Chapter 4, City Culture: Experimental and Entrepreneurial DNA). Indeed, Qianhai's developing journey evolves and reflects many social, cultural and political conflicts and battles between Hong Kong and Shenzhen, which will be discussed in the following chapters of this book from different angles. This chapter focuses on government planning and key development stages of Shenzhen. Qianhai is undoubtedly positioned to bridge entrepreneurial communities from Shenzhen and Hong Kong together, which can be easily seen from various Hong Kong style restaurants in the Qianhai Shenzhen–Hong Kong Youth Innovation and Entrepreneur Hub. Qianhai's development poses some regional integration challenges: It is possible to conduct institutional planning, while it takes unimaginable humane and institutional efforts to implement the actual integration and combination of Shenzhen and Hong Kong's industrial advantages when the social and cultural factors are subtly dynamic.

Conclusion

Returning to the Chinese saying, "Cross the river while feeling the stone," Shenzhen undergoes constant urban planning and changes. The vision to position it as an electronics-based, innovation-led city laid a foundation for its prosperity. Shenzhen has earned many labels: "The World's factory", "Maker's dream city", "The new Silicon Valley." David Li, the co-founder of China's first makerspace declared, "In the old days, if you wanted to be innovative, if you wanted to have the latest technology, you would go to Silicon Valley for electronics. But today, it's Shenzhen.[16]"

This chapter traces back to Shenzhen's urban economic planning as China's first special economic zone, stressing the point that local government planning played a critical role in shaping Shenzhen's industrial direction and development so that Shenzhen could focus on its "electronics focused, innovation oriented" industrialization. This planning is not rigid. As Lan (2024) argued in his book, *How China Works*, it is inevitable that Chinese government including the local ones played a crucial role in China's industrialization process since China's economic reform began as a planned economy. Unlike financial investment, industrial investment is a long-term process that constantly requires adjustment, input and management, which to some extent, requires local government officials' knowledge and vision in investing in certain industries. As figures and tables shown in this chapter, Shenzhen local government's R&D funding and municipal expenditure on science and technology exceeds other cities in Guangdong province in great deal. Global electronics production shift, from Hong Kong and Taiwan to the South of China (see Chapter 7, Shenzhen Grassroots Participatory Innovation) can be viewed as the beginning of information technology industry in Shenzhen and other cities in Guangdong. But large local government investment in R&D in high-tech industries in Shenzhen is seen as government intervention in industrialization and innovation. Can industrialization be managed by the government and can innovation be planned? Despite Shenzhen and China's technological breakthrough on the world stage, global south professionals (i.e., entrepreneurs, policymakers, and academics) still cast doubt on Shenzhen or China's innovation experience as it differs a lot from established theories on the success of western technology centers. What allowed Shenzhen to grow from a "fishing village" to a "tech paradise" that drives entrepreneurship and innovation? In any social phenomenon, lots of factors are complex and changeable which involve many variables such as culture, people, geography, and even luck. What is more, as Lan (2024) noted in his book, "only the final success can justify certain industrial policies, and even in that case, these policies are usually only successful in the eyes of their beneficiaries" (p. 124). Similarly, Shenzhen's present technological success can justify many of its successful industrial plannings and innovation implementations, in the eyes of its benefactors. Critics about special economic zones as well as criticisms of Shenzhen technological innovation cannot underestimate Shenzhen's unprecedented transformation from a special economic zone to a leading global innovation city, with its ever increasingly influential impact on global geopolitics and the technology world. What attracts people from across China to Shenzhen, a city with nothing in the early 80s? What draws entrepreneurs to establish private businesses in Shenzhen? Given Shenzhen's role as a global technological hub, the following chapters explore why and how Shenzhen has realized its city transformation into a vibrant innovative ecosystem today. Chapter 4 unpacks the perplexing investigation by examining Shenzhen's experimental and entrepreneurial culture: No matter how meticulously the economy and innovation is planned in government documents, can Shenzhen win the global innovation race if its people are conventional and risk-averse?

Notes

1. This slogan is first proposed by Yuan Geng when he led the construction and establishment of Shekou Industrial Zone. Information is retrieved from: https://cpc.people.com.cn/BIG5/68742/114021/114023/7282609.html.
2. Information is retrieved from: https://www.worldbank.org/en/country/china.
3. Primary, secondary and tertiary industries represent the different kinds of businesses in a country's economic setup. It is a universal industrial structure classification, but specific classification varies from country to country. In this chapter, 第一产业 primary industry, 第二产业 secondary industry, 第三产业 tertiary industry is categorized as below: (1) Primary industry refers to agriculture, forestry, animal husbandry and fishery, excluding agricultural, forestry, animal husbandry and fishery services in agriculture, forestry, animal husbandry and fishery; (2) Secondary industry refers to mining, manufacturing, production and supply of electricity, gas and water, construction, excluding auxiliary activities in mining, repair of metal products, machinery and equipment in manufacturing; (3) Tertiary industry refers to other industries except the primary and secondary industries. Information can be retrieved from: https://tjj.sz.gov.cn/saved_resource1/saved_resource(1)_xq.html.
4. Information is retrieved from: 《古代深圳简史》, edited by Shenzhen Museum, published in 1997.
5. Information is retrieved from: https://cpc.people.com.cn/BIG5/n1/2018/0419/c87393-29936856.html.
6. Information is retrieved from: https://tjj.sz.gov.cn/zwgk/zfxxgkml/tjsj/tjnj/content/post_3086000.html.
7. Central state-owned enterprise, 央企, is one kind of state-owned enterprises in China.
8. Information is retrieved from: http://politics.people.com.cn/BIG5/n1/2016/0201/c1001-28099323.html.
9. From 《李灏深圳工作文集》, in translation to English,《The Shenzhen Work Collection of Hao Li》, published in 1999 in Mandarin Chinese by Central Party Literature Press, 中央文献出版社。
10. Light industry (轻工业), according to National Bureau of Statistics of China, refers to "the industry that produces consumer goods

and hand tools. It consists of two categories, depending on the materials used: (1) Industries using farm products as raw materials. These are branches of light industry which directly or indirectly use farm products as basic raw materials, including the manufacture of food and beverages, tobacco processing, textile, clothing, fur and leather manufacturing, paper making, printing. (2) Industries using non-farm products as raw materials. These are branches of light industry which use manufactured goods as raw materials, including the manufacture of cultural, educational articles and sports goods, chemicals, synthetic fiber, chemical products for daily use, glass products for daily use, metal products for daily use, hand tools, medical apparatus and instruments, and the manufacture of cultural and clerical machinery."

11. See Chapter Two. Documented in Memoirs of Gu Mu, in Chinese, 《谷牧回忆录》, published in 2009. "杀出一条血路", in translation, "to kill a bloody road" was a popular slogan when economic development just started in China in the early 80s.
12. Li Guo Ding, in Chinese, 李国鼎, was born in Nanjing, China. He went to Cambridge University to study and was the student of Nobel Prize Winner in Physics, Ernest Rutherford. In 1948 after the Civil War, he went to Taiwan as the Nationalist Party and served as one of the committee members in Taiwan Economic Stability Commission. Li, fought against the Japanese invaders to Chinese Mainland during World War II.
13. Information is retrieved from Guangdong Provincial Statistics Bureau, 2004 Guangdong provincial report: http://stats.gd.gov.cn/tjgb/content/post_1430086.html.
14. Original document can be retrieved from: https://www.gov.cn/zhengce/2019-02/18/content_5366593.htm#1.
15. In the 2016 Statistical Yearbook, this figure is 72150. In the 2024 Statistical Yearbook, the figure is 72120.
16. Interview can be retrieved from news article, *A Look Inside Shenzhen's High-Tech Empire:* https://www.forbes.com/sites/wadeshepard/2016/07/14/a-look-inside-shenzhens-high-tech-empire/?sh=6da88b54f361.

CHAPTER 4

City Culture—Experimental and Entrepreneurial DNA

Cities have the capability of providing something for everybody, only because, and only when, they are created by everybody.
—Jane Jacobs, Author of The Death and Life of Great American Cities

Shenzhen Dream

The "Shenzhen Dream", a term I coin in this chapter, dates back to the 1980s when Shenzhen was established as the first special economic zone in China. My fascination and curiosity about Shenzhen traces back to my childhood when I first heard of the word: Xia Hai (下海). It refers to a group of people who quit their "Iron Rice Bowl" (铁饭碗) institutional jobs in protected Chinese government systems. Instead, they went to explore wealth creation business opportunities on their own. "Shenzhen Dream" instills a particular set of values and beliefs associated with economic mobility and entrepreneurial opportunities when the rest of China was operating under its planned economy. Shenzhen presented Chinese people with a vision of success and happiness that was disassociated with familial status but self-adventures and industriousness: China's first special economic zone, market opportunities, vast untouched lands. The idea of "Shenzhen Dream", or to some extent, China's economic dream in the implementation of a Shenzhen experiment in the 80s,

G. Y. Wang, *Dragon Innovation: Shenzhen*, Governing China in the 21st Century, https://doi.org/10.1007/978-981-95-9637-9_4

emphasizes on the significance of its self-realization. People do not seek their dreams elsewhere but in Shenzhen, with their own creations, which highlights the fundamental difference between the success of Shenzhen Dream and the failure of national development ambitions of some colonial states. For instance, anthropologist Benito Vergara (2009) notes a "long discontent" among Filipinos at being forced to seek their fortunes and futures elsewhere. Farm owners in the western United States and Hawaii recruited rural workers from the northern provinces of the Philippines in the 1930s due to the United States Congress's passing of nativist immigration laws which provided Filipinos with legal status to work in the USA (Sallaz, 2019). Sociologist Jeffrey Sallaz defined the *Philippine Dream* in his book, *Lives on the Line: How the Philippines Became the World's Call Center Capital*: "culling together sufficient resources to allow at least one child or dependent to obtain a postsecondary degree and thus a good job, ideally abroad" (Sallaz, 2019, p. 77). Differing from the Philippines state which failed to lift its people out of poverty because of its heavy reliance on external political influence,[1] Shenzhen Dream is built on Chinese state, local developmental state as well as its citizens and civil society. "We earned higher salaries compared to our counterparts in other cities in China," Alex,[2] President of an American non-profit organization, who immigrated to the United States decades ago shared with me about his working experience in a state-owned company in Shenzhen in the early 90s. Shenzhen was the first Chinese city to implement labor and wage reforms, and the salary was attractive across China (Fig. 4.1).

My interviewee, Su,[3] was also one of the young Chinese people in the early 80s who came to Shenzhen and realized his Shenzhen Dream. "I went to college in Zhengzhou, Henan province. I had no idea where Shenzhen was, but I kept seeing propaganda-like posts on the billboards of my college campus," Su recalled, "Pretty much in all the posts, they call for young college graduates to go to Shenzhen for economic development and China's national revitalization." With no professional networking support or familial links to the city where his college was at, in Mandarin Chinese, guan xi (关系), to help him prosper and climb the career ladders in his local area, Su decided to go to Shenzhen with his college degree in architecture and urban design. Guan xi, similar to social capital in the western context, usually refers to connections and relationships among people in society. However, in Chinese context, it often implies preferential treatment given to people in order to gain easy access to limited resources or opportunities (Lee et al., 2001; Wang, 2022). In

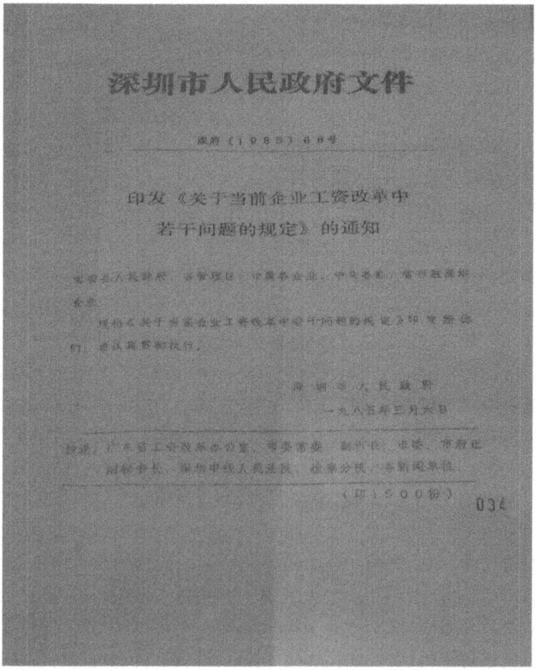

深圳市人民政府文件

印发《关于当前企业工资改革中若干问题的规定》的通知

Fig. 4.1 Shenzhen government document on wage reform in 1985 (*Note* Photo taken by the author at Shenzhen Museum)

the early 90s of Shenzhen, individual ambitions, hard work and skills are valued and awarded more than "guan xi" in the newly opened market-oriented economy in China. Young adventurous Chinese like Su went to pursue their Shenzhen Dream and to explore pioneering opportunities. Their escape from their hometowns and other Chinese cities to Shenzhen reflects a cultural similarity between Shenzhen Dream in China and Silicon Valley adventures in the United States. William Foster, co-founder of Stratus Computer, a company headquartered in Massachusetts, once compared the East Coast (i.e., Route 128 in Cambridge) in the United States with Silicon Valley in the West Coast:

> On the East Coast, everybody's family goes back generations. Roots and stability are far more important out here. If you fail in Silicon Valley, your family won't know and your neighbors won't care. Out here, everybody would be worried. It is hard to face your grandparents after you've failed. (Saxenian, 1994, p. 59)

Shenzhen Dream in China in the early 80s provided Chinese with a possibility of success and (or) failure, without letting both their families and neighbors know, to some extent, which motivated some people to take risks and to explore the unknowns. Standing in front of his calligraphy and Chinese painting exhibition held in a prestigious government villa community in Shenzhen, Su was content with his pursuit of Shenzhen Dream and pleased with his accomplishment. "I even could not afford a hard seat train ticket down to Shenzhen when I first graduated from college. I lived in urban village[4] when I first moved here. The apartments in those villages back then were in even worse conditions than what they look like today. People call it Tie Pi Fang (铁皮房), which is a kind of buildings built with cheap iron sheet and stainless-steel plate." Su started to talk about his life when he first came down to Shenzhen. He met college graduate students from all over China there, who probably heard of the city the same way as he did. Some of those friends returned to their hometowns after years of work, because they could not adjust to the subtropical weather in the humid summer of Shenzhen, or because they wanted to go home to unite with their families. But Su stayed, and has been in Shenzhen ever since, largely due to his adaptability to Shenzhen's climate and the local demand for skilled migrant professionals like him. When he initially arrived at Shenzhen from Zhengzhou, a province located in central China, he got a job working at a local urban planning and architecture institution, a job considered as "Iron Rice Bowl" in the traditional sense. No one loses a job once they are granted an "Iron Rice Bowl" since people are protected by the government system. Talent in urban design and planning were in high demand due to the needs of city infrastructure and urban development (see Chapter 3, China, the New Development). Su's excellent work and industrious attitude attracted attention from a more senior official who told Su that he could make more money if he went to work for a private design firm or started to do private design contracts. Su followed his advice and began taking on private contracts and worked from 7 a.m. to 3 a.m. every day voluntarily. Differing from the often condemned 996 working cultures in China in recent years, Su broke his back to get extra work done out of self-choices. He made ten times more for each outside design project than from his institutional job. "Shenzhen had to collaborate with many inland Chinese cities for raw materials and human resources, so I went on business trips frequently.[5] In the early days, every time I returned to Shenzhen from travelling, I was surprised to see a new building even did not exist before my business departure half a year ago." Su said to me while he was busy showing me a book collection of Shenzhen architecture with his designs in it. His hard work paid off. Within five years, he bought three apartments in the core center district in Shenzhen, each of which was worth about 500,000 RMB (yuan) by the early 1990s.

Different from Su's financial and professional returns on being a urban design practitioner in Shenzhen in the 1990s, Eric Orlander, the editor-in-chief of the China—Global South Project, who first went to Shenzhen in 1991 and commuted from Hong Kong to Shenzhen frequently, was shocked at the burst of buildings in the city, "In 1993, the Chinese built so many buildings in Shenzhen, but no demand was there. A lot of people say that China has this ghost city." Driven by curiosity about China, Eric Orlander went to Beijing in 1989 before he worked and lived in Hong Kong. "I went to Shenzhen in 1993 for the second time after Deng Xiaoping's southern tour, and I even took pictures at where Deng spoke," vivid memories emerged during my interview with Eric in October 2024. In his recall, some westerners in Hong Kong thought there were some dumb, stupid Chinese people who did not know what they were doing by wasting lots of money and resources to build those empty buildings. "At that time, we [the westerners in Hong Kong] still could not see what is happening [in Shenzhen]," Eric added when I asked him if he ever believed Shenzhen could turn into a successful development project and a leading global tech hub.

In the 90s, native Chinese like Su who worked on those "empty buildings" even could not have visioned what Shenzhen would become, let alone people from the outside. During my casual chats with Su, he shared with me that some of his male friends returned to their hometowns instead of staying in Shenzhen in the early days because of the lack of opportunities of finding a partner and getting married. "My wife was my pen pal. She was from a city in the northwest part of China. Somehow, she was curious about Shenzhen and ended up coming." More than thirty years have passed since Su came to Shenzhen. His realization of his Shenzhen Dream not only earns him a reputation as a well-known local designer and artist but also enriches him. Su's professional recognition and accumulation of wealth, in particular through his early purchase of residential properties in Shenzhen, satisfies him, an ordinary Chinese who makes a pleasant life for himself and his families through knowledge and hard work.

More than money attracts people to Shenzhen. Shenzhen took the lead in China in establishing a talent service agency in 1984.[6] It is the only city in Guangdong province that does not require its migrants and city residents to speak Cantonese since most people there are migrants from other Chinese cities who speak Mandarin Chinese.[7] "You do not have to know how to speak Cantonese to live and to work in Shenzhen." A native of Hunan province, Li[8] quit his government job and migrated to Shenzhen with his wife and daughter decades ago. "I do not know how to speak Cantonese, and I still don't know how to. Does it matter? No. However, you probably cannot survive in Guangzhou (the capital city of Guangdong province) if you can't speak Cantonese." The lack of Cantonese language barrier in Shenzhen has equipped migrants with a sense of belonging to a new city and an invisible confidence to work hard to better their own lives which differs from other Chinese metropolitan cities like Beijing, Shanghai and Guangzhou. In those three cities, local residents know immediately if someone is native or not simply by judging their accent or their mastery of local dialect. Li, a top-ranked city government official and an economics professor, came to Shenzhen to pursue his political career in the early 1980s. The first time Li visited the southern coastal city, he was amazed. He had never seen a Chinese city with subtropical green trees on wide and clean streets before. After touring the city, he went back to work in Hunan. "Upon my return, I started to talk to my supervisor regarding my resignation." Li was in a comparatively high position at his job in Hunan provincial government. However, he could not transfer to a parallel government position in Shenzhen. So, he quit his job to come to Shenzhen and started again at an entry level position in Shenzhen city government system. Nobody in his family supported his decision except his wife. "You see that man in the picture? I worked as his secretary when I first moved here at the age of 35." Li pointed at a picture while we were touring Shenzhen History Museum, a place he insisted on taking me to visit because he thought it would be beneficial to my research. Li was proud of his decision to rebuild his career in Shenzhen. He took his new government job seriously, priding himself on his role in the advancement of Shenzhen's economic development success while continuing to be part of it. He kept a foldable bed in his office where he could take naps when necessary. "Do you often work at weekends? Is it paid?" I asked him since Li accepted my interview on a Saturday as he was swamped with his work on weekdays. He laughed at my question and told me that his work at weekends was never paid but he loved to devote himself to his job. "Do you see the land over there? The next financial epicenter of Futian district." Li pointed outside to skyrocketing buildings and trestles surrounding his office building. Futian district, considered as a financial district in Shenzhen, differs from Nanshan district, which is named as "China's high-tech district." At the end of our interview, Li gifted me a book he wrote on Shenzhen's modernization, and ensured me that this city will continue to thrive.

Local government officials like Li embody a sense of competition and advancement spirit shown through their optimism and confidence in Shenzhen and their Shenzhen Dream. The detailed analysis of Shenzhen local government's role in its urban development and technological innovation is presented in "Chapter 5: Local Governance—Bureaucratic Entrepreneurs." Shenzhen's experimental and entrepreneurial city culture explains the reasons for the making of entrepreneurial bureaucrats in the city, especially in the early days. Possibility, prosperity, and fortune all seem reachable there as long as you work hard, which applies not only to people seeking business opportunities, but also to people looking to advance their political careers. In other metropolitan cities in China, people tend to be proud of their local Hukou (household permit, where they were originally born or their household registration). By contrast, people in Shenzhen are more likely to take pride in their achievements. People like Su and Li grew with Shenzhen since the early 90s and they were benefactors of the collective Shenzhen Dream in spite of their personal struggles in the early days. Meanwhile, they inherit Shenzhen city culture from the past to the presence. Su and Li's self-transformation stories in Shenzhen and their devotion to the advancement of its future development, remind me of the words of Wilf Corrigan, founder of LSI Logic: "There are a lot of people who come to work in the morning believing that they work for Silicon Valley."[9] The pursuers of Shenzhen Dream as well as the believers who work for Silicon Valley share their respective collective identities in spite of historical, cultural, social and political differences. Differently, people like Su and Li who went to Shenzhen in the early 80s not to become technological entrepreneurs, nor to invest in technology startups. The earlier generation of Shenzhen Dream chasers differs from entrepreneurs and technology investors who come to Shenzhen nowadays to achieve their financial gains and adventures in the startup world. They, as migrants to Shenzhen, even are different from the current wave of migrants who hold advanced degrees from overseas universities hoping to reside in the first-tier metropolitan Chinese city to continue their international-level lifestyles and fancy careers. People like Su and Li, the previous generation of Shenzhen migrants, arrived at a city with nothing. In a follow-up interview with Su, two years after our in-person conversations tracing back to 2019, I sought after his clarification on his hukou status when he first moved to Shenzhen. He replied back through texts: No one can even imagine what kind of people came to Shenzhen in the early 90s of China. For us, who held "Iron Rice Bowl" in other Chinese cities, we were considered as "gan bu (干部)." We had to give up our gan bu hukou status to obtain a lower socio-economic status "gong ren (工人)" hukou in order to legally stay and work in Shenzhen. Su's first-hand migration experience to Shenzhen reveals the complexity of Chinese hukou system and complements the existing scholarly literature and international media conversations on the study of hukou system which mainly focus on the analysis and examination of rural–urban migrations and agricultural and non-agricultural hukou status. It is interesting to note here that during 2024–2025 when I returned to live in China, I happened to interact with several local Beijing residents who went to Shenzhen in the early 80s and 90s as part of the "Xia Hai" wave. None of them settled down in Shenzhen. Though reasons may vary for personal choices and individual destinies, Su's migration experience reflects Shenzhen's evolutionary and experimental progress in many aspects, as China's first special economic zone. Until July 6th, 1983, the Shenzhen Municipal People's Government issued the "*Notice on Temporary Provisions for the Issuance of the Shenzhen Special Economic Zone Resident Permits and Temporary Residence Permit*,[10]" (《深圳经济特区居民证》and《深圳经济特区暂住证》) which enabled early Shenzhen migrants to start to have legal city identity and resident rights. It is quite possible that, back in the 80s and 90s, those local Beijing residents mentioned above viewed "Beijing Hukou" much superior to temporary Shenzhen residence permits. Thus, early Shenzhen Dreamers like Su, moved from any urban Chinese city to Shenzhen with the lowering of their hukou status essentially represent Shenzhen DNA: experimental and entrepreneurial. They are Shenzhen dreamers, but more importantly, they are city builders. The relationship they had with the city was symbiotic: They built and realized their personal dreams in Shenzhen, at the same time, Shenzhen grew and prospered on those citizens' individual transformations. The inspiring stories of my interviewees made me wonder: How does Shenzhen's city culture make people feel this way? Does Shenzhen city culture remain the same from forty years ago till now?

From Past to Present: Possibility, Prosperity and Success

It was a humid summer night in Shenzhen in 2019. The air was damp, and I was adjusting to the moist subtropical summer weather sitting outside a trendy tea shop whose Chinese name intentionally reflects an exotic Japanese linguistic association to romanticize the tea as an elevated lifestyle experience. My interviewee, Zhang, insisted on taking me to this tea shop. This desire to share was typical of Chinese hospitality, but also showed that she was eager to introduce me to as many of the cosmopolitan aspects of life in Shenzhen as possible. As we began our conversation, she said that this particular tea shop was founded in Shenzhen in 2015 to promote and revive a tea culture that originated in China long ago. Tea became a popular drink for social occasions in Tang dynasty (618–907 CE), one of China's most brilliant and prosperous dynasties in history.[11] The founder, a migrant professional, and her husband believe that there is a need for high-end tea shop targeting young professionals, in particular well-off young women between 20–35 years old who are willing to treat themselves well in a metropolitan Chinese city like Shenzhen. Zhang notes that people call this tea shop "new style tea", and describes how buying and drinking tea has become a sort of lifestyle experience modeled after the luxury consumption models of western style coffee shops.[12] "Influenced by western culture, Created in China" seems to be a dominant mindset among people in Shenzhen, and they take pride in their unique variations of established consumer trends.

It was about 8:30 p.m. on a summer night which was relatively early for Shenzhen residents. We ordered tea and sat outside watching people walk by. Most of them seemed to be young city dwellers or migrant professionals who just got off work in the nearby business district, others had just finished dinner in the mall. "It is normal that people leave their work around 8 p.m. to 8:30 p.m. every day," she said. "Yes, I can feel that people in Shenzhen, regardless of their socio-economic status and educational backgrounds, work very hard compared to people in most other Chinese cities." I acknowledged that her insight helped me understand this city. Zhang's hometown is Hunan, a landlocked province in south-central China not far from Shenzhen. I encountered and interviewed many migrants who came from Hunan province to settle down in Shenzhen in spite of their generational gaps. Geographical proximity between

Shenzhen and Hunan is one key enabler for massive inter-regional migration. Zhang went to college in her province. "I worked in Shanghai at an advertising firm right after college, however, I didn't stay there long enough since the rent near my company in the city center of Shanghai was too expensive on my meager salary as a new college graduate," she shared with me.

Because Zhang did not think she was able to make a living while chasing after her dreams in media, marketing, and advertising industries in Shanghai, she moved to Shenzhen in 2015. When asked to compare rental prices in these two cities, Zhang told me a term that immediately caught my attention: Cheng Zhong Cun (城中村). This is a term for urban villages[13] in Shenzhen. There are five major inner villages in Shenzhen: Bai Shi Zhou, Gui Miao Xin Cun, Nan Shan Cun, Shang Xia Sha and Huang Gang Cun. These five villages all are located in the core business and commercial districts in Shenzhen which makes living in those areas convenient and desirable. More importantly, since all the buildings in Cheng Zhong Cun are comparatively old and shabby, with occasional crime related dangers, the rent in Cheng Zhong Cun, is cheaper. Cheng Zhong Cun is a priority housing option for migrant workers and even migrant white-collar professionals who come to Shenzhen to find work and pursue their dreams. "I think there are more possibilities for me to work and to live in Shenzhen rather than in Shanghai," Zhang added. The belief that there were more opportunities and possibilities in Shenzhen was consistently emphasized in my fieldwork interviews with engineers, technocrats, taxi drivers, small business owners and entrepreneurs. Zhang also noted that one of her relatives from a rural area in her hometown Hunan province made his fortune from scratch by selling electronics components at Hua Qiang Bei electronics market almost ten years ago. Her relative never graduated from college but worked hard in sales and then established his own telecommunications equipment trading company. He got married, had kids, and bought two apartments in Shenzhen by the time he was 35. Zhang's emphasis on her relative's lack of a college degree showed that she was confident that she could do better in this city than her relative did as she was working on her master's degree in business and finance from the Shenzhen campus of Peking University. "You know, it is much easier for me to achieve the 'first-tier, metropolitan city' dream in Shenzhen than in Shanghai or Beijing.[14] Once I establish in Shenzhen, my kids will no longer worry about their 'first-tier, metropolitan city' dream when they grow up." We talked for more than two hours outside the tea shop. When she departed from the Metro, I noticed we were at the Bai Shi Zhou metro stop. I smiled goodbye and marked down Bai Shi Zhou in my cell phone, one of the urban villages she had mentioned.

I had conducted research fieldwork in Shenzhen more than four times when I interviewed Zhang. She was the first person who mentioned the cheap rent at Cheng Zhong Cun in Shenzhen though my other interviewee Su briefly mentioned his staying in urban village almost thirty years ago. Later, I found that many of my interviewees who made their fame or fortune had once lived in Cheng Zhong Cun as I started to ask them if they had ever lived there when they first came to Shenzhen to chase after their dreams. Reluctance to voluntarily bring up Cheng Zhong Cun among some migrants who later become extraordinary figures is unknown, however, no one denied their memory of living there when asked. I interpret this as a collective memory of the Shenzhen Dream. If Cheng Zhong Cun is a major reason that enables migrant workers and migrant white-collar professionals to move to Shenzhen, to stay and work in the city due to its low rent and physical proximity to city centers, what does it look like? I decided to visit Bai Shi Zhou, the same urban village that Zhang lived in. Bai Shi Zhou is said to be the biggest urban village in Shenzhen. It is in a desirable location in Nanshan district, "China's high-tech district." People describe Bai Shi Zhou as "the Africa of Shenzhen" while depicting the outer and peripheral area of Bai Shi Zhou, the high-tech concentrated business district and Shenzhen's OCT as "the Europe of Shenzhen." Stereotypical perception of Africa as an underdeveloped and poor region among many Chinese makes Bai Shi Zhou earn the name "the Africa of Shenzhen." In contrast, Shenzhen OCT, *Overseas Chinese Town*, was an electronics manufacturing base before it was turned into a local art and creative design center. Bai Shi Zhou was under massive demolition when I visited in the summer of 2019, and the destruction was widespread. I was told by local residents that Bai Shi Zhou enjoys a prime location, and its land has been planned for commercial usage and residential housing development for many years. The tensions between local government and the land's indigenous owners still exist, though I was not sure if it was the main reason that celebrated Shenzhen migrants were unwilling to mention "Cheng Zhong Cun" voluntarily. Besides, one local informant told me that there were some "mistresses" in urban villages bordering Hong Kong. It is a phenomenon that is secretly prevalent among some working-class Hong Kong men who frequent Shenzhen which reveals the complexity of urban villages in the social and cultural aspects. Interestingly, my local guide added during our Cheng Zhong Cun walk: "But, you know, time has changed." He was reluctant to elaborate on the exact meanings of change, but my conversations with other interviewees clearly indicated many Shenzhen residents' attitudes towards Hong Kong nowadays: Shenzhen's rising economic power and its technological innovation opportunities have changed many people's impressions of Hong Kong as an international trade center and a land of opportunity. In Bai Shi Zhou, construction trucks parked in between residential buildings. Logos and banners such as "舍小家为大家", in free translation to English, "sacrifice your own happiness and interests to achieve collective social advancement and development" are prevalent. Despite Bai Shi Zhou's destruction for new urban development, people were still living and doing businesses in grocery stores everywhere. In a news stand, a young woman named Xiao Xiao, a graduate of nearby Shenzhen University in Nanshan district had rented an apartment in Bai Shi Zhou for nearly two years since her college graduation. She worked at an internet company near her place which provided her with cheap rent and saved her from time-consuming daily commutes.[15] Cheng Zhong Cun is still accommodating many migrant workers and young white-collar professionals in the city even though Shenzhen has evolved into a global metropolitan city and a technology innovation hub in more than forty years.

Walking around Bai Shi Zhou, I saw rental ads on billboards and understood how cheap the rent was. In the center of the urban village, rental ads for studios, one bedroom one bathroom, two bedrooms one bathroom and three bedrooms one bathroom abounded. Price ranges roughly from 800 to 1000 RMB for studios, 1500 RMB to 2000 RMB for one bedroom one bathroom, depending on the property arrangement and condition. I saw rental ads on billboards with prices that would be equivalent to finding a one-bedroom apartment in Silicon Valley for less than $300 a month. However, the cheap rent comes with a trade-off. There is almost no sunlight or privacy in the rooms. Building walls are thin and tenants share limited communal space. David Da Wei Wang, in his book on Cheng Zhong Cun, observed that the appearance of urban villages is a result of the social, cultural, and economic diversity of migrants, both rural migrant workers and migrant white collars with college degrees. The crammed apartment buildings in urban villages offer countless units of rooms as the cheapest accommodation options that people could find (Wang, 2016). In Du's book (2020), she quoted a social media comment from someone who lived in Bai Shi Zhou for three months on arrival at Shenzhen: "It stirs my memory every time I go past the village, of those days that I was fresh to the city and struggled without thinking too much. For those who live outside Bai Shi Zhou, looking at the villages is a kind of satisfaction; But for those who live inside Bai Shi Zhou, looking out is a goal" (Du, 2020, p. 269, Kindle Version). Zhang, the interviewee who took me to the popular new style tea shop, was like this. Perhaps she felt embarrassed to tell me that she has lived in Bai Shi Zhou, since getting out of Bai Shi Zhou means possibility, opportunity, prosperity, and success to anyone who holds a Shenzhen Dream. The distance between "the Africa of Shenzhen" and "the Europe of Shenzhen" is not merely physical, but a gap between realities and dreams that are built on possibilities: the probability to succeed or the likelihood of failure. No migrant arrives at a new city with the belief of self-failure having left behind their families, friends, familiar surroundings, and established networks. Those migrants are open to risk-taking, opportunities, and experimentation (Figs. 4.2 and 4.3).

Migrant Culture and Individual Ambition

Migrants move for a variety of reasons, but they sometimes share similar traits: seek freedom, entrepreneurial and risk-taking. "For a better life" usually is the reason that motivates domestic migrants to leave for a new city or attracts foreigners to emigrate to a new country. Though "a better life" is subject to personal perceptions and standards, the U.S.—born scholar Richard Florida noted in his book, *Cities and the Creative Class* (2005) that talented people are drawn to places that have thick labor markets, culturally open and tolerant. The adventurous and welcoming culture in Shenzhen, particularly in its early days, opens doors for Chinese people who want to explore their futures for a superior, different yet unknown life, just as Silicon Valley attracts entrepreneurial spirits from across the globe. Richard Florida (2005) created the Composite Diversity Index, which is a sum of the Gay Index, the Bohemian Index and the Foreign-born Index to measure the connection between cultural tolerance and U.S. metropolitan areas' economic growth and high-tech success, with a theoretical conclusion that social and cultural diversity lowers barriers to human capital entry, attracts talents and ultimately stimulates technological growth. However, Shenzhen's uniqueness, as

Fig. 4.2 Rental ads billboard picture in Bai Shi Zhou, Shenzhen (*Note* Photo taken by the author)

a long-standing Chinese migrant city, challenges this western standard on the measure of diversity since the three key indicators in the above Composite Index fail to explain the Shenzhen migrant case.

In Jane Jacobs's book (1961), *The Death and Life of Great American Cities*, she argued that great cities are places that attract people from diverse backgrounds to turn their energy and ideas into wealth and innovations. Diversity of hope, possibilities, options and opportunities regardless of gender, socio-economic class, educational backgrounds, seem to be the main driving forces behind the pursuit of Shenzhen Dream. Back in the early 80s, there is a popular slogan in Shenzhen that: If a man wants to get married, he should look for Shenzhen Kai Da factory girls (娶女就娶凯达妹). "Kai Da" (凯达)is one of the first toy factories invested by Hong Kong businesspeople in Shenzhen. "Kai Da factory girls" represent money-making, hardworking, independence, and modernity. Take Zhou Qunfei, a self-made successful businesswoman for

Fig. 4.3 Residential buildings in Bai Shi Zhou (*Note* Photo taken by the author)

example. Ranked No. 3 in Hurun Global Female Rich List in 2020, also named as the 20th Most Outstanding Businesswoman by Forbes China,[16] she is the CEO at Lens Technology, a one-stop integrated manufacturing solutions provider established in Shenzhen in 1993 whose clients include Apple, Samsung and Huawei. In spite of her humble beginnings in Shenzhen as a factory girl from rural Hunan province, Zhou Qunfei went to night school for classes while working at a watch glass processing factory in the daytime. In sociologist Ching Kwan Lee's book *Gender and the South China Miracle* published in 1998, she interviewed young women from rural villages of China who went to Shenzhen or other cities in the South of China. Quite different from the conventional wisdom that those female migrant factory workers came to the city for economic opportunities, a lot of them admitted that they wanted to write their own destinies. It is true that many of them sent their earnings back to their families to ease the burdens in the left-behind rural areas, more importantly, Lee discovered that those women came to work in the factories to avoid being agricultural labors at home but also to escape their families' plan for their lives, usually made by their fathers and brothers in a patriarchal society (Lee, 1998). One of Lee's interviewees, Chi-Ying, noted that money is not the top priority for her to leave the village for factories. In fact, she paid back the young man, whom her parents chose for her marriage. She feels young, modern, and free in the city (Lee, 1998; Rivoli, 2005). Factory women (or factory girls in some circumstances) in Shenzhen or nearby cities, for instance, Dongguan, were documented both by scholars and by journalists. Similar to Ching Kwan Lee's description of young migrant female workers with entrepreneurial ambitions in 1998, former WSJ journalist Leslie Chang observed that the lives of factory girls are taken up by computer, English, and business classes (Chang, 2008). The New Yorker writer, Peter Hessler, also noted in his article published in 2001 *Boomtown Girl* that one of his former students, Ma Li, from Sichuan province, left her hometown and went to work in a jewelry factory in Shenzhen. In Ma Li's own words, she said: "Teaching is a good job for woman, and it is easy to find a husband, because men like to have teachers as their wives. It could have been a very comfortable life. But, if it is too comfortable, I think it's like death."[17] Peter Hessler paid a visit to Ma Li in Shenzhen to learn about how a 24-year-old migrant factory girl was doing in a city. He found that Ma Li had fallen in love and broken factory's curfew. She also stood up to her boss. But she was still doing fine.

Shenzhen, as a representative migrant Chinese city, enjoys its unique culture in addition to how a city makes rural migrants feel free, modern and young, as described above. This city continues to embrace its culture of openness, open-mindedness, and tolerance to attract diverse human capital, a key component of a city or region's capacity to not only attract but to keep developing the high-tech industries (Florida, 2005). "I feel less like an outsider in Shenzhen," said my interviewee who spoke highly of Shenzhen's welcoming city culture. Emily[18] graduated from a prestigious university in Beijing and then went to the London School of Economics and Political Science to pursue her master's degree. After finishing her studies in London, she earned another master's degree at Stanford and a doctoral degree at other renowned university in the West Coast of the United States. With her impressive educational background, Emily could easily have gone to Beijing or Shanghai to work, but instead, she chose Shenzhen. Emily told me that she would feel a bit isolated in Beijing as a non-native Beijinger, even absent the quota of Beijing hukou assigned to employers each year. The hukou quota system in China is similar to the permanent residence system in the United States. Hukou system created in Chinese Mainland in the late 1950s was originally designed to restrict rural–urban internal migration and to preserve social stability in China. Hukou system still remains as a barrier for social stability and protection in some metropolitan Chinese cities where it is hard for migrant workers and migrant professionals to obtain legal status to further gain access to public resources in spite of personal wealth, for instance, good-ranking public schools. Only residents with local household permits are eligible to purchase properties, to enjoy municipal healthcare benefits and to send their children to local public schools. Employers like corporates, universities, government agencies, have limited assigned quota for household permit applications every year. Some of my informants shared with me that the ownership of wealth does not necessarily contribute to the obtainment of a hukou in Beijing which is a reason many wealthy parents send their children to overseas high schools since they lack access to good local public schools in first-tier Chinese metropolitan cities. Compared to Beijing and Shanghai, it is relatively easy for non-residents to apply for Shenzhen household permit thanks to its welcoming culture and talent attraction policy (see Chapter 9, Human Capital and National Competitiveness). More realistically, Shenzhen has placed fewer limitations on property purchases, for instance, according to *2025 Shenzhen Real Estate Policy* (深圳房地产新政实施), for non-Shenzhen hukou residents, they are qualified to purchase residential property in Shenzhen as long as they have one-year individual tax proof,[19] compared to five-year tax evidence in Beijing.[20]

Open Window: East and West

"Once you come to Shenzhen, you are a Shenzhener" (来了就是深圳人), is a slogan Shenzhen uses to position its city culture and to attract human capital. When I first arrived at Shenzhen Bao'an airport many years ago, a banner with this city slogan was everywhere. The welcoming city culture helps attract talent and ideologically shapes people to be ready to fight for their own lives and futures from nothing. According to 2020's World Population Review, the development and advancement of high-technology, financial services, and cultural industries all contributed to Shenzhen's population growth since its establishment as a special economic zone four decades ago.[21] Shenzhen was voted as China's most dynamic city and the city most favored by migrant workers in 2014. It was selected as one of the top ten cities in China for expatriates. Expatriates choose it as a place to work and settle because of the job opportunities and Shenzhen's cultural tolerance and open-mindedness. UNESCO's report on *10 Things to Know about Shenzhen* (2009) named it as China's largest migrant city with the youngest population, with an average age of 30.8. With an estimated 1/6th of China's graduating doctoral students in Shenzhen, many of the young people that move to the city can be characterized as well-educated. Since 1980s, Shenzhen local government officials have sought to cultivate a special city culture that is welcoming to migrant workers and migrant professionals with different provincial and cultural backgrounds. The China Urban Vitality Research Report (2017–2019),[22] ranked Shenzhen as the top city in China in terms of its attractiveness. The adjacent city, Guangzhou, has been ranked in second for three consecutive years from 2017–2019. Table 4.1 shows Shenzhen's attractiveness index figure from 2017 to 2019, as compared to Beijing, Shanghai and Guangzhou. Table 4.1 indicated that Shenzhen's population attractiveness index increased from 9.925 in 2017 to 10.109 in 2019 while the index figure of Shanghai's did not exceed 8 for three years. Table 4.2 shows that Shenzhen also ranked No. 1 among all cities in China in youth population attractiveness. The top three youth population[23] attractive cities, Shenzhen, Guangzhou, and Dongguan are all located in Pearl River Delta, Guangdong province, where the Greater Bay high-tech and financial circle is planned for the next stage of China's technological and economic development. The unique city characteristics forged in Shenzhen, *Admire creativity, Encourage diversity, and Be tolerant of failure*, continue to play an important role in attracting talent and workers. Mandarin speaking in Shenzhen is a frequently mentioned key reason why people choose to work in Shenzhen instead of in other cities in Guangdong where residents are required to master Cantonese. "It is not like I cannot learn Cantonese. There is a cost and benefit analysis. If I can find an awesome job in Shenzhen where I enjoy absolute living convenience with no language barrier, why do I want to waste my time learning a dialect to just work and live there?" An employee at a major Shenzhen technology company noted. She moved from her hometown Hunan province to Shenzhen instead of nearby city Guangzhou after college. She stressed that Shenzhen's reliance on

Mandarin speaking without knowledge of Cantonese was a key reason in her decision to move there. Shenzhen Population and Growth Rate, in Table 4.3, shows that its population has grown dramatically since 1980, peaking in 1990 at 35.28% and continuing to grow in the time since. In fact, according to China's Seventh National Population Census conducted in 2020, Shenzhen's resident population has reached more than 17 million, outgrowing the projected number of 13 million city population by the end of 2030. Table 4.4 shows the breakdown of Shenzhen's demographic landscape in terms of age range, of which 79.53% of its resident population lies in the age range 15–59. In comparison, city resident population percentage of 15–59 in Beijing, Shanghai, and Guangzhou accounts for 68.5%,[24] 66.85%,[25] and 74.72%[26] respectively, while the national average is 63.35%.[27] These figures demonstrate that Shenzhen has skyrocketed its population and grown into an urban city with a hyperscale population from a ghost empty city with nothing, as described in earlier paragraphs. Most importantly, the Seventh National Population Census highlights Shenzhen's characteristics in comparison to other well-known metropolitan cities in China, the density of labor force in the working age group. Those are critical statistics since they demonstrate Shenzhen's continuous potential to grow its innovation to drive economic growth with a pool of appropriate labor force.

Table 4.1 2017–2019 Shenzhen, Guangzhou, Beijing, and Shanghai's city population attractiveness ranking

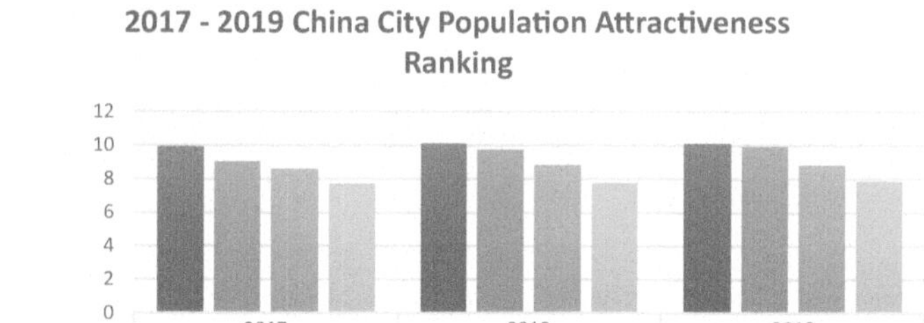

	2017	2018	2019
Shenzhen	9.925	10.102	10.109
Guangzhou	9.022	9.739	9.913
Beijing	8.582	8.821	8.816
Shanghai	7.713	7.779	7.857

Note Chart information is organized from 2017–2019 China Urban Vitality Research Report, 百度中国城市活力研究报告

Table 4.2 2019 China's top five cities ranking in youth population attractiveness

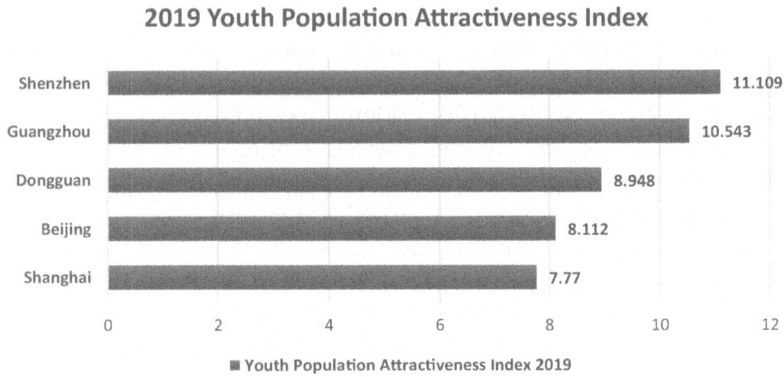

Note 2019 China Urban Vitality Research Report, 2019 中国城市活力研究报告

Table 4.3 Shenzhen population and its growth rate from 1975 to 2020, five year as an interval

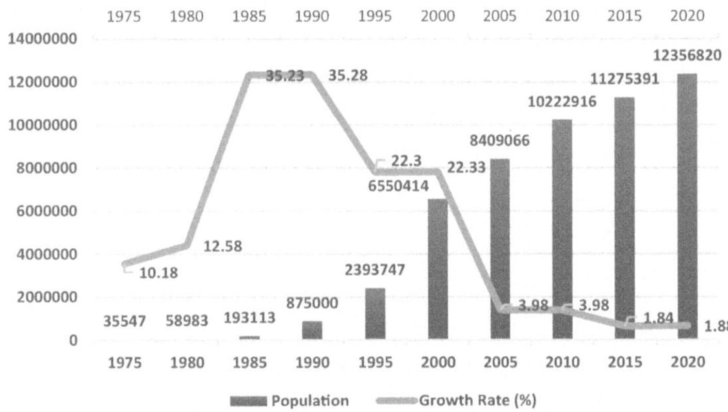

Note Shenzhen's population in the table is calculated based on urban area
Source World Population Review: Shenzhen

The influence of Hong Kong and western cultures contributes to the openness of Shenzhen through its geographical location. Eric Orlander, the editor-in-chief of the China-Global South Project, who had been going back and forth between Hong Kong and Shenzhen in the 90s once

Table 4.4 The seventh national population census—Shenzhen resident population age breakdown, 2020

Age	*Population number*	*Percentage*
Totality	17,560,061	100
0–14 age	2,653,381	15.11
15–59 age	13,965,964	79.53
60 and above	940,716	5.36
65 and above	565,217	3.22

Note Information is organized from Shenzhen Statistics Bureau

shared his comparative impression of these two cities. "Going to Shenzhen felt like going to China," though Shenzhen left different yet exotic impressions on many Chinese from other cities in the early days including my grandfather (see Chapter 1, China Innovation Path), "everybody [westerners] felt more comfortable with Hong Kong because Shenzhen was not that modern yet. It did not have all the conveniences, the movie theaters, the restaurants, the cafes, the community and international sports." In the early 1990s, Shenzhen and Guangzhou, were usually the first few cities in China to get pop music and western films through Hong Kong. The exchange and convergence of eastern and western cultures further led Shenzhen into a culture of openness and tolerance though it initially lacked cultural facilities that amused westerners. In fact, the famous American fast-food restaurant McDonald opened up its first 500-seat store in Shenzhen in the October of 1990, as its commercial entry to the Chinese Mainland market. At that time, McDonald's signature Big Mac hamburger was not affordable to most Chinese though McDonald is usually considered as cheap fast food in the United States. It is said that in the early 90s, the monthly salary of Chinese urban residents in major cities was 120 RMB (yuan) to 130 RMB (yuan) (about $17.54), while a Big Mac alone costed 10 RMB (yuan). In spite of the exorbitant price of a McDonald hamburger, many Chinese still flocked to the store to enjoy the cheeseburgers, French fries and milk shake. The success of the first McDonald shop in Shenzhen invoked its expansion to the rest of China since 1990. It is difficult to conclude that it was Shenzhen's welcoming and open city culture that contributed to the first McDonald outlet's success; however, what is certain is that the average annual salary of employees in Shenzhen was far more than the national average which enabled workers and residents in Shenzhen to consume at

McDonald at that time. According to Shenzhen Statistics Bureau, Shenzhen workers' annual salary was 4304 RMB (yuan) on average and their monthly salary was 359 RMB (yuan)[28] compared to a 1510 RMB (yuan) national average in China back in 1990.[29] As noted by Yunxiang Yan in his articles on McDonald, the American fast-food restaurant represents a form of liberation from hierarchical constraints and Chinese customers did not go to McDonald's for food, but for American experience and the taste of modernity (Yan, 2006). Deborah Davis also argued in her edited volume, *The Consumer Revolution in Urban China*, "Eating a Big Mac will not bring down a dictator, but it can send a million daily messages that old ways have changed" (Davis, 2000, p. 22). In the case of Shenzhen city culture, it is hard to determine if it is the Big Mac that has changed "old ways" or "traditional mindsets" of those young Chinese who migrated to Shenzhen to explore their futures. In *Making Capitalism in China* (1998), Hsing emphasized on South China's long tradition in foreign trade which attracted people from the southern provinces to seek opportunities in nearby Asian countries, especially in Southeast Asia. Adventurous spirits thrive in South China. In "Chapter 2, The Genesis of Shenzhen," some early descriptions of commercial activities in Xin'an county which included both Shenzhen and Hong Kong are depicted. The culture of openness, open-mindedness, tolerance, and diversity influenced how Shenzhen grew from its beginning, with its city government officials playing a unique role in fostering its culture since Shenzhen bureaucrats themselves embodied a sense of entrepreneurship and adventurous spirit no matter if they chose to come to Shenzhen or were dispatched to work there when Shenzhen became the first special economic zone.

This chapter examines Shenzhen city culture and highlights how migrant and welcoming culture plays an essential role in the formation of its city spirit. The analysis begins with Shenzhen Dream and further delves into Shenzhen's diverse and open culture. In retrospect, Shenzhen's tolerant culture is the reason why migrants hold a Shenzhen Dream, particularly in the early days: free of judgement, lack of traditional Chinese constraints and societal bureaucracy, as well as its relative freedom to fight for one's own destiny. Shenzhen's diversity as a typical Chinese migrant city, challenges western standards on the measurement of regional diversity, since racial and national diversity are not accounted in the Shenzhen case, especially when the Open and Reform policy was initially implemented. It is important to note that though Shenzhen is similar to Silicon Valley to the extent that migrants (or immigrants) account for its major regional demographics, this cultural analysis does not reflect the entrepreneurial culture as well as its technological innovation ecosystem in Shenzhen (see Chapter 6, The Entrepreneurial Ecosystem). A thorough understanding of Shenzhen's experimental and entrepreneurial DNA is conducive to other regions and countries that try to inspire its citizens for development and innovation. "Chapter 5, Local Governance: Bureaucratic Entrepreneurs" will reveal how city cultural characteristics impact Shenzhen local government officials and further examine the significance of local governance and the roles Shenzhen city and district government officials play in its development to reflect institutional and political impact on Shenzhen's development and innovation.

Notes

1. Before liberation, Philippines was colonized by Spain and then the United States.
2. Alex is a pseudonym.
3. Su is a pseudonym.
4. The "urban village" mentioned here is referred to Cheng Zhong Cun (城中村) in the later paragraphs.
5. "Shenzhen - Inland collaboration model" is documented in the Chapter 5: Local Governance: Bureaucratic Entrepreneurs.
6. 1984年，深圳市人才服务公司成立。In 1984, Shenzhen Talent Service Company was established. Information is retrieved from: https://www.szdag.gov.cn/dawh/tqssn/content/post_927051.html.
7. Cantonese is a dialect that is mostly spoken among native residents and speakers of Southeastern China, Hong Kong, Macau as well as overseas early Chinese immigrants. In Chinese Mainland, Cantonese is the dominant language in the province of Guangdong (广东) and its neighboring area, Guangxi (广西).
8. Li is a pseudonym.
9. Article titled, Silicon Valley May Have Lost its Way, is retrieved from: https://www.nytimes.com/1992/09/28/business/silicon-valley-may-have-lost-its-way.html.
10. Information is retrieved from: https://www.sz.gov.cn/szstory/202302/content/post_10432750.html.

11. A comprehensive book on tea is written by Lu Yu (陆羽), an author from Tang dynasty. The name of the book, 茶经, was first translated into *All About Tea* by William Harrison Ukers (1873–1945).
12. Nayuki, 奈雪的茶, founded in 2015 by a millennial couple and is headquartered in Shenzhen, Guangdong province.
13. Urban villages, or villages within the city, is a unique existence during China's urbanization. Farmlands were formerly owned and cultivated by the villages and then turned into urban land for development by the government.
14. Beijing, Shanghai, Guangzhou and Shenzhen, jointly called 北上广深 in Mandarin Chinese, are first tier cities in Chinese Mainland.
15. Information from news article, 深圳白石洲拆迁背后. Retrieved from: https://new.qq.com/omn/20190927/20190927A0361P00.html.
16. Information is retrieved from: https://www.hunanmingren.com/details/17.html.
17. Retrieved from The New Yorker, *Boomtown Girl* by Peter Hessler: https://www.newyorker.com/magazine/2001/05/28/boomtown-girl.
18. Emily is a pseudonym. After roughly about two years after Emily's stay in Shenzhen, she pursued a research fellow position in Beijing. The reasons she left for Beijing were not explained, but the quality of university in Shenzhen might contribute to her departure. She has been looking for university jobs mainly in Beijing and Shanghai when I had the chance to talk to her for the last time.
19. Information is retrieved from: http://bsy.sz.bendibao.com/bsyDetail/623733.html.
20. Information is retrieved from: https://zjw.beijing.gov.cn/bjjs/xxgk/ztzl/bjgfzn/gfzgsq/index.shtml.
21. World Population Review, Shenzhen city: https://worldpopulationreview.com/cities/china/shenzhen.
22. China Urban Vitality Research Report is released annually since 2017 by Baidu.
23. The age of the young population, defined by China Urban Vitality Research Report, is from 18–34.
24. Information is retrieved from: https://tjj.beijing.gov.cn/zt/bjsdqcqgrkpc/qrpbjjd/202105/t20210519_2392982.html.
25. Information is retrieved from: https://tjj.sh.gov.cn/7renpu/index.html.

26. Information is retrieved from: https://www.gz.gov.cn/zwgk/sjfb/tjgb/content/post_7286231.html.
27. Information is retrieved from: https://www.gov.cn/guoqing/2021-05/13/content_5606149.htm.
28. Information is retrieved from: http://sz.bendibao.com/szsi/2008227/si62700.htm.
29. Information is retrieved from: http://www.gov.cn/jrzg/2013-11/06/content_2522445.htm.

CHAPTER 5

Local Governance: Bureaucratic Entrepreneurs

Shenzhen City and District Government Officials

Eliminating institutional elements that hinder innovation is more important than technology realization itself.

—Zhou Luming[1]

Without government creating a good city environment, enterprises cannot develop and prosper.

—Li Zibin, former Shenzhen mayor[2]

Local Government Officials: Bureaucratic Entrepreneurs

Efficacious and operative government work in Shenzhen plays a significant role in building a welcoming, business-friendly city environment that can better advance technological innovation and entrepreneurship. Experimental and entrepreneurial culture in Shenzhen (see Chapter 4, City Culture—Experimental and Entrepreneurial DNA) influences how local bureaucrats work, while local government officials play a critical role in encouraging and supporting Shenzhen's culture of technological innovation. At a Shenzhen academic event, the opening ceremony speech was made by a city government official in charge of the education division in

G. Y. Wang, *Dragon Innovation: Shenzhen*, Governing China in the 21st Century, https://doi.org/10.1007/978-981-95-9637-9_5

Nanshan district, Shenzhen's high-tech district. Lu[3] was one of my interviewees, and she invited me to catch up over dinner, where she introduced me to a professor and a businessman in the creative technology industry. Earlier that day, she had met with a German-Chinese professor and scientist interested in establishing a research lab in her district to facilitate advanced technology development in collaboration with the Shenzhen local government. She asked for my assessment of the potential success of such a collaboration. Later, she invited me to local government meetings on science and research development, hoping to get my international perspectives to help her understand Shenzhen's education and innovation in a broader context.

In the dedication to her work, her enthusiasm in attracting top scientific research teams, and her understanding of the key elements for building a world-class technology innovation hub, Lu is typical among Shenzhen local government officials. Yet Shenzhen city leaders seem ahead of officials in other regions and cities in China. Another city official in charge of Shenzhen's science and innovation division observed: "I think my cultural awareness, along with the knowledge and understanding of the global economy and technological development, exceeds many of my counterparts in some developed countries." He further made a critical comment based on his trips to the United States and Europe for trainings and high-tech innovation seminars: "Their [western government officials] mindsets are western-focused and do not know about other developmental models." This government official spoke highly of Deng Xiaoping, the so-called economic master of China's Open and Reform policy. He regarded Deng as a brilliant politician who had the foresight to plan China's modernization at a particular historical moment and who designed an appropriate path for the country's economic development. Deng Xiaoping, who put an end to the argument about capitalism and socialism in the early 80s, remarked that it does not matter if a cat is black or white, as long as it can catch mice, it is a good cat (see Chapter 2, The Genesis of Shenzhen). Chinese economist, Keyu Jin (2023), argued in her book, *The China Playbook*, that "the idea that a market economy could be compatible not only with capitalism but also with socialism was a breakthrough that set the nation on a course of economic liberalization (Jin, 2023, p. 6)." In fact, as Jin argued that China's economic model, a special blend of the state and the market economy, does not fit into any existing economic category. So is China's development model, as the Shenzhen city government official commented above. Indeed, Shenzhen, as China's first special economic zone, demonstrates a unique governance structure which contains political centralization and local autonomy in China's developmental path. In spite of the fact that there are many new "Silicon Valley" springing out in China nowadays, Shenzhen, as a national pilot program since 1979, has pioneered in various aspects in private enterprises, institutional innovations and technological regulations. Chinese scholar, Lan Xiaohuan (2021) wrote in this book, *How China Works*, that the relationship between Chinese central and local government has been documented and studied extensively in Chinese history and politics. Maintaining a unified strong country needs central leadership, meanwhile, China's vast geography and cultural scale and diversity require the daily business of administration and governance at the local level. Though Keyu Jin argued that "mayor economy" symbolizes the unique interactions among central government, local officials and Chinese entrepreneurs, Shenzhen case, as documented detailedly in this chapter, indicates how local government officials act as bureaucratic entrepreneurs to complement its nascent institutions and immature regulations at the beginning of its economic development and in the process of the ongoing technological innovation (Fig. 5.1).

Province	**Provincial Level**
Municipality	
Autonomous Region	
Special Administrative Region	
Prefecture-Level City	
District	**County Level**
County-Level City	
County	
Town	**Township Level**
Township	
Subdistrict	

Fig. 5.1 Administrative divisions of the people's republic of China (*Note* Statistical table of administrative divisions of the people's republic of China. http://xzqh.mca.gov.cn/statistics/2020.html)

My impression of Shenzhen city government officials differed from the stereotypical view of Chinese bureaucrats as dull, rigid, impersonal, and authoritative. Entrepreneurial local officials had been assets in Shenzhen's rapid economic development and technological innovation since the 1980s. During my fieldwork, local officials generously provided historical stories and updates on current development policy, but they also sought my answers to their questions. They wanted to know how to develop and advance Shenzhen as a world-class technological innovation hub. They asked me about building technology centers and looked for my feedback regarding how Shenzhen can improve its ability to attract world-class talent globally. They were eager to learn external perspectives, and in that way, they differed from some other regional bureaucrats I happened to interact with in China. One of my informants told me that the spirit of Shenzhen city government officials is reflected in the flat-topped city hall building: Abandon conventional hierarchical ideology and serve the people. He further asked me if I thought Shenzhen city leaders are service-oriented.

My experience of this unique researcher and bureaucrat interaction called to mind You-Tien Hsing's (1998) fieldwork in South China investigating the shoe industry and foreign trade in Pearl River Delta in Guangdong. Local officials offered researchers information while also looking to secure business opportunities and collaborations through researchers' overseas connections. This kind of interaction was especially noticeable when access to outside information and business opportunities was not easily obtained as it is today. Hsing described the local bureaucrats in South China as different from stereotypical socialist bureaucrats. They acted as entrepreneurs in the newly opened Chinese economy in the early 1990s. The economic decentralization policies provided local government officials with economic autonomy and authority over their own city's development. In Evans' book (1995), *Embedded Autonomy*, he emphasized "autonomy" by arguing that state officials need some of the critical aspects of Weberian bureaucracy to insulate them from outside pressures. At the same time, these government officials must be engaged with the networks that link entrepreneurs, technologists, and capital. Entrepreneurial Guangdong officials followed the mantra "Move quickly when the green light is on; move slowly when the yellow light is on; find a detour when the red light is on" (Hsing, 1998, p. 119).[4] Examples of bureaucratic entrepreneurs are abundant in Shenzhen. One corporate group that started in 1992 as a pharmaceutical company grew into a group of more than ten companies involved with the pharmaceutical, printing, food processing, electronics, hotel, and apparel industries. Its chairperson, a local party secretary with a military background, relied on *The Art of War* (孙子兵法) to run his business with the idea that the marketplace is like a battlefield. He approached business like fighting a war.[5]

"Shenzhen government is highly efficient," said a Chinese tech investor based in Silicon Valley. Government efficiency has a significant impact on entrepreneurs' business adventures and experiences. Entrepreneurs do not want to waste their time on business registration. They want to seize the opportunity to enter the market as fast as they can. On August 1st, 2013, the Shenzhen city government implemented a fully online process for business registration, which improved efficiency greatly. An enterprise can complete its business registration online in one day.[6] In comparison, Shanghai has not enabled a complete online business registration until 2021, partially because of Covid-19 lockdown.

Business efficiency in Shenzhen is supported by local government officials, whose management attributes can be credited to executive training and constant learning. Government officials who pursue effective policies need to grasp the capacity to think independently about the technologies and related aspects that enable the realization of technological innovation. "Different from government delegates from other cities or provinces in China, Shenzhen city government delegates are more concerned about learning and arming themselves with knowledge when they are here. They tell us specific topics that they are interested in such as artificial intelligence and advanced manufacturing," said a project manager in charge of senior executive government training programs with the city government at a Tier One U.S. research university in California. "We ask them to evaluate our courses at the end of the training. They really made serious comments on their satisfaction or dissatisfaction with the course contents." This one-month executive training program is expensive, but Shenzhen government employees were regularly sent to the training that they were a major revenue source for this university department. For more than a decade, a senior executive government training program with Shenzhen city government took place at this university before escalating U.S.—China tension scuttled it.[7] (see Chapter 11, Research Note, Emerging Sensitive Research, *A Non-western Female Perspective*).

Shenzhen city officials embrace an entrepreneurial spirit and learn pragmatic management styles. A CEO at a bio-tech startup, who is a native

Chinese woman and a John Hopkins finance graduate, praised Shenzhen city government officials' tolerance for risks and their welcoming attitude toward new technology and fresh ideas. "They are supportive and reliable," she shared with me. Bureaucratic entrepreneurs' willingness to embrace new knowledge is consistent with Deng Xiaoping's 1978 speech at the Third Plenary Session of the 11th Central Committee: "We must learn to manage the economy following economic and scientific methods. If we do not understand it, we should learn from people who know it and learn from advanced foreign management methods" (see Chapter 2, The Genesis of Shenzhen).

Shenzhen local government officials constantly learn new knowledge, advanced scientific management styles, and more importantly, they put theories into practice and their governmental services. A Brazilian doctoral graduate who found one job in Shenzhen and one job in Zhejiang province after his graduation in China in 2024 not only praised Shenzhen government's working efficiency, but also applauded Shenzhen government's autonomy in issuing work permits for foreign citizens. In his description, he had to return to his home country Brazil while he was waiting for the completion of a work permit in China if he took the job offer in Zhejiang. Nonetheless, he did not need to return to Brazil while waiting for his work permit if he took the Shenzhen job offer. He ended up with the job in Shenzhen since it only took local government three weeks to finalize his work permit, whereas, it cost him three months to have received the work permit from that Zhejiang sponsoring employer.

Institutional capacity matters in both macro and micro governmental management. "I think China operates in a unique sense that the bureaucrats, the people in power actually work for the people." Muhammad Nidhal, a policy researcher at the Center for Indonesian Policy Studies said to me during our interview in July 2025 when I questioned him if he thought China's economic success and technological breakthroughs are attributed to its authoritarian regime, as many western media and academics criticized. "It is the institutional capacity that China has, but other countries, many of them in the global south, do not have," Muhammad further commented that he read in Indonesian media outlets and other published texts that many high level leaders in Chinese central government have years of working experience in rural and remote areas in China, which, in his view, is beneficial for politicians to understand developmental problems in local contexts. The frustration over impossibility for central government leaders to understand local developmental struggles as well as the misalignment between central and local government has been brought up several times during my conversations with policymakers, and academics especially from the global south. Like many policy researchers and practitioners in the global south countries, Muhammad is amazed at China's unique state capacity to pilot a policy or a program at the regional level before implementing it at the national level. "Well, Shenzhen, the first special economic zone, a leading global tech hub nowadays, is exactly what you described as a pilot program over forty years ago." I told Muhammad, who has been working on regulatory sandboxes in the digital sectors in Indonesia. He expressed the necessity and need for Indonesian policymakers to come to China to learn how to design sophisticated national policy after successfully piloting programs at the regional level.

Institutional Pioneer—From 1979 till Now

Shenzhen is the pioneer of China's private economy. Local bureaucratic entrepreneurs are also bureaucratic venture capitalists, to the extent that, they must bear and accept the uncertainties when formulating new enterprises and science & technology government policies, and also deciding if they should continue to support the implementation of certain policies and measures when they are outdated. Consistent with the municipal urban development planning strategy, the city government instructed and guided the Shenzhen Science and Technology Development Center (深圳市科技发展中心) to organize, coordinate, direct, and manage scientific and technical personnel to establish private scientific and technological enterprises. In addition to Shenzhen Science and Technology Center, under its governing structure, Shenzhen Technology Transfer Advisory and Review Committee was founded in 1986, whose major members included government officials, local enterprise management and technical personnel. Committee members with a technical background played a critical role in this consultancy as the official document indicated that: Technology import projects that are deemed technically unfeasible concluded by the Advisory and Review Committee shall not be approved by all levels of departments in principle.[8] In 1987, the Shenzhen city government issued *The Interim Provisions of the Shenzhen City Government on Encouraging Scientific and Technological Personnel to Establish*

Private Technology Enterprises ("Shenzhen Technology Enterprise Identity Card"), known as the "1987 Document," which made Shenzhen the first Chinese city allow private technology enterprises to be established. Private technology companies were allowed to obtain mortgages, secure loans from national banks, and apply for loans from foreign banks if approved by the Shenzhen city government. Companies were allowed to absorb shares of state-owned enterprises and collective enterprises under mutual agreements. They were also permitted to absorb shares of foreign-related enterprises and to raise funding from overseas investors. In addition to capital, intangible property such as patents and technical skills were counted as shares and not limited by the number of employees. Private scientific and technological enterprises were permitted to exercise their management rights independently; meanwhile, they enjoyed the same corporate rights as other types of companies, including state-owned and collective ones. To encourage the establishment of private scientific and technological enterprises, the taxation department allowed for the reduction or exemption of corporate income tax for one to three years depending on a company's operations.[9] Along with the "1987 Document," flexible and experimental taxation initiated and approved by Shenzhen local government officials laid a solid foundation in the early 1980s for Shenzhen's development as China's first special economic zone (Fig. 5.2).

In 1998, the Shenzhen city government issued *Notice of Shenzhen Municipal People's Government on Issuing Several Regulations on Further Supporting the Development of High-Tech Industries*,[10] namely "22 lists." It calls for governmental support for high-tech industries such as information technology, biotechnology, and new material science. Specific measures were implemented mainly via increased local government budget spending in science and technology, corporate tax reduction, hukou allocation for technical talents and free land use transfer fee for high-tech companies. Simplified travel application procedures to Hong Kong and overseas for personnel in high-tech enterprises and those working on related high-tech projects were also included in the implementations, to maximize regional information and technology exchange (see Chapter 3, China, The New Development). This document not only laid a foundation for the development of high-tech industry in Shenzhen but also it served as an exemplar for other cities in China, including Beijing and Shanghai to explore high-tech industry development path.

Fig. 5.2 Shenzhen takes the lead in China's modern enterprise system (*Note* Photo taken by the author at Shenzhen Museum)

In 1999, the Shenzhen city government issued a revision of the 1998 document.[11] Known as the "1999 Revision," this document addressed Shenzhen's weakness in developing high-tech industries, particularly with respect to talent and resources. To make up for the shortages of local colleges and universities, Shenzhen government groundbreakingly proposed to establish Shenzhen Virtual University (深圳虚拟大学园) back in 1999 to facilitate effective university—industrial collaborations (see Chapter 8, Shenzhen R&D Ecosystem). More importantly, the "1999 Revision" proposed to hire domestic and foreign experts to constitute Shenzhen's science and technology advisory committee (深圳市科技顾问委员会):

> To promote the industrialization of Shenzhen's high-tech achievements, to effectively and rationally allocate government resources, and to enhance the effectiveness of industry-oriented government decision-making, the

> city government hires well-known domestic and foreign experts in science and technology, economics, finance, management, and law to enrich the Shenzhen Science and Technology Advisory Committee. The funding of the Science and Technology Advisory Committee will be arranged under a special municipal financial division. The advisory committee plays a role in the evaluation, consultation, and the formulation of Shenzhen's high-tech industry development planning and major high-tech investment activities.[12]

The stress of hiring foreign experts in the Shenzhen Science and Technology Advisory Committee is consistent with Shenzhen's urban development Stage Two, from 1993–2003, "open window to the international world." As noted in "Chapter 3, China, the New Development," Shenzhen local government constantly revises its city development objectives to adapt to the municipal development needs as well as the external business environment. One outcome of this high-tech private enterprise initiative was to attract technical talent, drawn to Shenzhen to realize their entrepreneurial dreams. For example, Deng Qinghui, a senior engineer at a state-owned television factory in nearby Jiangxi province, came to Shenzhen in 1987 to establish a television research manufacturing company. He started a business with more than five people, which he was not allowed to do in his hometown where was still operating under the planned economy like most of the rest of China in the early 1980s to 1990s. In an interview in *Shenzhen Stories*, a documentary aired on the CCTV network, Deng said, "I heard on a business trip to Shenzhen that technical people could establish their own private tech enterprise. I was too excited to fall asleep that night and gathered in a hotel with other engineers to discuss our possibilities."[13] Young and ambitious, Deng made his own way in the quasi–market economy. In less than one year, the color televisions manufactured by Deng's company were exported overseas, and he became a successful technology businessman.

Wang Chuanfu, founder and CEO of BYD (Build Your Dream) Automobile and BYD Electronics, shares a similar story. After working as a government chemistry researcher in Beijing, Wang came to Shenzhen, which was said to be the best place for tech innovation and entrepreneurship in China because of the market economy experiment and advanced telecommunications infrastructure. Armed with a dream of entrepreneurship and his expertise, he quit his Iron Rice Bowl government job in Beijing and went to Shenzhen to establish a battery manufacturing company in 1995, when he was not yet 30 years old. With no familial connections or powerful relatives, Wang believed that he would be able to realize his engineering dream through entrepreneurship and business in Shenzhen.[14] BYD became the world's largest manufacturer of hybrid and electric vehicles, and it has surpassed Tesla to become the world's largest producer of pure electric cars.[15]

In addition to attracting tech entrepreneurs like Deng Qinghui and Wang Chuanfu to Shenzhen, the "1987 Document" "1998 Document" and "1999 Revision" also provided people who were struggling financially with opportunities to get out of financial obstacles by establishing private enterprises. Ren Zhengfei, CEO and founder of Huawei, was one of them. Ren came to work at Shenzhen Nanyou Holdings Ltd. in 1982. Five years later, at the age of 43, Ren started Huawei telecommunications company, which sold phone switches, to repay his debts. Unlike hackers or tech entrepreneurs in the west who are driven to pursue their technology and entrepreneurship dreams through creativity and innovation, Ren repeatedly mentioned in public interviews regarding his personal struggles to pay off his debts when he started Huawei. Later, after he resolved his financial struggles, he and his founding team aimed to use their technology research and development patriotically, to build China's own telecommunications equipment.[16] Ren's dream has come true in Shenzhen. Since Huawei's founding in 1987, it has grown into a leading global provider of information and communications technology infrastructure and smart devices (see Chapter 8, Shenzhen R&D Ecosystem).

Enterprise, Market and Government

The institutional support created by Shenzhen city government allowed people with technical skills, business acumen, and entrepreneurial aspirations to start private enterprises when the rest of China was operating under a planned economic system. Shenzhen's market economic experiments boosted the local economy and industrial modernization. Between 1994 and 1999, the city's total industrial output value increased from 72.3 billion RMB to 202.6 billion RMB, the fourth highest among cities in China. The value of high-tech product output rose from 14.6 billion RMB to 81.9 billion RMB, an increase of 4.6 times, with an annual growth rate of 42.6%. The value of high-tech exports increased from $990 million to $5.19 billion.[17] Since the establishment of the Shenzhen special economic zone and the beginning of Shenzhen's industrialization, the city government had a clear vision of the path toward economic development direction and its guiding principle: ***Enterprises as the main body, market as the basis, and government as the backing support***. The emphasis on enterprise and the de-emphasis of government interference shaped Shenzhen's image as an entrepreneur's paradise in China. China Ping An Group[18] and Skyworth Group,[19] both founded in 1988, and the Kingdee International Software Group, established in 1993,[20] are all products of the groundbreaking institutional documents that paved the way for innovation and development. These companies developed into national brands in their respective fields and have, until today, continually contribute to the technological innovation and development in Shenzhen and China.

Shenzhen local government progresses with these private enterprises founded in this entrepreneurial city, albeit technology ones or not. Table 5.1 shows industrial enterprises in Shenzhen classified by its registration in 2009, and a total of 3795 are private enterprises, followed by companies funded by businesspeople from Hong Kong, Macau and Taiwan. In recent years, Shenzhen continues to lead in economic reforms and institutional innovations in China with regard to private economy and technological innovations that suit its regional development needs, while setting national regulatory exemplar. China's Private Sector Promotion Law, the first fundamental law dedicated to promoting the private

Table 5.1 2009 industrial enterprises in Shenzhen grouped by registration

Registration type	*Number of registered enterprises*
内资企业 Domestic investment Enterprise	4440
国有企业 State-owned	47
集体企业 collective-owned	40
私营企业 Private enterprises	3759
港澳台投资企业 Funded by entrepreneurs from Hong Kong, Macao and Taiwan	2949
外商投资企业 Foreign funded	1024

Note Information retrieved from: https://tjj.sz.gov.cn/zwgk/zfxxgkml/tjsj/tjnj/content/post_3086000.html

economy was passed on April 30th, 2025 and came into effect on May 20th, 2025. The law aims to optimize business environment for the private sector and promote the growth of China's private economy and private entrepreneurs. Two years before 2025, in early 2023, the Shenzhen government introduced several measures to promote the expansion, improvement, and strengthening of its local private economy by setting up a national pilot demonstration to advance comprehensive reforms. Shenzhen's pilot policy measures introduced in 2023《关于促进民营经济做大做优做强的若干措施》[21] set a foundation for *China's Private Economy Promotion Law*, encouraging domestic private enterprises to participate in national science and innovation projects, to take the lead in establishing industries that match with the international standards and trends, as well as to expand in the overseas market by shaping a market-oriented international business environment governed by a sound legal framework. Shenzhen's measures, in essence, show that the city is actively playing its role as China's first special economic zone and accelerating China's economic transformation and upgrading of private enterprises to achieve high-quality national development.

Besides Shenzhen's private economy regulations in 2023, on November 1st, 2020, *Regulations of Shenzhen Special Economic Zone on Science, Technology and Innovation* (《深圳经济特区科技创新条例》[22] is officially implemented. The 2020 regulation highlights the importance of strengthening the cooperation in scientific and technological innovation between Shenzhen and Hong Kong in the backdrop of the development of a world-class innovation cluster, the Guangdong—Hong Kong—Macao Greater Bay Area. Many initiatives are the national first to continue Shenzhen's innovative competitiveness. For instance, if the ownership of scientific and technological achievements is granted to the individual or team that completes the achievement, the individual or team can agree to joint ownership or shared ownership. If shared ownership is agreed upon, the share held by the individual or team must be no less than seventy percent. In this way, scientific researchers and technical personnel are incentivized to commercialize their laboratory discoveries. Besides scientific product commercialization, this regulation supports the establishment of nonprofit intellectual property service platforms in Shenzhen to provide higher education institutions, research institutes and enterprises with intellectual property information, training, consulting and assessment which reflects the demand for standardization that match the international levels as Shenzhen pioneers its innovation path in China.

> Without the Hi-Tech Fair in Shenzhen, there would be no Tencent today.
> —Pony Ma Huateng, CEO of Tencent

> To promote economic and technological cooperation between China and other countries in the world, the Chinese government has decided to hold the China International Hi-Tech Fair every year in Shenzhen.
> —Zhu Rongji, former Premier of China

Platform Government Officials: Matchmakers

Shenzhen local government officials act as bureaucratic entrepreneurs, experimental risk-taking venture capitalists, institutional innovators, and most importantly, they are resourceful adventurers who are people in action. In Shenzhen in the early 1990s, it was hard for tech entrepreneurs who lacked funding and capital early on to launch their enterprises. Startups in high-tech industry are risky. Return on investment is uncertain. It is difficult to research and develop technological products without strong financial backing. Pony Ma Huateng, CEO of Tencent, the most highly valued internet company in China, attributed his company's survival to the first China Hi-Tech Fair, held in Shenzhen in 1999. In an in-person interview with Ma in 2019, he emphasized the important role Hong Kong played in attracting international capital to Shenzhen; he also noted that city government's efforts to hold the 1999 China Hi-Tech Fair were important in bridging capital, enterprises, and talents:

> Most of the internet companies were in Beijing at that time, so were venture capital firms and private equity companies. There was no advantage in launching and operating internet startups in Shenzhen. There were only a few internet-related companies here. No venture capital firms came to Shenzhen so it was difficult for small businesses to get access to capital.

On the edge of his company's failure, Pony Ma Huateng and his team searched for funding opportunities at the 1999 Hi-Tech Fair. Fortunately, the little penguin (Tencent's logo) attracted the attention and interest of IDG Ventures China (the Hong Kong office of the U.S. - based venture investor International Data Group) and PCCW, a Hong Kong–based information communication technology corporation. Tencent received

$2.2 million in initial venture capital funding and then $4.0 million in follow-up funding from both IDG and PCCW.

Ma and his founding team described the money as Jiu Ming Qian 救命钱 ("lifesaving money") and repeatedly emphasized the significance of the 1999 Hi-Tech Fair in Tencent's history and success: "The Hi-Tech Fair helped make Shenzhen known to the outside world as a city developing in the direction of high-tech and innovation." Ma described the "matchmaking" role that this fair played, providing tech entrepreneurs like Ma with access to capital. In addition, the exhibition facilitated information exchange among technology enterprises, researchers, and venture capital firms despite the physical location constraints. "Because of the Hi-Tech Fair, they [venture capital firms] started to pay more attention to Shenzhen. This event made it much easier for us to get in touch with them," said Ma.

Over a decade has passed since Tencent received its venture capital investment. By 2019, China was the second-largest global venture capital market, as calculated by capital invested in 2018,[23] but venture capital came to the Hi-Tech Fair before many people in China had even heard about the concept. *Guangzhou Daily*'s news report during the exhibition on October 7th, 1999, commented on what venture capitalism meant.[24] Interestingly, in my interview with him, Tencent's CEO Pony Ma Huateng shared that he and his cofounders had never heard of the concept "venture capital" before they secured the funding from IDG Ventures China and PCCW. Tencent's Chinese corporate biography, 《腾讯传》, documented how this tech giant decided to turn to venture capitalism after the failure of selling their company. Liqing Zeng, one of Tencent's founding partners, suggested to the founding team members that they should talk to a different group of people regarding fundraising. That "different group of people" is exactly those who initially invested in Tencent, the venture capitalists who bet on the future.

Responsive to the market and quickly adaptative to local enterprises' needs, the city government during the second Hi-Tech Fair in 2000 issued regulations on venture capital investment in Shenzhen's high-tech industries, China's first official government regulation on capital investment.[25] This regulation on venture capital investment ensured a healthy high-tech developing market; it also enhanced the variety of funding resources to boost industry dynamics. In addition to venture capital investment, industrial information and technical knowledge were important. Therefore, the Shenzhen Hi-Tech Fair organizing committee invited domestic and international scientists, economists, and financial experts to give speeches and present seminars from the fair's early days. Patrick Joseph McGovern, IDG's founder, recalled that some people once laughed at his craziness to invest in China, though he knew there was something the others did not understand about China in its media, technology business. Besides the win on Tencent, IDG bought Chinese search engine Baidu in \$2 per share before selling it \$100 a share.[26]

Shenzhen - Inland Collaboration Model

The 1999 Hi-Tech Fair was a milestone in Shenzhen's technological innovation development. The city government tried diligently to gain support from the central government in Beijing. With Beijing's approval of the fair, Shenzhen was able to market itself to attract business, foreign investment, venture capital, and entrepreneurs. Consistent with the Shenzhen Urban Development Strategy, the city government followed the *electronics-based, innovation-led industries* as local economic direction (see Chapter 3, China, the New Development). More than 31 cities and provinces sent local government delegates and enterprises to Shenzhen. A total of 2856 enterprise exhibitors, 4150 high-tech related exhibition projects, 955 capital investors, 5 foreign government delegates, 32 major high-tech multinational companies, and 22 universities from Chinese Mainland, Hong Kong, Macau, and Taiwan participated in 1999. The value of investment and transactions were reported to reach billion dollars.[27] Foreign technology transfer deals were made during the event. Reportedly, Jiangsu Provincial Government Investment Bureau signed an agreement with an American telecommunications company worth \$150 million to introduce telecommunications engineering projects to Jiangsu Province.

Since 1999, Shenzhen has hosted the annual high-tech industry event to create a bridge between capital, entrepreneurs, governments, universities, and other agents in the exchange of knowledge and information and the building of technological innovation networks in Shenzhen and China. For instance, the city government formalized the high-tech talent collaborative training program with Wuhan University during the second Hi-Tech Fair in 2000, with each entity aiming to help the other deepen technology research and development: Wuhan University provided Shenzhen city and local enterprises with scientific and engineering talent and with intellectual properties, while companies in Shenzhen offered technology spillovers and products manufacturing.[28] Andrew Schrank and Josh Whitford (2011) wrote that most new technologies develop as a result of collaborations, first among different groups of scientists and engineers working in different organizations (Block & Keller, 2009) and then among different firms to bring the product to market. The *Shenzhen - inland collaboration model* I summarize in my words has promoted Shenzhen's technological development and innovation, building on the respective advantages of Shenzhen and other cities or provinces. At the start, this collaborative approach made up for Shenzhen's lack of research-focused scientific talent while the city actively looked for the best and the most suitable technological development path for itself. Shenzhen's realization of its corporate scientific research and development also relied on the shift of global electronics manufacturing networks from Taiwan and Hong Kong due to the industry shift in the 1990s (see Chapter 7, Shenzhen Grassroots Participatory Innovation: Let the People Make). For instance, the executive chairman of Taipei Electrical Appliance Trade Union said at one Hi-Tech Fair that high-tech entrepreneurs from Taiwan would not simply relocate low-level electronics manufacturing to Chinese Mainland while maintaining advanced scientific research and development at home. Taiwan technology entrepreneurs wanted to explore new development models to benefit both sides. Of all Chinese cities, Shenzhen most interested Taiwan entrepreneurs because of its openness and proximity to Hong Kong (Fig. 5.3).[29]

Connect with the Global Markets

As the popularity of the Hi-Tech Fair increased, it became an effective platform for encouraging and boosting high-tech industry development locally and worldwide. It consequently started to serve two purposes for the local government and Chinese corporations: to establish business connections with domestic and international players and to attract global business to China. For instance, the 2011 fair theme was "Promote International Innovation Cooperation, Accelerate the Development Transformation." Subconferences in Israel and Hungary preceded the fair's official opening in Shenzhen in October. The overseas subconferences gave Chinese companies an opportunity to travel outside China to expand their foreign markets and to seek potential talent and business

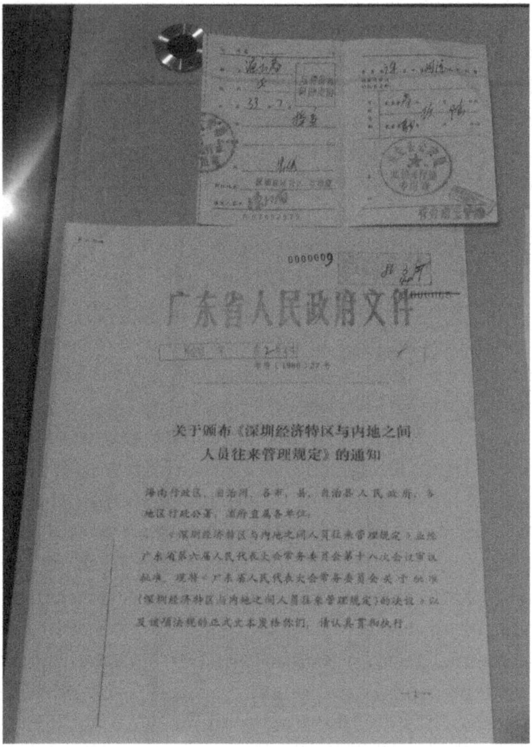

Fig. 5.3 Guangdong government official document: Regulations on personnel exchanges between the Shenzhen special economic zone and the rest of Chinese Mainland (*Note* Photo taken by the author at Shenzhen Museum)

collaborations, like foreign investment or the establishment of Sino-foreign joint ventures. For example, subconferences held in Austria in 2005, Spain in 2007 and 2014, Belgium in 2008 and 2014, Finland in 2008 and 2016, and Germany in 2009 and 2017 facilitated government-level collaborations and strengthened the relationship between Shenzhen and foreign technological centers at the local level. Since the establishment of a sister-city relationship between Shenzhen and Helsinki, Finland, in 2013, the Sino–Finnish design park in Shenzhen has become a tech incubation nexus that attracts European tech entrepreneurs and industrial designers. Further, the design park acts as a symbolic technological ambassador to European entrepreneurs: there is a base in Shenzhen where tech enthusiasts and adventurers from Europe can work. Hi-Tech Fair subconferences in Europe have generated rewarding consequences, as European exhibitors being the top 1 overseas exhibitor group in 2019 and 2020, as shown in Table 5.2. More recently, the 26th China Hi-Tech Fair in 2024 featured fast-growing sectors, such as artificial intelligence, robotics, clean energy, semiconductor display and integrated circuit, environmental protection and green & low carbon. The China IP small-medium enterprises (SMEs) helpdesk IP business advisor visited the trade fair to advise EU SMEs as more EU business entities make efforts to update themselves about the Chinese industries, markets and standards.

The annual event has attracted significant global investment in Shenzhen companies and it has become a major Chinese and international tech event. In 2008, Warren Buffett's investment firm, Berkshire Hathaway, invested HK$1.8 billion (about $232 million) in BYD automobile.[30] Berkshire Hathaway's investment helped with BYD's strategic product development and innovation. Most importantly, this high-profile investment enhanced BYD's visibility as an early player in the electric vehicle industry in China and the world. The Hi-Tech Fair's reputation and attraction have grown since 1999. The number of exhibits at the fair rose from 2856 in 1999 to 16,299 in 2013, an increase of 82.5%. More importantly, the number of investment institutions and individual investors attending the event increased from 955 in 1999 to 3812 in 2015 (see Table 5.3), which improved the chances for tech entrepreneurs to secure investment in their new products and services. A report on the 2017 Hi-Tech Fair broke down the attendees: Enterprises accounted for 78.67%, research institutions 8.16%, and universities 2.96%, as shown in Table 5.4. Table 5.5 shows that in 2019, enterprises and research institutions constituted 80.43% and 9.74%, respectively, a slight increase from 2017 for both groups. In addition, 75.3% of the enterprises in the 2019 fair were returning attendees. Among participating enterprises, information technology companies topped the list, followed by enterprises in advanced manufacturing and in new materials and energy saving (Table 5.6). In Table 5.7, *Industries Represented by Shenzhen Hi-Tech Fair Enterprises Participants in 2023,* big data & cloud computing and internet+ are two industries missing in the 2017 participants breakdown, accounting for 3.29% and 3.78% respectively, which implicitly demonstrate China's high-tech industrial development and directions.

The Hi-Tech Fairs have become a matchmaking platform, in China and globally, for information exchange, business cooperation, and capital investment since 1999. The reasons for attending the Hi-Tech Fair alter as this matchmaking platform gain domestic and global recognition across industries and geographies with the time passing. "Corporate promotion and branding" "promotion of products and projects" as well as "look for business partners" become three top reasons for companies' participation. It is interesting to note that "obtain industrial development trends" and "seek for investment" are no longer the essential reasons that attract domestic companies to attend this fair.

"Shenzhen, compared to Beijing, Shanghai or Guangzhou, actually has its extremely unique international collaboration advantages since private small to medium enterprises concentrate in the city. It is quite flexible for local SMEs to establish cooperation with international partners directly," said Tina Tu, chief representative in Shenzhen and the Greater Bay Area at China Britian Business Council, "International SMEs come to China mainly for two purposes, market and supply chain, which differ from renowned multinationals whose China entry or presence revolves much around government relations." In the past before China achieves its technological prominence on the world stage, companies attending the fair offer indications and directions for Shenzhen local policymakers and government officials on industrial development trends with state-of-art technologies and innovation products and services. Building on information from the Hi-Tech exhibition, the Shenzhen city government adjusts its industrial policy and tries to invest in promising local companies that build new technologies and innovative products. Nowadays, Shenzhen Hi-Tech Fair has a new function: to provide international companies, many of them from advanced economies, to learn from Shenzhen and China's high-tech development. In 2024, on the 26th Hi-Tech Fair, the Australia Trade and Investment Commission brought seven Australian companies to learn about China's green development, environmental protection, and new energy to foster cooperation with local businesses.

Tracing back to 1999, Shenzhen local government officials would never have imagined that Shenzhen could become a hot hub for exhibitions. By the time of writing in the first half of 2025, there are over thirty regional and international level specialized exhibitions with key words including manufacturing, electronics and artificial intelligence were hosted in Shenzhen. As argued by Chinese economist Keyu Jin (2023) in her book, *The China Playbook,* it is local government officials who push for local economic development, optimize municipal business environment, attract foreign investment and promote municipal images. Jin (2023) argues that in the mayor economy, local governments are incentivized to help business overcome barriers and attract resources. But why

Table 5.2 2019 and 2020 Shenzhen Hi-Tech Fair overseas exhibitor breakdown

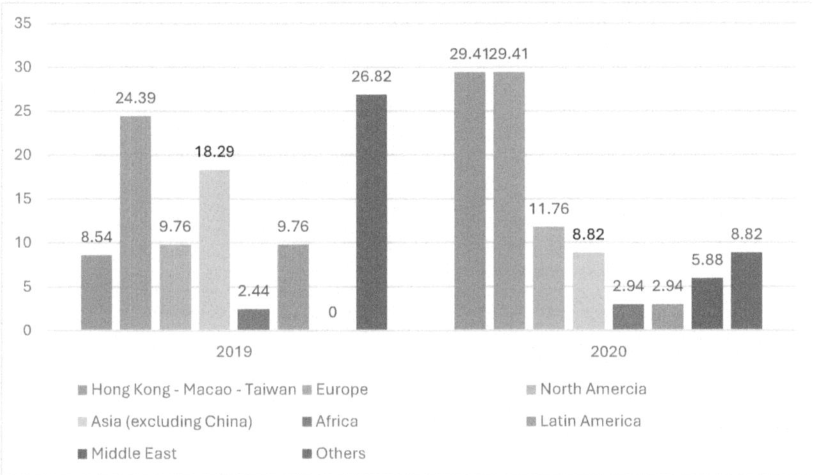

Note China high tech fair report

has Shenzhen become a world-class special economic zone and a leading technological hub? What are the recipes for Shenzhen's technological growth and breakthrough? In fact, district governments within Shenzhen compete for high-tech companies registered and created in their administrative areas. The Nanshan district government emerged as the "macro incubator" by leveraging and expanding its administrative capacity in the technological development and innovation process and achieved remarkable results. The next section considers how the Nanshan district government advances technological innovation particularly through the funding process.

Incubator and Monitor: Nanshan District Government

Nanshan district is known as "China's high-tech district" because internationally famous Chinese technology companies, such as ZTE, Huawei, Tencent, and DJI, were all founded there.[31] The choice made by these companies to establish their business in the same district explains

Table 5.3 Number of investment institutions and investors at Shenzhen Hi-Tech Fair, 1999–2015

Note Data compiled from Shenzhen Hi-Tech Fair archives

Table 5.4 Shenzhen Hi-Tech Fair participant demographics, 2017

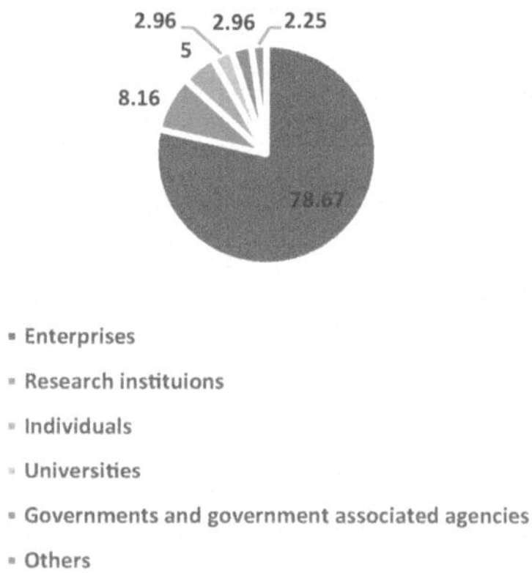

Note China high tech fair report

Nanshan's advantages in attracting startup businesses. According to a government-initiated research report conducted by Guangdong Academy of Social Science, Nanshan district in Shenzhen and Zhongguangcun in Beijing are ranked, respectively, as the top one and two high-tech districts in China in terms of regional startup incubation capacity.[32] During the 2017 Hi-Tech Fair, the Nanshan district government released the 2016 *Shenzhen Nanshan District Science and Technology Finance Development*

Table 5.5 Shenzhen Hi-Tech Fair participant types, 2019

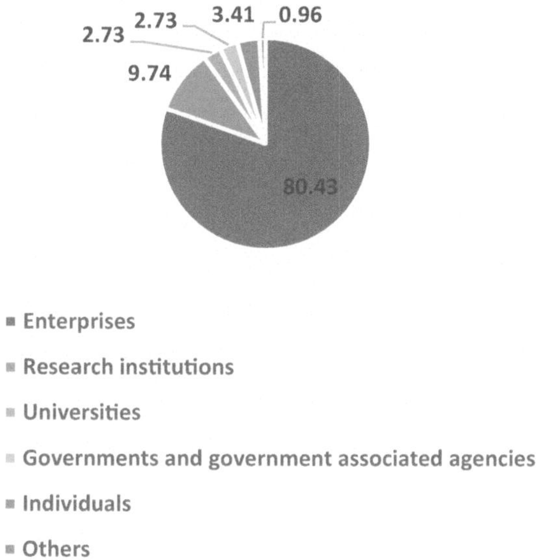

Note China high tech fair report

White Paper, summarizing its efforts to support high-tech companies created in the district since 2008. The number of national tech enterprises in Nanshan rose from 677 in 2010 to 3579 in 2018 (Table 5.8). The new free-trade zone within Shenzhen, Qianhai (前海), is located on Nanshan's periphery. In 2018, the district's gross domestic product (GDP) reached 5018 billion RMB, number one citywide, with its tertiary industry[33] accounting for 59.2% of its total GDP. Consistent with Shenzhen's urban economic development strategy, the Nanshan district government has identified technological innovation as an important engine for the development of its district. It has further created its own *Technology Finance Online Platform*, described as "1+1+3+9": one platform, one system, three financial modes, and nine funding and investment products (see Fig. 5.4).

The former director of the Science and Technology Finance Center in Nanshan district told me in an interview that the district government uses this platform to support small and mid-size enterprises in high-tech industries. Nanshan district government utilizes its networking ability to

Table 5.6 Industries represented by Shenzhen Hi-Tech Fair enterprises participants, 2017

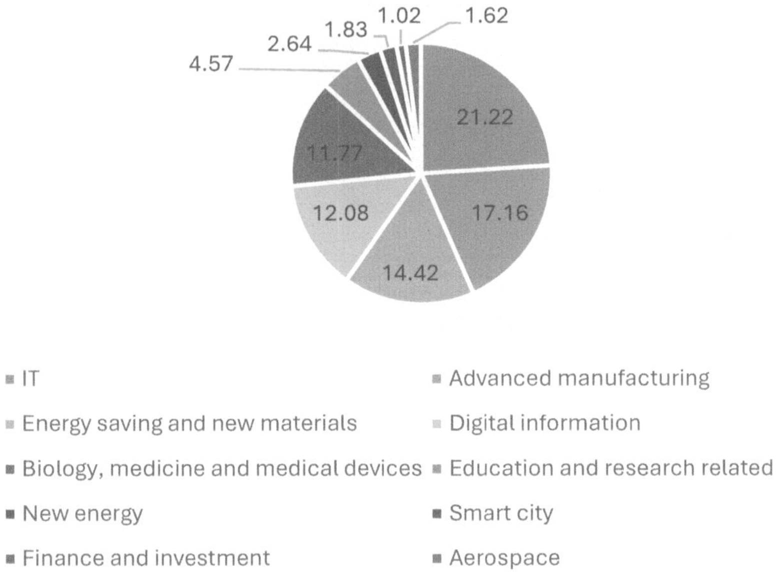

Note China high tech fair report

help technology firms and banks which reduces network failure in innovation process. Andrew Schrank and Josh Whitford (2011) point out that markets and states often fail because technologists or firms could not find the partners or fundings they need, or those partners lack the competence or mutual trust for successful collaborations. "Nanshan's government serves as the medium between banks and enterprises," my interviewee said, explaining that state-owned banks do not understand high-tech enterprises and relevant industries which make them reluctant loan tech entrepreneurs money or help the companies grow. So the Nanshan district government collaborated with Peking University's Shenzhen Research Institute to develop the *Small- to Medium-Size Technology Enterprise Rating System Index*. The rating index considers the concerns of financial institutions and the district government together. Financial institutions, the lenders, care most about a company's financial situation, which is its ability to pay back loans. The Nanshan district government

Table 5.7 Industries represented by Shenzhen Hi-Tech Fair enterprises participants, 2023

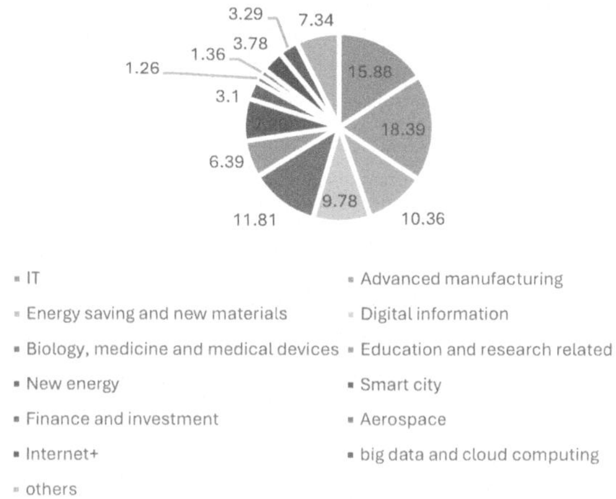

Note China high tech fair report

focuses more on the contributions a high-tech enterprise might make to enhance the technology industry in the district.

The four rating indicators are enterprise management capabilities, innovation capabilities, business operation environment, and business financial situation. A company's ability to innovate and its potential to produce innovative products or services is the critical consideration. The Nanshan district government filters out companies that score poorly and connects high-scoring enterprises that need funding with local banks. Banks have more confidence in lending to these companies after the government's prescreening. In effect, the district government is the guarantor, and no company will risk "messing up with the government," as the director jokingly said to me. There also is a monitoring system on the *Technology Finance Online Platform*; companies that fail to pay their mortgages are added to a blacklist. Blacklisted companies cannot apply for other government enterprise incentives. "It is like the district government has created a protection umbrella for the banks," the Science and Technology Finance Center's former director explained (see Fig. 5.4).

Nanshan's district government uses the information it collects on high-tech enterprises to guide technological industrial development through its funding choices. Table 5.9 shows loan distributions among science and

Table 5.8 Number of High-Tech enterprises registered in Nanshan, 2010–2018

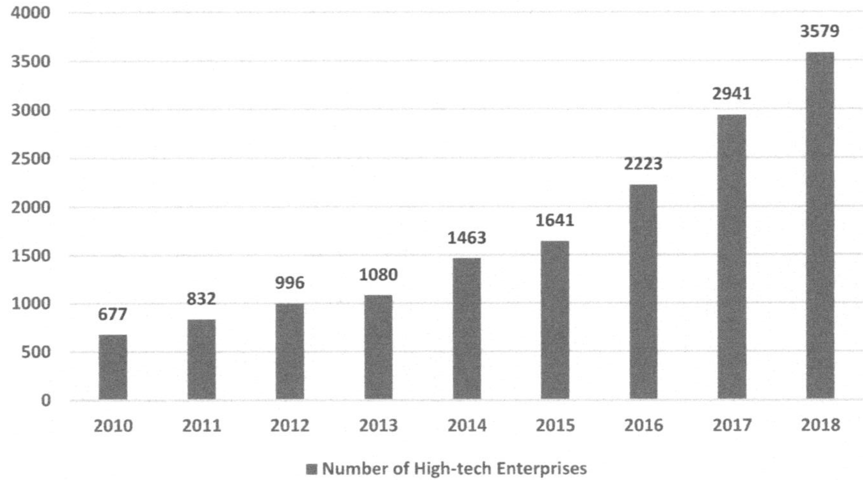

Note Data from national economic and social development of nanshan district over the years, translated into Chinese: 南山区历年国民经济和社会发展统计公报

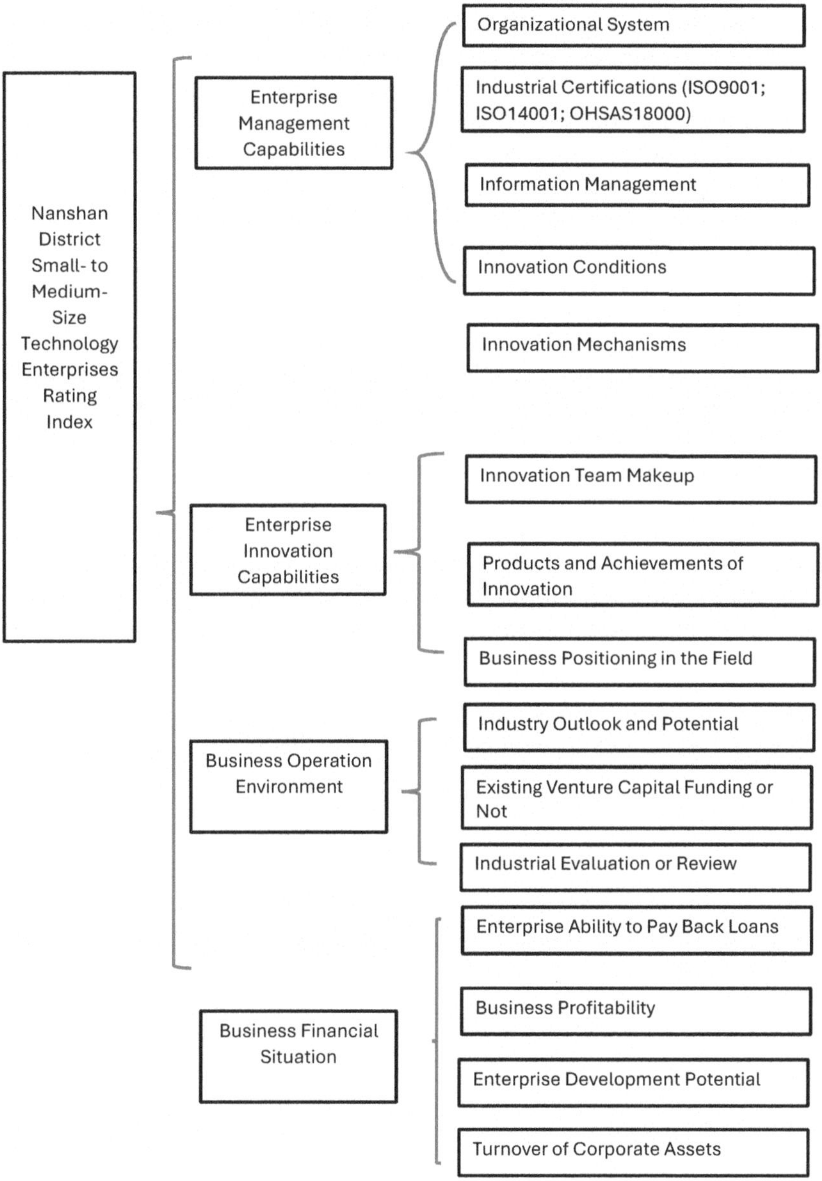

Fig. 5.4 Nanshan district small to medium sized technology enterprises rating index

technology enterprises in 2018. Small- to medium-size companies in new information technology and telecommunications industries received the most money (49.4%), followed by internet, energy saving, and environmental protection industries. Tech entrepreneurs in Shenzhen are inclined to establish information technology and internet businesses, perhaps because these are more mature sectors. The Nanshan district government and banks know more about these two industries and so prefer to invest in them. These sectors differ from aerospace engineering and new material industries, which require a tremendous amount of funding to purchase and continuously upgrade high-cost equipment. By contrast, the amount of startup money needed to develop an internet or information technology company is comparatively small. Table 5.10 shows the number and the total amount of loans from 2008 to 2018 annually. Those enterprises did not receive loans directly from the district government, though the government rating results and referrals affected their success in securing bank loans.

During our interviews, the former director of the Science and Technology Finance Center stated that the educational level of a company's chairperson and various factors related to its technical personnel are important in funding decisions. Educational level, particularly that

Table 5.9 Industry distribution (as percentage of total financial loans) of Science and technology loans in Nanshan district, 2018

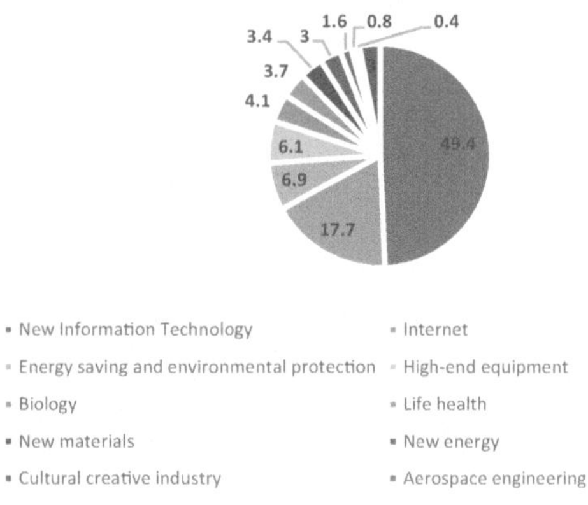

*Note*2019 Shenzhen Nanshan District Technology Finance Development White Paper, p. 31, in Chinese: 深圳市南山区科技金融白皮书

Table 5.10 Number of loans and loan amount held by Hi-Tech enterprises in Nanshan district, 2008–2018

Year	*Number of loans (number of supported enterprises)*	*Loan amount (10,000 RMB)*
2008	7	2500
2009	52	56,000
2010	33	10,000
2011	79	46,000
2012	108	65,000
2013	144	79,000
2014	262	124,000
2015	324	181,034
2016	552	348,468
2017	713	425,088
2018	886	518,600

Note Data from 2018 Shenzhen Nanshan science and technology finance development white paper

of technical personnel, demonstrates the enterprises' organizational and technological expertise, which may help district government officials in deciding whether the investment will be successful. The *2018 Shenzhen Science and Technology Finance Development White Paper* shows that among the funded enterprises on the Technology Finance Online Platform, most founders graduated from Tier 1 Chinese research universities, 93.9% of chief technical personnel graduated from Chinese domestic universities, and only 6.1% of technical personnel were trained in the United States or other overseas universities. The statistics reflected in these educational backgrounds demonstrate two key points that distinguish technological development and innovation in Shenzhen from that in Beijing or Shanghai in the past. First, as I indicated in my article on talent migration, Chinese overseas returnees prefer Shanghai over Shenzhen because of Shanghai's internationalism, cultural and living facilities, and city entertainment like nightclubs (Wang, 2022). Second, it is not surprising that the Nanshan district government incubates and finances companies whose founders or key technical personnel graduated mainly from Chinese universities. None of the CEOs or founders from Tencent, Huawei, or DJI graduated from foreign universities, with the only exception that Frank Wang, DJI's founder, obtained his doctoral degree from Hong Kong University of Science and Technology. It is possible that

Nanshan district government does not think an overseas educational background is critical to a technology startup's success due to historical proven records. It is also probable that founders who graduated from Chinese universities and rooted in the Chinese market are more likely to create startups that serve the local needs with potential success.

There are two types of Tier 1 research universities in China, 211 and 985.[34] These high-level research universities have direct central government funding augmented by provincial and city financial resources. Table 5.11 shows the breakdown of the universities attended by chairpersons, managers, chief technology personnel, chief marketing personnel, and financial personnel in Nanshan district's high-tech enterprises. In addition to the educational background of senior management and technical personnel in funded enterprises, the district government tracks the patent ownership of companies on their platform. Table 5.12 shows patent holding distributions from 2016 to 2018 for all enterprises registered on the Technology Finance Online Platform. Most enterprises hold 1 to 15 patents, accounting for more than 60% of the total number of

Table 5.11 Education of key personnel in Nanshan district's Hi-Tech enterprises, by institutional type

University institutional type	*Chairperson*	*General manager*	*Chief technical personnel*	*Chief marketing personnel*	*Chief finance personnel*
211	19.9%	20.9%	21.5%	17.2%	12.7%
985	26.3%	28.0%	27.2%	17.1%	9.5%
Chinese domestic university (not 211 or 985)	46.0%	43.2%	45.2%	59.5%	75.3%
Top 100 U.S. and European university	2.0%	2.0%	2.1%	1.3%	0.8%
Top 30 U.S. and European university	1.7%	2.0%	1.4%	0.6%	0.2%
Other overseas university	4.0%	3.9%	2.6%	4.2%	1.5%

Note 2019 Shenzhen Nanshan District Technology Finance Development White Paper, p. 43, in Chinese: 深圳市南山区科技金融白皮书。

Table 5.12 Patent filing by Hi-Tech enterprises in Nanshan district, 2016–2018

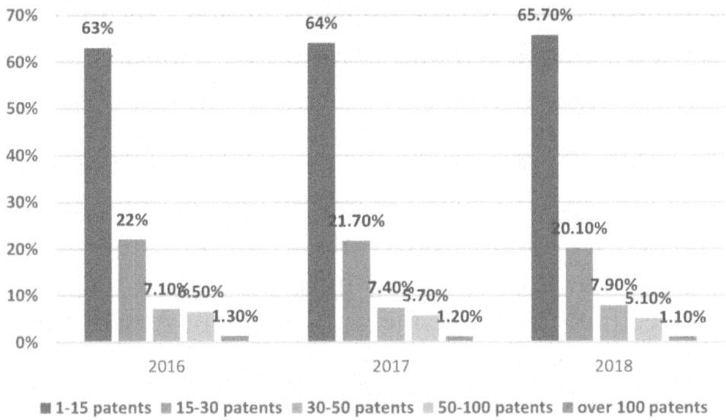

Note 2019 Shenzhen nanshan district technology finance development white paper, p. 50, in Chinese: 深圳市南山区科技金融白皮书

enterprises in each year from 2016 to 2018. The percentage of companies holding 1–15 patents increased from 63% in 2016 to 65.7% in 2018, and the percentage of companies with 30–50 patent holdings accounted for 7.90% in 2018, compared with 7.10% in 2016. The figures indicate that the number of patents held by an enterprise or its technical personnel plays a significant role in influencing government funding decisions.

In a follow-up conversation, my interviewee told me:

> Government is still doing the white paper every year, but more and more tech companies get access to venture capital and other funding resources in the market. Time has changed. Funding is no longer the obstacle for many tech startups in Shenzhen. Even if some small enterprises need loans from banks in the seed stage, many of them can get venture capital money later. The white paper has become more of an industrial development portrait as government information database nowadays.

Conclusion

This chapter's analysis of the characteristics of city- and district-level government officials has shown the roles these officials play in Shenzhen's economic development and technological innovation. Original Chinese archives and in-depth interviews aided my analysis and have demonstrated the overarching role that local government officials have had in technological advancement since the early 1980s. Are all Chinese telecommunications or internet companies funded by the government? This popular view is incorrect, and it would be a mistake to assume that all companies in these sectors are funded by the government. Tencent received its first round of funding from investors in the U.S. and Chinese Hong Kong, IDG and PCCW, with investment followed by South African media company Naspers. China's participation in the global economy networks predated its joining the World Trade Organization (WTO) in 2000. That said, it is clear that government has played a significant role in establishing technology companies in Shenzhen. Absent the policies set forth in the "1987 Document" "1998 Document" and the "1999 Revision," skilled technical people could not have flocked to Shenzhen to start their tech companies and pursue their entrepreneurial dreams. Without the city government's initiative and lobbying to launch the Hi-Tech Fair in 1999, Shenzhen likely would have missed the opportunity to develop in the electronics and technology sectors. It is critical to note that government funding and support in technological innovation even happened in the United States in the 1980s when the U.S. semiconductor industry competed against the Japanese. For instance, SEMATECH (Semiconductor Manufacturing Technology) was a consortium started in 1987 with initial funding from the U.S. government to aid private research in semiconductor industry. The involvement of public resources and public officials facilitates mutual trust among entrepreneurs, firms, and research entities particularly in the process of creating or shaping industrial development. As Lan (2024) argued that it is impossible to understand Chinese economy without understanding government. So are its technological development and innovations. The mix of public and private resources (i.e., funding, land) in the process of economic development and industrialization is not a simple division between the government and the market. The two are deeply intertwined.

It is undeniable that the Shenzhen local government has promoted the growth of robust enterprises for the benefit of local bureaucrats as well as for the prosperity of local businesses. Local government officials benefit themselves by helping local enterprises. One of my interviewees laughed when I asked, "Did Huawei ever receive any government support?" as I tried to gather and confirm information from multiple sources. He explained the level of help involved in facilitating certain Huawei employees' application for Shenzhen hukou (residential permit). My interviewee burst into laughter at my question because our conversation happened at the time the U.S. media criticized Huawei's government connections. I interpreted that my interviewee did not tend to laugh at me or my question but at the sentiment. The city government eliminated barriers to innovation activities with support from the Chinese central government: Cross the river while feeling the stone.

Shenzhen's many experimental policies have emerged from Chinese politics. As Castells (1998/2000/2010) noted:

> A state is developmental when it establishes as its principle of legitimacy its ability to promote and sustain development, understanding by development the combination of steady high rates of economic growth and structural change in the productive system, both domestically and in its relationship to the international economy (p. 287).

The Chinese state encouraged "experimenting with policies" in Shenzhen, initially for survival, and then for development and technological modernization. The city government sets an example as a regional developmental state (Castells, 1998/2000/2010). Shenzhen officials held fast to their mission to set a successful example for the rest of China as the first special economic zone. Shenzhen's failure would have meant that they, as government officials, had failed. It also would have indicated a failure of China's market-oriented experimental economic development. The drive to eradicate poverty and revive the Middle Kingdom's technological capacity fueled the officials' confidence in themselves and their faith in their ability to build a new city. Patriotism, in the form of national identity and cultural heritage, has been embedded within all the efforts.

This chapter's analysis of the role of local government officials in developing Shenzhen's technology industry demonstrates that the regional developmental state (in this context, the Shenzhen city government and its district governments) is flexible enough to navigate the developmental process between government, entrepreneurs, and businesses. Shenzhen's innovation process shows that unlike the Silicon Valley innovation model or the Finnish welfare state information society (Castells & Himanen, 2002), the Chinese state, especially city and district governments, plays a critical role in providing "backing support." That backing support ranges from policy and a culture of city autonomy to tangible support such as information exchange and financial backing.

Still, what do tech entrepreneurs think of Shenzhen's local government? Do they feel supported? Do they agree with the local government that Shenzhen's business environment is friendly and welcoming? With China's recent economic growth and urban development, more and more cities aim to develop their local technology industries. For instance, Hangzhou, where e-commerce giant Alibaba is located, and Kunshan, where many Taiwan electronics companies established their factories at. Shenzhen is no longer the only city in Chinese Mainland that operates with a market economy. How is Shenzhen's entrepreneurial culture compared to Silicon Vallay's? Do Shenzhen local government officials help local private enterprises grow and prosper? Do members of the younger generation, born in relatively affluent modern China, share the same patriotism as their parents or grandparents? What motivates the new generation's drive in creating tech startups? To unravel the puzzles, I next analyze the entrepreneurial ecosystem in Shenzhen.

Notes

1. Zhou Luming, former chairman of Shenzhen Science and Technology Association. This quote is retrieved from his article published in Mandarin Chinese: https://news.sciencenet.cn/sbhtmlnews/2019/9/349539.shtm.
2. This excerpt is from Li Zibin's book published in Mandarin Chinese, 《我在深圳当市长》, titled translated to English, 《Being a Mayor in Shenzhen》:https://weread.qq.com/web/reader/0a2321f0720930550a252ba.
3. Lu is a pseudonym.
4. Translation into Chinese, summarized as 遇到绿灯快步走，遇到黄灯慢步走，遇到红灯绕道走。
5. In Hsing (1998)'s book, *Making Capitalism in China*, page 119, she cited Lin's work published in 1993 in *China Times Weekly*. Since Hsing noted it was work in Chinese, I searched "China Times Weekly" in Mandarin but could not find it online. According to Hsing's bibliography, Lin's work appeared in *China Times Weekly*, no. 73, May 23–29, pp. 17–20.
6. From a Mandarin Chinese research report: 深圳与国内其他主要城市创业成本比较研究, translated into English, A Comparative Study on the Cost of Entrepreneurship between Shenzhen and Other Major Cities in China.

7. According to the project manager, the program was shut down because of increasing U.S.—China tensions. However, during my 2019 research visit to Shenzhen, I specifically asked former participants of the executive training program and the local training organizer about the reasons for the suspension. I was told that the collaborative program with this U.S. university was ended when the party leader who had initiated the training a decade earlier retired.
8. Information is retrieved from: https://www.szdag.gov.cn/attachment/0/90/90210/1150507.pdf Original document, in Chinese is titled: 关于设立"深圳市技术引进咨询评议委员会"的通知。
9. Shenzhen City Government issued the 1987 document: 《深圳市人民政府关于鼓励科技人员兴办民间科技企业的暂行规定》. This original government document can be found at: http://www.asianlii.org/chi/cn/legis/gd/laws/fb7f7d76bc84dddc2975d00cb9d0cf0725d00785/.
10. Shenzhen City Government issued the first version of the document in 1998, translated into Chinese: 《关于进一步扶持高新技术产业发展的若干规定》Document can be retrieved from: https://www.sz.gov.cn/zfgb/1998/gb135/content/post_10115835.html.
11. Document can be retrieved from: https://www.sz.gov.cn/zfgb/1999/gb175/content/post_10097943.html.
12. The excerpt was translated from the original document in Chinese. In the 1999 document, this committee is named as 深圳市科技顾问委员会, which differs from the 1986's 深圳市技术引进咨询评议委员会.
13. The interview was recorded and aired at CCTV documentary, *Shenzhen Stories*: https://www.scbochen.com/m/view.php?aid=1037
14. Information is retrieved from: http://www.xinhuanet.com/photo/2020-10/09/c_1126586101.htm
15. Information is retrieved from: https://economictimes.indiatimes.com/news/international/us/this-chinese-company-has-overtaken-tesla-as-worlds-largest-maker-of-pure-electric-cars-heres-how-it-outsmarted-elon-musk/articleshow/116947090.cms?from=mdr
16. Information is retrieved from: https://ee.ckgsb.com/faculty/news/detail/157/6866.html.
17. From an article written by former Shenzhen Mayor, Li Zibin. Information is retrieved from: https://www.ca-sme.org/content/Content/index/id/15999.

18. China Ping An Group, founded in 1988 in Shenzhen, developed into an international company involving financial technology, real estate, and investment: https://www.pingan.com/us-en.shtml.
19. Skyworth Group has evolved from a TV manufacturer to a multinational electronic and smart devices company: http://global.skyworth.com/
20. Kingdee International Software Group Company Limited: http://www.kingdee.com.hk/en/
21. Information is retrieved from: https://www.sz.gov.cn/cn/xxgk/zfxxgj/zwdt/content/post_10790391.html.
22. Information is retrieved from: https://www.sz.gov.cn/szsrmzfxxgk/zc/gz/content/post_9453824.html.
23. Pitchbook, the premier data provider for the private and public equity markets, released its report *Venture Capital in China* in 2019: https://pitchbook.com/media/press-releases/china-became-second-largest-venture-capital-market-by-total-capital-invested-in-2018-according-to-pitchbook-report.
24. The news report is retrieved from: http://www.chtf.com/liaojiegaojiaohui/lijiehuigu/chtf1/news/201508/t20150825_5567.html.
25. Information is retrieved from: http://www.chtf.com/liaojiegaojiaohui/lijiehuigu/chtf2/
26. Information is retrieved from: https://www.forbes.com/global/2010/0208/companies-patrick-mcgovern-china-idg-scores.html.
27. Information is retrieved from: http://www.chtf.com/liaojiegaojiaohui/lijiehuigu/chtf1/.
28. Information is retrieved from: http://www.chtf.com/liaojiegaojiaohui/lijiehuigu/chtf2/news/201508/t20150824_5515.html.
29. Reported by Chinanews in 1999, article retrieved from China Hi-Tech Fair website news archive: http://www.chtf.com/liaojiegaojiaohui/lijiehuigu/chtf1/news/201508/t20150825_5563.html
30. Information is retrieved from: https://www.forbes.com/sites/miriamtuerk/2018/08/16/why-warren-buffett-is-right-about-china/#18226cc41bff.
31. Huawei was originally founded in Nanshan district but relocated its Shenzhen headquarter to Longgang district afterwards.
32. Original Chinese report: 《中国区域孵化能力评价研究报告2016》, in translation to English, 2016 Chinese Regional Incubation Capacity Evaluation Research Report.

33. The three-sector model in economics classifies the primary sector as raw materials, the secondary sector as manufacturing, and the tertiary sector as service industries.
34. Project 211 (211 工程), or simply 211, was initiated by the Ministry of Education of China, with the intent of raising research standards of high-level Chinese universities. The name comes from an abbreviated slogan "In preparation for the 21st century, successfully managing 100 universities." Project 985, or simply 985, was announced in 1998, to promote the development of China's higher education system by founding world-class universities in the 21st century. This project added 33 universities to the existing Project 211 universities. The 33 universities were selected to support urgent needs in the state's development, particularly in scientific or engineering subjects.

CHAPTER 6

The Entrepreneurial Ecosystem in Shenzhen

> Shenzhen's most famous local specialty is its entrepreneurs.
>
> —Chen Zhilie, Founder of EVOC[1]

Silicon Valley of Hardware: Fast Speed and Action

"People in Silicon Valley just bullshit. It is more about storytelling in the Valley. Chinese companies are not good at storytelling, but they deliver. People deliver in Shenzhen." My interviewee, TE, cofounder and CEO of a Swiss security robotics startup, accepted my interview invitation via LinkedIn. His willingness to respond to my cold-call message and his agreement to converse about his Shenzhen startup experience interested me. We scheduled a Skype call. I was eager to find out why he described Silicon Valley's long-praised marketing strategies as "bullshit" while also highly endorsing Shenzhen.

TE is a serial entrepreneur from Switzerland and was a researcher in field and space robotics before his startup adventures. "It was a quick decision to go to Shenzhen," TE recalled. "My team and I met an associate from [the hardware accelerator] HAX and SOSV [the San Francisco venture capital firm of which HAX is a part] at an event in Switzerland. He said that HAX could help us prototype our product and enter mass production in Shenzhen." With no experience working in China

G. Y. Wang, *Dragon Innovation: Shenzhen*, Governing China in the 21st Century, https://doi.org/10.1007/978-981-95-9637-9_6

and no knowledge of Mandarin Chinese, TE and his two cofounders left for Shenzhen in December 2015 to "give it a shot." They stayed with HAX, which had been founded in Shenzhen in 2011, for six months, working intensively on prototyping to create agile robots to perform security and safety monitoring of industrial sites, saving people from working in uncomfortable, risky environments. TE described their time in Shenzhen as crazy and intense. "We devoted ourselves to working every day in those six months as we stayed away from home, families, and friends. We sometimes hung out with other startup teams, but every team was as swamped and stressed as we were with their own product development." TE repeatedly emphasized the convenience of the hardware supply chain at Hua Qiang Bei electronics market, where HAX is located. "We finished our product prototype in Shenzhen and began to do product demonstrations at local startup events as well as at tech exhibitions in Shanghai. Our first client was a small company from Jinan, Shandong province. This company remains our client; we helped them enter and grow in the European market." TE seemed satisfied with the "product-making" to "client-selling" experience his team had in China. "Hardware startups can move to the production line quickly in Shenzhen as most suppliers are there."

When I asked him to describe his Shenzhen startup experience in a few words, he told me without hesitation: work and speed. TE did not see a major difference between the Chinese entrepreneurs he met at HAX and European entrepreneurs. Both are extremely hardworking and aggressive: Work is central. As a cofounder of a hardware startup, TE cared more about the function and quality of his products than storytelling. Silicon Valley had proved fruitless for him: "We went to Silicon Valley as part of a HAX cohort in 2018 to seek funding. We got some funding through SOSV's investor networks, but our major funding resource is from a Swiss investment fund." TE seemed unimpressed with his Silicon Valley trip. "It is impossible for us to enter the U.S. security market. It is protected and fragmented. Our major markets are in Europe and China."

Many people echo TE's opinion about Shenzhen's startup ecosystem. From sourcing, supply chain, prototyping, and industrial design to manufacturing and marketing, the city is a part of the action, according to Benjamin Joffe, a general partner at HAX. This action amazes hardware startup entrepreneurs like TE who aspire to rapidly produce real products, to test them in broad potential markets, and to constantly enhance their products. HAX's determination in growing hardware startups and companies makes Shenzhen indispensable in the global hardware startup ecosystem. HAX receives more than 2000 applications worldwide every year, from which it selects two batches, about 30 startup teams. According to Cyril Ebersweiler, SOSV's general partner, hardware venture requires a different scale and strong technical skill (Ester, 2017). However, these skills alone would not make a hardware startup successful. Founders and engineers need to deal with suppliers, manufacturers, and distributors, and this is one reason why HAX requires the selected teams to spend nearly six months at HAX Shenzhen finalizing their product prototyping before mass production. In other words, creating a hardware startup is a supply chain issue, in contrast to a software startup in an engineer's garage. And Shenzhen can single-handedly remove the obstacles to those hardware companies' potential success. Why is Shenzhen able to provide TE with suppliers and markets in an area traditionally viewed as "low manufacturing hub" in South China? What makes Shenzhen the Silicon Valley of Hardware and a paradise for tech entrepreneurs? Do foreign entrepreneurs like TE get help and support from local government officials? Building on interview data, this chapter describes the characteristics of Shenzhen's startup ecosystem. Its unique entrepreneurial environment grew from its hardware supply chain networks. The comprehensive electronics market has enabled foreign and domestic entrepreneurs to experiment freely to build their products and to innovate through combination and recombination. The vast Chinese market provides tech entrepreneurs with opportunities to test new products.

In June 2019, I interviewed Emma,[2] a program supervisor from HAX. She jokingly described herself as "the Chinese mom" at HAX since many foreign tech entrepreneurs know nothing about China and do not understand Mandarin Chinese. She helps them with everything, including opening bank accounts and securing apartment rentals. Securing an interview with a HAX representative had been more difficult than arranging visits to other Chinese incubators or accelerators because local government officials in charge of tech startup incubation had little interaction with the hardware accelerator though some officials heard of HAX due to its well-known reputation. I was eventually connected with HAX through a seasoned Chinese American angel investor who had had business interactions with SOSV in Silicon Valley. This demonstrated the role of connections and the international networks in globalized business and everyday life.

"After the founding of HAX Shenzhen, we had no contact with the local government until 2015 when the Mass Innovation, Mass Entrepreneurship initiative was launched. Then, Futian district government officials came to visit our accelerator. That is pretty much it." Emma's inadvertent response to the lack of government involvement before the 2015 entrepreneurship policies is consistent with what I learned in my interviews with local government officials: Shenzhen local government does not often interfere with foreign entities and only tries to be of service. The city and district governments adhere to the principle that government is the backing support for local enterprises. Emma confirmed that "the business environment in Shenzhen is friendly and supportive. We do not need to maintain government relations for the sake of maintenance." Emma told me that HAX was started when the SOSV managing partner from the United States decided to open a hardware accelerator in Shenzhen in 2011 to take advantage of the city's hardware manufacturing. It is the first, and by far the largest hardware accelerator in the world. They recruit startup teams (mostly working on hardware) globally and gather the teams in Shenzhen for intensive product development and prototyping, typically for four to six months. The HAX program helps entrepreneurs with electronics components sourcing and puts them in touch with appropriate and reliable local suppliers. "As an accelerator, we have our own structural, mechanical, and electrical engineers as well as designers," Emma told me. "We help those startup teams with batch production and then advise them on mass production and manufacturing." Startup teams tend to work closely with HAX, to get help with products and manufacturing and to gain access to SOSV's investors networks, both in China and overseas. Foreign teams at HAX mainly come from United States, Canada, the European Union, South Korea, Japan and Southeast Asia. Some teams, like Canadian tech college teams, come to HAX with Canadian government-sponsored funding. Tech teams at HAX have their own regional characteristics. For instance, software-oriented startups are more concentrated among teams from Southeast Asian countries. After China's 2015 Mass Innovation, Mass Entrepreneurship initiative, a national development strategy promoting the integrated development of large, medium-sized and small enterprises in order to drive economic growth, people working at HAX noticed a trend of promising young native Chinese startups (see Chapter 7, Shenzhen Grassroots Participatory Innovation: Let the People Make). Emma explained to me how foreign and Chinese startup teams differ in their fundraising: "Our Chinese startup teams rarely have problems securing investment from Chinese investors since venture capital firms in China like to invest in local founders who know the Chinese market well. In addition, because most Chinese startup founders develop products tailored to Chinese enterprises and customers, they do not need to go overseas for funding." Emma's comment was especially true during the Mass Innovation, Mass Entrepreneurship period.

During my interview with Emma, I mentioned that I had taken the metro and arrived at the Hua Qiang Bei electronics market almost 40 minutes before our scheduled meeting. However, I had gotten lost in the "electronics jungle", a giant market plaza full of stores piled with all kinds of electronics components. Emma kindly laughed at my experience: "No one would believe HAX is located in a place with plain office setup in this giant electronics market." The office is located on two floors filled with desks, computers, machines, and most strikingly, fast-walking entrepreneurs. This location has practical advantages: "For some of the assembly parts we need, we can order in the morning and get them delivered in the afternoon. We built a robot that we can get out in about a week," said the twin brothers Chen who are avid table tennis players. They were accepted to the HAX program in 2016 after building their first table tennis robot in a garage in 2011. Harrison Chen went to the United States for college but dropped out after one year and returned to China to pursue this entrepreneurial path.[3] The Chen twins called their robot Trainerbot. They dream of building a portable table tennis robot that can play anytime, anywhere, at any level of competency. "HAX Shenzhen does not place excessive demands on the entrepreneurs' research and educational backgrounds," Emma told me. Instead, they put more emphasis on the applicants' practical ability and their products' market potential. Indeed, the number of young Chinese entrepreneurs, like Harrison Chen, who are pursuing a tech innovation and entrepreneurial path has increased. "This phenomenon has been especially true since the national Mass Innovation, Mass Entrepreneurship initiative," Emma explained. "At the central government level, entrepreneurship is encouraged through policy support. At the university level, colleges—either alone or in collaboration with enterprises—run tech entrepreneurship competitions to encourage students to try out their ideas, to create new inventions, and to start businesses." This welcoming entrepreneurial environment, supported by government policies and university encouragement, seems to have gradually changed college students' career pursuits, away from the conventional aim to become a government civil servant or to join a state-owned enterprise for social prestige and secure benefits. According to Emma, "The pursuit of entrepreneurship is now a recognized goal. Even if the entrepreneurs fail, their experiences and lessons learned in this process will likely benefit their future jobs." The Mass Innovation, Mass Entrepreneurship initiative, she acknowledged, had been significant in creating this shift. Though Emma's observation and interactions with young Chinese entrepreneurs happened before the Covid-19 hit and the global economy slowed down, the hidden cultural change among young Chinese generation has been obvious: Do what you love, has become a social acceptance.

Chinese Companies Born with Global DNA

One notable beneficiary of the Mass Innovation, Mass Entrepreneurship initiative and rising social recognition of entrepreneurship as a pursuit among young Chinese is Dorami,[4] a provider of robotic solutions powered by artificial intelligence (AI), founded in 2015 by a group of young entrepreneurs. Dorami, as a case, represents a new entrepreneurial venture among younger Chinese generations growing out of the Mass Innovation, Mass Entrepreneurship initiative: founders' native Chinese background, global research and development (R&D) networks, domestic venture funding. When I visited the company in June 2019, it had just celebrated its fifth anniversary. According to its official website, the company "provides end-to-end solutions for logistics, express, e-commerce, seaports, airports, manufacturing, and other scenarios." Its solutions include computer vision, motion planning, mobility, and deep learning. "What does your company name mean?" I asked my guide while staring at various robot arms, legs and other machines. My interviewee, who led public affairs and government relations, explained that Dorami reflects the company's young spirit and creativity. "Our cofounder and chief technology officer is a tech geek who is a huge fan of a Japanese sci-fi cartoon," my guide explained to me about the origin of their company's name. When I visited, it had just completed its fourth round of funding from major domestic Chinese venture capital firms. I was told that they had won this investment largely because of investors' confidence in Dorami and their acknowledgment of the company's technological skills and products which turn out to be the enterprise's strength for its continuous global expansion and success. "At Dorami, none of our cofounders went overseas for science and engineering degrees, and none of them even went to study abroad," I was told. "Dorami is a 'Made in China' tech company."

Another "Created and Made in China" startup, MatataStudio, founded in 2017 in Shenzhen, shares a similar story of how the company's name came into being. Its Chief Operating Officer, Tony Xiaoxiong Zheng, was inspired by the Disney global blockbuster, *The Lion King*. "Hakuna Matata is the phrase where I got my inspiration from. I hope Matata, [our company] could provide children with a way of learning that is free of worries." Tony explained to me when I paid a visit to their company in November 2025. Located at Xinghe World industrial park in Longgang district in Shenzhen, MatataStudio is an AI enabled technology startup that provides STEAM (science, technology, engineering, art and mathematics) educational solutions. I was no stranger to the concept of STEAM as well as its importance in encouraging students' creativity and their abilities to solve scientific problems because of my long-term education in the United States. What surprised me is that none of its CEO, Su Rongxing and its COO, Tony Xiaoxiong Zheng, went abroad for studies. However, their devotion to creating a STEAM oriented educational startup mainly stems from their desire to revolutionize the traditional way of learning in China. "I attended Tsinghua university for undergraduate program as a high school student from Shandong province," Su said to me in their conference room, while I acknowledged his emphasis on a national college exam candidate from Shandong province, one of the most competitive places in China with a large number of college entrance examination candidates. "Though I aced the games in the traditional education system, I did not feel like learning enough skills and training creative way of thinking that are beneficial to my life-long education," he continued. Su's self-reflection of Chinese education as well as his belief in technology's power in transforming education on the global scale made him co-found MatataStudio with COO, Tony Xiaoxiong Zheng.

Similarities between technology startups in Shenzhen, such as Dorami and MatataStudio do not merely lie in their creative and westernized English names as well as their founders' Chinese educational background. Most importantly, they are founded by new generational Chinese entrepreneurs that grew up in a period when non-Chinese cultures in the format such as Disney movies and Japanese cartoons were flooding to China and gained their popularities. Economic globalization and cultural globalization become part of those entrepreneurs' DNA even unconsciously, which mark those startups an epochal characteristic: Chinese companies born with global DNA. For instance, MatataStudio started their product development and educational curriculum design initially with American publishers, and then with European education experts at different stages. "Our Little Q robot in the Tale-Bot Pro series went through multiple rounds of design and correction," COO Tony Xiaoxiong Zheng at MatataStudio described to me about an evolutionary journey of one of their products, "a renowned Dutch child education psychologist pointed out that we should use dotted line rather than straight line for two key buttons in case not to cause child players any confusion." (see Fig. 6.1) Amazed at the Dutch expert's attention to details, the Matata team accepted the suggestion without fully understanding the psychological logic behind and started landing tests at thirteen kindergartens across the North America, Europe and the Asia-pacific. Users experience feedback confirmed the Dutch expert's insight which led to the final decision on the design of the product. It is no surprise to me that MatataStudio has gained high market penetration rate in countries such as France, Spain, Estonia, thanks to those global education experts' feedback in their product R&D design process as well as Matata's willingness to implement the feedback.

Given the diversity of national education systems and value differences, I was eager to figure out how a Chinese company could favor schools, educational organizations and teachers that differ drastically from the Chinese ones. MatataStudio's CEO, Su Rongxing pointed out that mutual selection matters. "I think our products truly win them [those partners] over. As an educational technology company, we'd like to choose global partners that share the same [educational] values with us regardless national, cultural and political differences." Su's words to me demonstrated his confidence in their products, "the globalization of Chinese enterprises has two distinctive advantages, namely the supply chain and our product development and design." A member of the European Schoolnet, a non-profit organization works to bring innovation in teaching and learning, MatataStudio now has access to this particular network, being able to get engaged with schools, teachers, researchers, and industry partners across thirty-four European countries . "Who your friends are reflects who you are," COO Tony Xiaoxiong

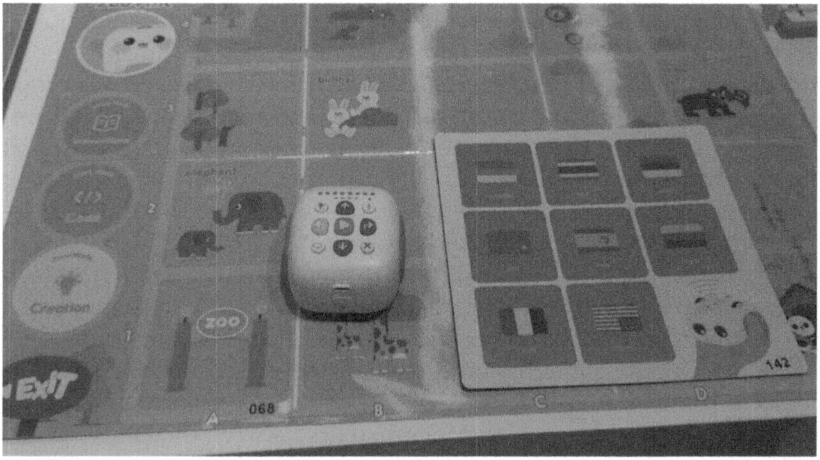

Fig. 6.1 Picture indicates global expert's feedback (*Note* Photo taken by the author at MatataStudio headquarter)

Zheng commented with a sense of accomplishment. Indeed, becoming a member of the European Schoolnet network signals the acceptance of China innovation and Chinese companies with global DNA.

In addition to partnering with likeminded global education experts in product design and development, MatataStudio has their in-house curriculum design education expert who holds a doctoral degree in education from the United States. Thorough understanding of STEAM education and child psychology in the United States and Europe requires international level talents. "We hire this kind of in-house expert to establish our company's reputation in connecting with our global counterparts," COO, Tony Xiaoxiong Zheng shared with me while showcasing a collection of case studies and academic papers published by European school teachers and researchers. "We were not aware that some kids love our little Q robot so much that they even hold it to sleep. Our company learned about those real examples and applications from the papers and case studies published by foreign experts we did not even know." Tony's words demonstrate the "globalized humanity" in the politicized anti-globalization wave.

Besides product design and R&D, "starting as global" as a mindset when creating new Chinese technology companies, leads to both the company and city government having an open and international attitude, which facilitates organizational and cultural change in either corporations or governmental organizations. My Dorami interviewee was proud of the company's ability to attract non-Chinese international talents: "We have many foreign employees, who say they are happy working at Dorami. You know, foreigners usually care more about the comfort of working space than their Chinese counterparts do." Indeed, the majority of employees were foreign at their robotic research and development (R&D) office space. Of Dorami's 170 employees, 85% are technical personnel. Of these, 35% come from more than 20 countries, including the United States, Russia, Australia, Canada, Israel, Spain, India, and Argentina. Dorami's international strategy and expansion helps with its global tech talent recruitment. Amazon Robotics Challenge, an annual event sponsored by Amazon to strengthen ties between the industrial and academic robotics communities, is a key recruitment source for robotic talent, according to my informant. The company also has four foreign employees through the Peacock Talent Program, a Shenzhen city government project meant to attract overseas talent, including foreign passport holders (see Chapter 9, Human Capital and National Competitiveness). The importance of global knowledge and talent networks is manifest in both Chinese tech startups like Dorami and established enterprises such as Huawei, the leading telecommunications company (see Chapter 8, Shenzhen R&D Ecosystem). The local government's role in providing backing support was emphasized again by my interviewee: "City government is quick to provide us with assistance when processing foreign talents' residential permits or visa matters, which allows our foreign employees to start working quickly." Local bureaucrats seek corporate collaboration to advance government-funded university research since academic R&D is considered as a local disadvantage. One of my interviewees at Dorami left to meet a visiting Chinese scientist during our interview meeting. "Too many visits and research collaborations inquiries" were her last words to me (Fig. 6.2).

Smart Hardware Paradise

The broad-gauge hardware supply chain in Shenzhen is an important factor pushing many tech startups to move forward quickly. Shenzhen is a hardware paradise. People can place an order, and it will be delivered within the next day. If the product does not meet their expectations,

Fig. 6.2 World's first robotics 6S store in Longgang district Shenzhen city (*Note* Photo taken by the author)

they can simply take a taxi to Hua Qiang Bei's electronics markets and get a replacement within hours. Entrepreneurs who locate their companies in Silicon Valley still order the exact same electronics components from Shenzhen. However, it takes two to four weeks for the packages to be delivered, which is extremely inefficient. It is said that Dorami can iterate one version of its products per week, while it takes more than three months for foreign companies.

Convenience and efficiency are two unbeatable advantages in establishing startups in the smart hardware industry in Shenzhen. "I worked in Shenzhen and relocated to work in Shanghai afterwards. When I decided to pursue my entrepreneurial adventure in creating MatataStudio, I returned to Shenzhen because of industry relevance and Shenzhen's smart hardware cluster strength." MatataStudio's CEO, Su Rongxing thought the determining factor for his decision in creating Matata in

Shenzhen relies on its mature cluster effect since most of their electronics suppliers are in surrounding cities such as Dongguan, Huizhou and Zhongshan. It is said that one of Matata's original equipment manufacturers is a listed company in Zhongshan exploring new growth engines in working with startups.

Smart hardware cluster effect in Shenzhen and the broader Greater Bay Area is frequently mentioned by multiple local small-mid enterprises. Shenzhen Zhi Hui Lin Network Technology is a medium-sized innovative technology company that focuses on researching and developing next-generation artificial intelligence technologies and their applications. Taking advantages of their location in Shenzhen, surrounded by traditional manufacturing companies such as toy manufacturers, Zhi Hui Lin provides those enterprises with their AI solutions, to help conventional industries realize their industrial upgrading. Shenzhen's hardware supply chain not only attracts hardware startup entrepreneurs and international hardware incubator such as HAX, it also interests scientists who embrace entrepreneurial ambition. A chief scientist at a global Fortune 500 company in charge of its AI and robotic development noted in an interview:

> I do not think good technological inventions or products will happen just in research labs anymore. We need the markets to test out our ideas and products. I think only China can offer that right now, though many people would say "the Chinese opportunity" exists because of a lack of regulations. I am a scientist and an entrepreneur. I am inventing new products. Of course, there is not much regulation on things that have not happened yet.

He joined his firm as chief scientist while operating his own robotic lab in Shenzhen. In essence, he argued that "scientific development and innovation is moving forward at the same pace as the government regulatory implementations." By contrast, an interviewee from another robotic startup said, "Institutional constraints on research and development are heavy. Companies must follow all codes of conduct." She never explained the nature of these constraints.[5] (see Chapter 11, Research Note: Emerging Sensitive Research).

At the end of my afternoon at Dorami in 2019, an American undergraduate walked me out. Back then, he was a student in Georgia

Tech-Shenzhen, a joint program between Georgia Institute of Technology with Tianjin University in Northern China. He was completing his last semester in Shenzhen. "I take courses at Shenzhen college town and do my internship at Dorami since my study concentration is robotics. It is good to see how the process works, and I can learn better from the real hands-on applications," he told me. "In my application to Georgia Tech, I expressed my interest in Asia. Someone from the admissions office called me to see if I would be interested in their joint program in Shenzhen. Here I am." His internship at Dorami had gone well, and although U.S. - China geopolitical tensions made his situation uncertain, he expressed his hope to stay at the company and in China to further his study and internship at Dorami: "I do not need Chinese permanent residency, but if I have a longer business visa, that would be ideal." When this American intern made this visa comment, there is no K visa in China yet. His words indeed reflected obstacles that foreign talents and students were faced with at that time (see Chapter 10, New Innovation Hubs are Possible).

The intern hangs out mostly with other foreign friends or Chinese overseas returnees in Shekou. The area was the first industrial export zone in Shenzhen, and multinational companies (and factories) historically set up their offices in that area, which link Shenzhen with Hong Kong, across Shenzhen Bay. Shekou is not in the city center, but its restaurants, facilities, and atmosphere are more tuned to a foreign taste and the area has an exotic ambience. "Foreigners know foreigners gather in Shekou, so we like to hang out here," the student explained. From his words, it seems that his social circle outside of school and his internship consists mainly of "foreigners" and returnees with whom he has no problem communicating in English (Fig. 6.3).

Platforms and Support System: Coworking Spaces, Incubators, Accelerators

The American undergraduate intern at Dorami faces a glass ceiling in Shenzhen because of language, culture, and mentorship. His inability to speak Mandarin restricts him from expanding his social or professional circle. The people he socializes with in Shenzhen are categorized not by their nationality but by their English language ability. Similarly, entrepreneurs' social circles in Shenzhen are stratified in multiple ways: by province, by industry, and by overseas returnee status. Among overseas returnee entrepreneurs, further sorting takes place according to the

Fig. 6.3 A blvd named Robot Blvd in Shenzhen (*Note* Photo taken by the author)

number of years overseas, alma mater, and the host country's international standing. For instance, returning from undergraduate study overseas implies that your family might be wealthy since four years of tuition is paid instead of a one or two-year master's degree program. In the entrepreneurial world, educational and family backgrounds suggest the possible funding and social networks brought to a fledging startup team.

This classification of entrepreneurs in Shenzhen's entrepreneurial ecosystem can be found in coworking spaces and startup incubators and accelerators. According to Thomas,[6] the manager of a coworking space I visited, "Rich second-generation entrepreneurs rent out our working space as our building is one of the tallest in Shenzhen Bay, and they are able to see the beautiful city view." This particular coworking space is affiliated with a tech giant in a province far from Shenzhen. It is part of the parent company's real estate division and does not represent a tech investment though some entrepreneurs who rent their spaces told me that they expected to meet people who can potentially fund their startup at this coworking space because of its affiliation with that tech giant. There are seldom grassroots entrepreneurs at this coworking space since it costs ¥2500 per desk per month. This is expensive compared with a lower end coworking space, which charges only ¥800 per desk monthly. "It is not hard to tell those startup kids' backgrounds when they first come to visit. I know they are not grassroots entrepreneurs with no money as soon as they first ask me about the services included in our coworking space." Thomas is well experienced in spotting entrepreneurs' backgrounds, which to some extent, benefits his work there as a manager.

When I further asked if the services offered by the coworking space include venture capital investment, he explained the differences between Shenzhen's many "coworking spaces" and "incubators":

> It is probably different from your understanding in the American context. There are three kinds of "coworking space" in Shenzhen. The first sort is like ours. We do not incubate any startups here. We are a real estate service provider. We rent out our space by desk or by room. There is a coffee shop, a gaming room, and conference rooms. We sometimes organize social events for the startups here, but our parent company does not incubate these firms, and we do not offer entrepreneurs any mentorship.

The manager acknowledged that some entrepreneurs came to set up office desks and rooms in this coworking space because of the celebrated name—owing to the parent company's reputation. Entrepreneurs hope to access the parent company's resources and networks in terms of investment and mentorship; however, none of that is possible there. Predictably, since most entrepreneurs who rent out space here are from relatively well-off backgrounds, they have their own connections, and they end up looking for potential investors on their own, while their expectations of the coworking space remain unrealized. This unrealized expectation causes dissatisfaction among some startup founders I talked to at that coworking space as their companies continue. Rich second-generation overseas returnees have no problem securing seed funding from their parents and relatives, however, as their businesses continue, the demand for funding increases correspondingly that they must fundraise.

As my research progressed, I saw serious confusion among city and district government officials, service providers, and even entrepreneurs about the differences between coworking spaces, incubators, and accelerators. Coworking spaces are based on a rental business model, no matter if the office space is sponsored by the government, affiliated with private enterprise, or is a rental coffee shop. Their main function or service is to provide entrepreneurs with office space, and their main income source is rent. Incubators, according to Prashant Shah, managing director of TiE LaunchPad, a Silicon Valley based accelerator begun by TiE for enterprise-focused startups, were initially built based on the idea of coworking spaces but may offer value-added services, such as investor networks and mentorship. Accelerators, however, do not involve real estate. They may offer their program participants free office space for a period, but they charge mandatory fees, not in the name of rent but consulting fee. They may also make money by taking equity, as does Silicon Valley's Y Combinator (Ester, 2017).

Specifically, incubators differ from accelerators in many ways in terms of entry, duration, funding, program intensity, teams, culture, and cohorts (Ester, 2017). In Peter Ester's (2017) book *Accelerators in Silicon Valley: Building Successful Startups*, he examined 23 accelerators by interviewing their founders' philosophy and understanding of accelerators. He reported that a large number of executives think incubators focus on very early-stage business ideas, while the primary motive of accelerators is to boost startup ventures that have already developed a product (even prematurely) and a business model. More concretely, incubators provide startups with limited support such as a small amount of money and office space where the startup can temporarily "stay." Accelerators, on the other hand, facilitate a startup's growth and success by providing management support, access to customers, and exposure to more investors or the broad markets.

Among the "incubators" that I visited in Shenzhen, those affiliated with prominent companies hardly received any mentorship. Some startup teams will get investment depending on the structural system within those incubators. For instance, at one incubator/coworking space founded in Nanshan district in 2016, the parent company hires an independent company to operate the incubator/coworking space. That company is in charge of creating media content, promoting and renting office spaces, and recruiting startup teams. But the operating company reports to the parent company constantly, even regarding what to post on their official WeChat account. What differentiates this incubator/coworking space from the office rental mentioned above is their startup team selection criteria: they seek to incubate potential "unicorns," so they have stricter standards in recruiting members and renting spaces. They ask whether (a) founders or cofounders have worked for major tech companies like Huawei, Tencent, and Alibaba; (b) founders or cofounders have an overseas educational background; (c) the startup team has a strong technical background; and (d) the startup teams' projects match well with the parent company's strategic development.

Coworking spaces, incubators, and accelerators have sprung up in Shenzhen in recent years, at least before Covid-19, in imitation of Silicon Valley. Admittedly, these spaces are essential elements of Silicon Valley's tech innovation ecosystem, but they are not silver bullets for innovation and startup success. Their significance does not lie in their office facilities or office locations but rather in the synergy of their members and the networks within them. They serve as a network and support system in the innovation ecosystem (Ester & Maas, 2016). These relatively new concepts differ from formal network systems like trade organizations and business associations; they also differ from restaurants, bars, and other informal gathering places, where Silicon Valley's Homebrew Computer Club met (Saxenian, 1994). As discussed in the book, the social and cultural dimensions of an innovative milieu are usually unique. The founder of Homebrew Computer Club posted the following sign: "Come to a gathering of people with like-minded interests. Exchange information, swap ideas, help work on a project, whatever" (Currid-Halkett, 2007, p. 73). People come to these informal gathering spaces to relax after work, but more importantly, they constantly seek exciting new work opportunities in a company next to their own or even potential business partners. According to Saxenian (1994), Homebrew Computer Club members have founded more than 20 computer companies over the past few decades including Apple, by Steve Jobs, and Microsoft, by Bill Gates. The informal social interaction outside companies and university research labs serves a critical role in Silicon Valley's technological and entrepreneurial success.

Coworking spaces and incubators can also play a role in gathering like-minded entrepreneurs to exchange ideas and information. However, this synergy was not obvious in the coworking spaces and incubators I visited in Shenzhen. Compared with Silicon Valley entrepreneurs' free exchange of ideas and information, Chinese seem more reserved in information exchange until they know each other better, one entrepreneur shared. A male entrepreneur, who is an overseas returnee, at a coworking space said,

"When I first came to visit their offices, they only had one office room available, and it was right next to the public corridor. I was concerned that people walking by would see our whiteboard information and business ideas." Despite his worries, he rented the office room as his team's designated space. He continued, "Then I thought it does not matter. Most of the innovation ideas are combined and recombined. Nothing [is a] breakthrough."

Yet his initial concern makes sense. The confusion about concepts—coworking space, incubator, accelerator—in Shenzhen is detrimental to entrepreneurs and the whole entrepreneurial ecosystem: Entrepreneurs do not know about their own expectations nor what is truly needed to enter a suitable coworking space or to succeed in an incubator. Most coworking spaces and incubators are rental real estate businesses. They do not balance their tenants' industries and sectors since their income depends on rent, not on the startups' growth and success. Invisible competition among startup teams at coworking spaces and incubators is therefore obvious. In addition, there may also be competition for talent. Engineers hired by one startup team may be lured to work at another company across the office if there is a higher chance of success and a bigger paycheck.

The absence of free information exchange and sharing in Shenzhen's coworking spaces and incubators could also be explained by the absence of effective mentorship. But, as defined earlier, both coworking spaces and incubators in Shenzhen rely on rent revenue, although incubators may offer value-added services. It is rather accelerators that provide entrepreneurs with access to mentorship, management and leadership training, investor networks, and potential markets.

For some people, coworking spaces or incubators are a way to make money because the city government, who owns the land, subsidizes these kinds of businesses. Businesspeople rush into this enterprise as it is easy to be a "landlord" and generate quick revenue. I was told by an informant that during the 2015, Mass Innovation, Mass Entrepreneurship week, in Shenzhen alone, there were even more "incubators" than startup projects. For others, though, coworking spaces represent more than just money. Thomas, the coworking space manager I interviewed, worked at that coworking space for over two years. He described himself as a type of "service person": "I like to help entrepreneurs at this coworking space to succeed, though my job at this place is basically a property manager. Startup journeys are full of challenges and risks. If sometimes I can help entrepreneurs by simply listening to their struggles and complaints, that is comforting to me." Three months after our interview, however, he left Shenzhen for his hometown. His last message to me before his departure is that he was going to create an education startup in his hometown after years' working in Shenzhen's startup ecosystem.

The entrepreneurial journey is lonely, with only a glimmer of hope in the early stage. A vibrant entrepreneurial ecosystem with good mentorship could greatly help entrepreneurs. Unlike Shenzhen's coworking spaces and incubators, many Silicon Valley accelerators offer coaching that contributes to startups' long-run success. Mentors are usually serial entrepreneurs, former startup founders, or entrepreneurs turned tech investors who possess the necessary experiences, knowledge, understanding, capabilities, networks, and resources to coach entrepreneurs and to help them face uncertainties, navigate pitfalls, and solve problems. Experienced mentors are the mainstay of accelerators' micro-innovation system (Ester, 2017). Mentorship offers practical business advice as well as mental support. Successful entrepreneurs and businesspeople are abundant in Shenzhen; however, whether they are willing to offer such mentorship is unclear. It is also possible that some successful businesspeople in Shenzhen are incapable of providing mentorship to young Chinese startup founders who aim to establish and to expand global technology startup firms due to generational gap. A successful and established businessperson in traditional food processing industry might not understand how global logistics industry or STEAM education works. One Shenzhen incubator founder, Huang, who focuses on startups' seed series, expressed his skepticism about mentorship during an entrepreneur conference:

> Why aren't we successful? Can we bear the loneliness during the entrepreneurial journey? For a good startup project to achieve success, it will take three to five years, or even longer. Many people who run incubators have impure motives. They do it because it is trendy, because they can get government subsidies; however, they do not mean to help entrepreneurs. Once government stops subsidizing them in three to five years with no successful returns, they quit.[7]

Entrepreneurs' motives for mentorship vary. However, long-term, sustainable startup success entails costs, which includes dedicated mentorship from experienced startup founders willing to spend their time and take risks on budding entrepreneurs. In Silicon Valley, many startup mentors do that pro bono because they want to give back (Ester, 2017). Susan Lucas Conwell, a Silicon Valley startup mentor expressed her interest in helping new companies because it keeps her sharp and alert to new developments in relevant industries. She does not think mentoring startups is just about money; seeing interesting startups grow is gratifying for her (Ester, 2017). Patience, faith, and joy from mentoring are rewarded by investment returns for startup mentors.

Mentoring in Shenzhen is less promising. Huang pointed to gaps: "Look at these empty offices. These so-called incubators are backed up by well-known VC [venture capital] firms or angel investors. I have never seen them come, not to mention working closely with entrepreneurs." In 2019, when I visited Huang's incubator, he was guiding one entrepreneur through improvements to e-cigarettes. That entrepreneur had come down to Shenzhen from Shanghai, met Huang at an event, added him on WeChat, and secretly "observed" Huang on friends' WeChat Moments (where people can share their updates, stories, and information) for over a year before he decided to come to Huang's incubator. This entrepreneur holds a master's degree in material engineering and was trying to develop a special e-cigarette that can soothe the throat. He told me, "When I came down to Shenzhen from Shanghai, I knew I wanted to follow a real mentor in doing a startup. I needed to see whether those investors genuinely believe in my product and dream." This young entrepreneur's discreet observations and careful decision-making, to some extent, may implicitly demonstrate young entrepreneurs' desire for effective mentorship in an entrepreneurial process.

Conclusion

The advantage of Shenzhen's hardware supply chain, a seemly entrepreneurial culture continues to play a role in the city's technological innovation and its private enterprise sector. Unlike the previous generation of tech entrepreneurs and business owners discussed earlier, younger Chinese entrepreneurs are motivated to create tech startups by their interests, passion, and creativity. Only not a long time ago, it would have been surprising that young Chinese dreamers would drop out of American colleges like Bill Gates or Mark Zuckerberg to build their own tech startups. For example, the Chen brothers created Trainerbot, the portable table tennis training companion, because they wanted to play table tennis anytime, anywhere. They were motivated to "Do what you love." Their pursuit of their passions and interests might derive from a relatively well-off upbringing in modern China, compared with that of their parents and grandparents. Thus, the economic path Deng Xiaoping chose for China met China's historical, social, and cultural needs: Let some people get rich first. Innovation, free thinking, and the freedom to create and innovate only occur when people escape extreme poverty.

In addition, global talents and capital networks facilitate innovation and enhance the quality and diversity of the entrepreneurial ecosystem in Shenzhen. From its earliest days, many local startups demonstrated the talent flow and the significance of global collaborations. Many young Chinese tech entrepreneurs have demonstrated their technical skills, their open and global mindset, and their international vision. They were born and educated in China; however, their international involvements take place on many international platforms. Founders or co-founders at Dorami or MatataStudio participated in international tech competitions or worked in multinational companies to get involved in the maker and hacker community even before their entrepreneurial adventures in Shenzhen. However, as analyzed in the last section of this chapter, compared to Silicon Valley, Shenzhen seems to lack entrepreneurial mentorship to a larger extent. Familial-based culture in China could be a partial reason for the lack of network or community centered entrepreneurial mentorship. Regardless, international talents and hardware startup founders in Shenzhen reinforce the point: Networks have connected like-minded people into a single new network.

One network that is evolving in Shenzhen and China grants a special "maker passport." The maker passport has come to represent a recognition of membership in China's creative and innovation community. Many early Chinese makers were scolded as producers of knockoff products, but they came from the very place that makes Shenzhen the Silicon Valley of Hardware: the Hua Qiang Bei electronics market. Dr. Wen Wen at Shenzhen University has mused on the question of knockoffs from her research interview: "How do you define knockoff products? When the first generation of iPhone first shipped to China, there [were] already precisely 'imitated' iPhones at our electronics markets."[8] Advocates for open-source innovation differ in their view of "knockoff." Some even believe great makers emerge from making knockoff products. The next chapter begins with an analysis of the grassroots maker innovation at Hua Qiang Bei electronics market. How does global manufacturing network turn Shenzhen into a new rising tech hub in the global south? Makers may be one of the hidden answers.

Notes

1. Information is retrieved from Chinese book publication, 创新高地, p.91.
2. Emma is a pseudonym.
3. Information is retrieved from Wired documentary: Shenzhen, The Silicon Valley of Hardware: https://www.youtube.com/watch?v=SGJ5cZnoodY
4. This is a pseudonym.
5. This interview was set up through a city government official who supervises all tech companies in that region. My interviewee kept saying, "Follow all the government instructions," which I interpret as her generic response to any interview or visit introduced by the local government.
6. This is a pseudonym.
7. Speech delivered at MIC2020 conference on November 15–16. Chinese link could be found at: https://news.pedaily.cn/20201119/7672.shtml
8. At the time of writing in 2019, interview retrieved from Wen Wen's unpublished Chinese book on maker culture in Shenzhen. Wen is an associate professor at Shenzhen University. Wen's book is later on published in Mandarin Chinese by Social Science Academic Press.

CHAPTER 7

Shenzhen Grassroots Participatory Innovation: Let the People Make—*Makers and Manufacturing*

> Lose control of the manufacturing or production process of your product, and you risk losing control of both the technology and the final markets.
>
> —Stephen Cohen and John Zysman[1]

City of Makers

"What is maker (chuang ke)?" asked former Chinese Premier Li Keqiang[2] when he visited Shenzhen's Chai Huo Makers Space for the 2015 launch of the Mass Innovation, Mass Entrepreneurship initiative. Eric Pan Hao, founder of Seeed Studio and a long-time leader in the global maker movement, explained, "Makers are technological innovators from civil communities with no institutional associations. In Chaihuo Makerspace (i.e., Chaihuo is a subsidiary of Seeed Studio), makers use their spare time outside of their regular working hours for open exchanges and innovative collaborations." Makers are significant in technological innovation. Reflected in the icon of Chaihuo Makerspace—a campfire—this maker space adopted a traditional Chinese proverb, "zhong ren shi chai huo yan gao" 众人拾柴火焰, which refers to the power of collective intelligence and strength. Unlike the top-down process of traditional R&D in scientific laboratory research, market environmental scanning, and product commercialization, maker innovation is less hierarchical and

G. Y. Wang, *Dragon Innovation: Shenzhen*, Governing China in the 21st Century, https://doi.org/10.1007/978-981-95-9637-9_7

more reversible. As Eric Pan Hao, an advocate for maker innovation and open source, further explained:

> If I am a maker, I will share my progress and my own achievements in this community. You can use my "wheels" to make your "cars," and you can likewise share your own discoveries and achievements. Maker innovation removes the barriers separating innovative individuals. The sharing and allocation of resources encourages overall innovation efficiency.[3]

"Let me add another log to the fire." It is said that former Premier Li Keqiang, with the new understanding of "maker," offered to register as the first Chai Huo member in 2015.[4] Since then, Shenzhen has remade itself as a City of Makers and has hosted its annual Shenzhen International Maker Week every June since 2015. Figure 7.1 shows the Maker Week sign, reading "City of Makers," at Shenzhen Entrepreneurial Plaza in Nanshan, the high-tech district in Shenzhen.

Eric Pan Hao is well known in the Shenzhen maker community. The program director I interviewed at HAX, Emma, said that Sean O' Sullivan, founder of the venture capital firm SOSV, contacted Eric when he first started the HAX hardware accelerator (see Chapter 6, The Entrepreneurial Ecosystem in Shenzhen). Native Chinese and educated in China, Eric is a maker who enjoys electronics assembly and making things. "I was hooked and made up my mind to start my tech company in Shenzhen after a tour at Hua Qiang Bei electronics market." Eric left Beijing for Shenzhen because Hua Qiang Bei had the best and the most complete electronics components supply chain. It is as if someone with a dream to act went to Hollywood, drawn by its resources, opportunities and social environment. In 2008, he founded Seeed Studio, with the belief that "electronics can be art," adding an additional "e" to "Seed" to represent electronics. Passion, interest, and enthusiasm for maker innovation motivated him and his team. By 2012, Seeed Studio was the largest open-source hardware manufacturer in China and one of the top three in the world.[5]

Eric is an influential voice in China's maker community. He recalled his 2010 trip to the United States: "People there knew us and liked our products, but nobody wanted to believe that we are a Chinese company. Nobody had thought that cool and innovative products could come of China."[6] After that trip, Eric started to add the label "Innovate with China" on Seeed Studio products. In 2012, Seeed Studio helped bring

Fig. 7.1 City of Makers sign (*Note* Photo taken by the author at Shenzhen Bay Entrepreneurial Plaza [Inno Park])

the Maker Faire to Shenzhen—Maker Faire's first introduction to Chinese Mainland, including the Hong Kong area.

The Maker Faire festival is a global event that partners with local collaborators to promote the maker movement and bottom to top grassroots innovation worldwide. *Make*, the affiliated magazine, has proved a valuable resource on innovation among global makers and the "do it yourself" creative culture. Shenzhen International Maker Week is sponsored by the city government; Maker Faire is more of a non-governmental event. Since 2012, with official authorization from Maker Faire, the annual Shenzhen Maker Faire has become a symbolic event for the maker community in both Shenzhen and its peripheral cities and beyond, even countries in Southeast Asia. Entrepreneurs, college students, academics, and families wishing to cultivate their kids' creativity attend Maker Faire. Global makers, exhibitors, and grassroots entrepreneurs seeking business partners also attend.

Like the San Francisco Maker Faire Festival begun in 2006, Maker Faire Shenzhen builds on Shenzhen's unique technological development's needs and expectations: *to the heart of the community, to the cluster of the industry* 回归社区，对接产业. The Shenzhen city government's Hi-Tech Fair, started in 1999, is more official and business oriented (see Chapter 5, Local Governance: Bureaucratic Entrepreneurs), whereas Maker Faire Shenzhen stimulates grassroots innovation and maker creativity, at the same time, searching for business potential. Unlike the San Francisco Maker Faire, which does not link the local maker community with industrial manufacturing, Maker Faire Shenzhen connects people in communities and business in industries. It leverages China's internet economy and manufacturing resources to attract enterprises and individuals. Days before 2019 Maker Faire Shenzhen, sales advertisements and promotions on limited-edition Maker Faire Shenzhen T-shirts, canvas bags, and magnets were listed on Taobao.com, WeChat, and other popular e-commerce platforms in China.

Dale Dougherty, founder and CEO of Maker Faire and *Make* magazine, stated that the early creative and maker culture in San Francisco has faded away. Even in San Francisco, everything has given way to money. Dougherty said, "I think we are missing and losing creativity and sort of the individual and small group magic that made this place special in the beginning."[7]

By contrast, Maker Faire Shenzhen remains vibrant and has become a symbolic maker event. Most importantly, the promotion of the maker movement and innovation is a radical challenge to traditional Chinese culture and education, which emphasizes memorization, standard answers, and high grades. A maker-inspired education, by contrast, encourages innovation, creativity, and the joy of exploration. This change is especially obvious in China's metropolitan cities. Chaihuo Makerspace, the organizer of Maker Faire Shenzhen, developed its own maker technology education system for young makers by using industrial resources and creative content platforms. Their system includes entry- and advanced-level curriculum and solutions for elementary school, middle school, and high school students. Kids in elementary school are called "innovation explorers" and "innovation trainees," students in middle school are called "innovation practitioners," and high school students are called "innovation leaders." Anyone with access to the internet can download the Codecraft coding software and use the hardware resources Chai Huo Maker Spaces provides to turn their ideas into real products.

A cofounder at Shenzhen Litchee Lab maker space shared a story shared a story about how an eight-year-old Chinese boy built a key sensor for his mom to prevent her from forgetting her keys whenever she leaves home.[8] Encouragement of innovation and creativity, facilitation of hands-on skills, and the supporting ecosystem to turn ideas into real products have gradually transformed conventional Chinese education. Exposure to fast-changing technology products and creative ideas opens the children's minds from a young age (Fig. 7.2).

Andrew Huang, an MIT-trained electrical engineering PhD graduate, and a controversial figure in open-source hardware and hacker culture, declared, "If you want to make stuff, you need to talk to people, and share ideas with people." Singapore-based Huang is an advisor to HAX hardware accelerator and a frequent contributor to *Make* magazine. He advocates for reverse engineering and open-source hardware innovation. "I like to wander around Hua Qiang Bei electronics market," Huang noted. In 2016, he published a crowdfunded book, *The Essential Guide to Electronics in Shenzhen*, to help English speakers navigate the Hua Qiang Bei marketplace in Shenzhen, one of the world's premier electronics marketplaces and production hubs. At a TED Talk on the innovative city, Huang described the famed electronics marketplace by playing off Tennyson's famous line, "'Tis better to have loved and lost than never to have loved at all" to create a Hua Qiang Bei analogy: "'Tis better to be produced and copied than never to have produced at all."

Fig. 7.2 An AI-maker exhibition store in Longgang district (*Note* Photo taken by the author. Words in the picture translated to English: Everybody is a maker; Everything can be AI-nized)

Hua Qiang Bei Electronics Market

China's largest electronics trading market.
Low cost, low quality.
Knockoff center hub (*Shan Zhai Zhong Xin Di* 山寨中心地).
Hardware paradise.

Hua Qiang Bei has many labels, good and bad. The electronics market is located in Futian district, near Futian Port and close to Lok Ma Chau in Hong Kong. It was the first electronics components market in Chinese Mainland. Its predecessor is a provincial military factory, Yue Bei Jun Gong Chang 粤北军工厂, located at a remote, converted site in Guangdong province. Since its relocation to Shenzhen, the military factory was transformed from producing military radio semiconductors to producing televisions, radios, and other consumer electronics. They named it Hua Qiang (华强), which means "China strong" in Mandarin Chinese.

The early rise and development of Hua Qiang Bei relied on several factors. As noted previously, with the 1978 Open and Reform policy, the Shenzhen city government strategically committed to developing its electronics industry. In 1985, China's Ministry of Electronics Industry set up a branch office in Shenzhen to integrate dispersed small-scale electronics companies and to promote market-oriented operations in the electronics industry. However, China did not yet have the scientific research ability and production capacity to develop these electronic components; they were, therefore, imported through Hong Kong. Hua Qiang Bei gradually developed into China's first import distribution center for electronics components and electrical parts in Shenzhen's market-oriented economy.

Hong Kong, as an international trade center, was important to the transactions and imports of electronics components to Shenzhen. However, aside from offering imports, capital, and timely information exchange obtained from the developed world before its ubiquity in Chinese Mainland, Hong Kong's contributions to Shenzhen's technological innovation are questioned. The conventional explanation for Shenzhen's successful economic development and technological rise is its locational proximity to Hong Kong. Yet one of my interviewees disagreed: "Did you ever hear about any technology brands made in Hong Kong? Not at all." A Canadian citizen, born in Hong Kong, Phoebe[9] commutes every day from Hong Kong to Shenzhen for work at a famous technology firm. She believes that the high-tech industry is far more developed in Shenzhen than in Hong Kong. "Factories, manufacturing, and hardworking talents are here." And she likes to learn and see new products coming out of Shenzhen by working there. My interviewee's acknowledgment of the competitive advantage of Shenzhen's technological development is reinforced in Dorami's strategic arrangement (see Chapter 6, The Entrepreneurial Ecosystem in Shenzhen). Dorami once located their manufacturing and research centers in Shenzhen and overseas while their marketing center was in Hong Kong. Some Shenzhen corporations, like Ping An Group, set their media and public relations center in Hong Kong to utilize its international media resources while keeping their headquarters in Shenzhen. MatataStudio, as described in Chapter 6, locates its headquarter in Shenzhen while having Hong Kong and Macao sales representatives. Those companies' strategic arrangement, both startups' and established corporations', again refute the conventional wisdom that Shenzhen's technological success relies on its physical proximity to Hong Kong. As argued in this book, Shenzhen's locational proximity to Hong Kong was only the necessary but not sufficient condition.

In the early 1980s, many electrical appliance manufacturers set up their manufacturing factories or research labs in the Hua Qiang Bei area to compete for the "premium" electronics components imported from Hong Kong.[10] In this way, Hua Qiang Bei gradually formed a complete electronics product development and production system, including production, research, and sales. One person in the documentary *Shenzhen: Silicon Valley of Hardware* described this place with excitement:

> People at Hua Qiang Bei all know each other. One person will only do one portion of the work, and they will give the other portion of the work to other friend to do, so they can finish the work very quickly. This is how Hua Qiang Bei works. Some people can design, other people can manufacture, and other people can sell. So everyone is working together. That is why it only takes two or three months for a product to be ready for the market.[11]

Hua Qiang Bei's complete electronics supply chain and its production system is a double-edged sword. Efficient manufacturing capacity enables fast production of electronics; however, since it was easy to make quick money by simple assembly and manufacturing, little advanced research efforts were put into the process. Still, the self-sufficient and mature production system opened a door for copycat (Shan Zhai) electronic products. From 2005 to 2010, Hua Qiang Bei allegedly became the hub for global copycat mobile phone manufacturing. Around 2005, the Chinese government loosened its policy and changed its national approval system for mobile phone production, which lowered entry barriers for mobile phone manufacturing. Hua Qiang Bei took advantage and started to produce copycat mobile phones. Mobile phones were exported to Dubai, Africa, and Southeast Asia. I was told during a visit to Huawei R&D campus in Dongguan, "The first appearance of dual-SIM-card smart phones were copycat phones from the electronics market."

In fact, dual-SIM-card mobile phone indeed is considered as an important innovation of Shenzhen's Shan Zhai (copycat) success. This innovative product draws on consumer insights to satisfy Chinese consumer needs. Dual-SIM-card mobile phones support two operator networks on one mobile device which enables phone users to avoid roaming charges. At the same time, it helps users separate work use from life-related use if phone users prefer to have two mobile numbers on the same device (Keane & Zhao, 2012). Domestic roaming fee in China is not canceled nationwide until September 2017 which demonstrates that this dual-SIM-card Shan Zhai phone, as an innovation, derives from Chinese consumer needs in China's local market.

Another often-heard Shan Zhai story is about the touch screen Nokia smart phone. Before the smart phone came out, a popular touch screen smart phone circulated at Hua Qiang Bei. Some phone factories built on the mature production system for touch screen MP4 and combined it with Nokia phone's keyboard. Thus the "touch screen Nokia smart phone" came out before iPhone's appearance in China. When the iPhone came to China, many electronics manufacturers started to produce power banks that could charge an iPhone anytime, anywhere. These were needed because the iPhone's big screen consumed its battery faster than other mobile phones. Hua Qiang Bei electronics market is like a naughty kid who kept working on "creations" that the big guys neglected. Its well-developed manufacturing supply chain, the clustering effect of hardware manufacturing and IT companies in Shenzhen along with Chinese national government's call for indigenous innovation contribute to the fast-growing Shan Zhai phenomenon in Shenzhen. As Tse et al. (2009) argued, Shan Zhai innovation results from both soft (Chinese culture, history and government regulatory) and hard (market supply and demand) factors. Shan Zhai phenomenon, from a cultural aspect, is not much different from hacker culture in the west in a way that they both emphasize on user-led networked innovation and the anti-authoritarian part, however, in the Chinese context, Shan Zhai culture provides the "information-less" with innovation and business opportunities rather than to the elites alone (Cartier et al., 2005; Keane & Zhao, 2012; Qiu 2009). But Shan Zhai mobile phones, or the Shan Zhai industry in general, face news challenges from government regulations and the formal economy. It is reported by Xin Hua News Agency in March 2011 that about one-third of nearly 3,000 mobile phone sellers in Hua Qiang Bei including Shan Zhai phone sellers have closed up their business operations due to Chinese government's initiative to improve intellectual property rights as well as the urge to develop indigenous innovation.[12] A founder of a maker technology company and president of a Shenzhen University entrepreneur association argued, "Niche markets or niche technology product markets may be the next economic growth opportunity as more and more people prefer to have customized items. It is a perfect combination of maker creativity and Hua Qiang Bei's efficient and mature electronics supply chain and production system."[13]

Manufacturing Networks

Hua Qiang Bei has gone through ups and downs because of its own business structure, the business environment, and external economic influences. Shenzhen is the center of distribution, design, application, and innovation in China's integrated circuit industry. Table 7.1 shows that in 2015 Shenzhen's integrated circuit design sales were about 38 billion RMB, accounting for 31% of the national total and ranking No.1 in China. Main electronics components produced in Shenzhen are integrated circuits, electronics components, semiconductor discrete devices, liquid crystal displays, semiconductor memory, and hard disk storage.

In the printed circuit board (PCB) field, Shenzhen boasts the most companies in China, most of which are large. It is the most important trading center for circuit boards in China, and more than half of Chinese PCB companies have established their operation and trading centers in the city. The 2014 China printed circuit board industry top 100 list included 27 Shenzhen companies (including foreign joint ventures), with an overall operating income of 45.308 billion RMB, accounting for 27.46% of the total revenue generated by China's 116 PCB companies. Table 7.2 shows the number of top 100 Chinese PCB enterprises located in Shenzhen.

Table 7.1 Shenzhen integrated circuit industry sales, 2010–2015 Unit Billion RMB

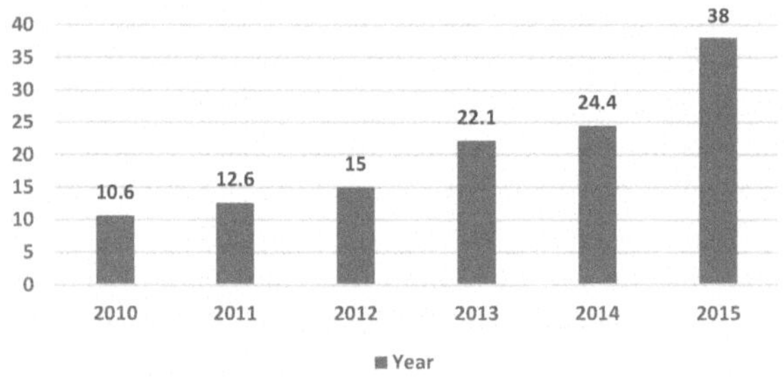

Note Data from China Semiconductor Industry Association

Table 7.3 shows sales revenues from 2008 to 2012 for the top 100 PCB companies in China and those ones in Shenzhen. The Pearl River Delta, where Shenzhen is located, is an important region for domestic and international PCB manufacturing and trading. Its PCB output value accounts for 55% of China's total. Also, among the top 10 integrated circuit design companies in 2019, three are from Shenzhen. Of these, Huawei's HiSilicon ranked first.[14]

As did the PCB industry, the electroacoustic industry saw rapid growth due to the development of mobile communications equipment worldwide. Miniature electroacoustic components and consumer electroacoustic products enabled the acoustic industry to grow annually by more

Table 7.2 Number of top 100 Chinese printed circuit board enterprises in Shenzhen

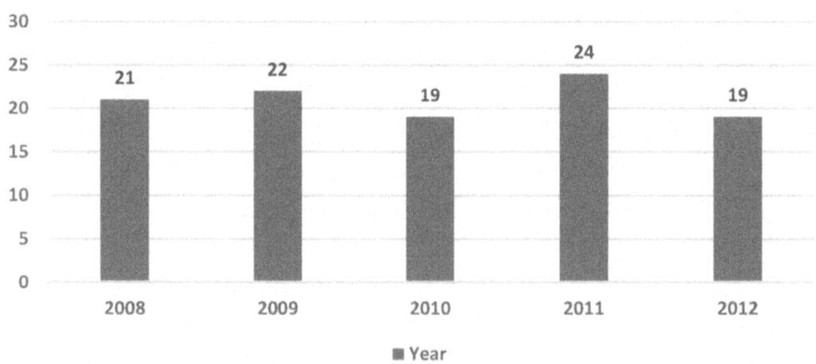

Note Data compiled from China Printed Circuit Association.[15]

Table 7.3 Revenues of top 100 printed circuit board enterprises in China and Shenzhen, 2008–2012

Note Data compiled from China Printed Circuit Association

than 15%. By 2013, the industry's output exceeded 10 billion units, with sales of 84 billion RMB. AAC Technology, founded in 1993, is a leading provider of sensory experience solutions and provides miniature components for consumer electronic products. As a major supplier to Apple, AAC Technology has nine major manufacturing bases in China, Vietnam, and the Philippines. Its Shenzhen production base is located in Longgang district, which is also home to Huawei's headquarters and Foxconn, Apple's major assembly factory. Although AAC is one of the world's largest acoustic industry manufacturers, one top management person expressed concern about its dependence on foreign precision production equipment in the global supply chain system.

East and Southeast Asia are important in the global production networks of IT contract manufacturing. Global electronics production and manufacturing are shaped by manufacturing as a global service through the international division of labor. Production networks produce a system that allocates different functions among developed and less developed countries and regions. Silicon Valley, the "Detroit of the information age" (Lüthje, 2001), boasted the largest number of contract manufacturers' headquarters and development and production centers. Singapore, Malaysia, and Chinese Taiwan were the low-cost contract manufacturing facilities for first- and second-generation Silicon Valley chip and computer manufacturers. China followed in the late 1990s (Lüthje, Boy, et al., 2013). In spite of China's late entry, the production of global IT contract manufacturing in Asia has a Chinese quality: Singapore, Malaysia, and Chinese Taiwan all have many tech leaders of Chinese heritage and have ethnic Chinese in management and technical circles, which leaves the impression of a Chinese business network (Hsing 1998; Yeung & Olds, 2000). Influenced by international geopolitical positions and national domestic industrial policies, Singapore, Chinese Hong Kong, and Chinese Taiwan became regional headquarters and major trading bases in electronics manufacturing for western multinational corporations in East Asia and Southeast Asia in the 1990s.

Under British rule in the 1960s, Hong Kong became the first offshore electronics industry center in Asia, with investments from Philips and other companies (Henderson, 1989/2002). Hong Kong's electronics manufacturing grew rapidly during the 1990s but declined after the 2000 financial recession. Some infrastructure remained, however, in the form of small- to mid-sized electronic factories that gave Taiwanese entrepreneurs a base from which to establish business relations with special economic zones in South China, especially surrounding Hong Kong. Shenzhen was one of them. Investments from Taiwan started to channel through Hong Kong to cities in the Pearl River Delta. Hsing (1998) noted that Taiwan entrepreneurs took advantage of the cultural affinity, common language (i.e., Mandarin Chinese), and family ties to cities in Pearl River Delta and began to establish small- to mid-sized companies. Meanwhile, with the decline of Hong Kong's electronics manufacturing, many electronics companies started to relocate their operation centers to Chinese Mainland, particularly to Shenzhen and its surrounding cities (Lee, 1998). Shenzhen's electronics industries developed initially under the combined forces of the local government's urban development strategy— "electronics oriented, innovation focused" (see Chapter 3: China, the New Development)—and Taiwan's and Hong Kong's industrial restructurings, taking advantage of the new special economic zone in Chinese Mainland.

Unlike Hong Kong, Taiwan benefited from the industrial restructuring in the wake of the 2000 financial recession. As a major hub of electronics contract manufacturing and original design manufacturing (ODM) companies in Asia, Taiwan cultivated a base of skilled engineers and contract manufacturers of electronic components. Its Hsinchu Industrial Science Park 新竹科学园, established in 1977, symbolized its government initiative in developing Taiwan's high-tech industry (see Chapter 8, Shenzhen R&D Ecosystem). Taiwan, a developmental state (Castells, 1998/2000/2010), provided strong support to its high-tech industry, including chips, printed circuit boards (PCBs), and optoelectronics. Sometimes, the government was the direct owner or shareholder in Taiwanese industrial groups (Amsden & Chu, 2003; Berger & Lester, 2015; Pohlmann & Lim, 2014). More importantly, "brain circulation" from the United States back to Chinese Taiwan, particularly of Taiwanese immigrant engineers and entrepreneurs from Silicon Valley, helped Taiwan establish and expand its global networks and enhance its overall engineering talent pool (Saxenian, 2002). In 2003–2004, following the 2000 crisis, multinational companies such as IBM, Apple, Motorola, and Siemens, either opened new technology sourcing centers or expanded their existing centers in Taipei (see Chapter 8, Shenzhen R&D Ecosystem).

Electronics manufacturers began to shift large amounts of production to Chinese Mainland in the 1990s. "Made in China by Taiwan" characterizes the phenomenon and the production networks linking Taiwan and Chinese Mainland. Foxconn, for instance, maintains research, development, and product introduction in Taiwan but shifted substantial product engineering to its manufacturing centers in Chinese Mainland to take advantage of the low-cost engineering workforce (Lüthje, Boy, et al., 2013). Taiwan businesspeople and entrepreneurs continued the same business and production models in both the electronics industry and the fashion footwear industry described by Hsing (1998). Taiwan has almost always retained the R&D divisions but shifted manufacturing production to the mainland. Table 7.4 shows that by 2006 several major electronics contract manufacturers had located in Chinese Mainland, mostly in Shenzhen or the Pearl River Delta. It shows that electronics manufacturing, especially in PCBA (printed circuit board assembly), is concentrated in Shenzhen.

Shenzhen Grassroots Participatory Innovation: Let the People Make

Global electronics production networks in Asia gradually shifted from the Four Asian Tigers (Singapore, Chinese Taiwan, South Korea, and Chinese Hong Kong) to Chinese Mainland in the 90s. Shenzhen and its adjacent cities (e.g., Guangzhou, Dongguan, and Zhongshan) emerged as the main locations for global electronics contract manufacturing. Hua Qiang Bei electronics market, for instance, has an integrated and comprehensive electronics supply chain, low- and high-end component manufacturers,

Table 7.4 Location distribution of major electronics manufacturing companies

Company	*Location and function(s)*
Foxconn	• Taipei, Taiwan—HQ, R&D, Log., Manuf • Shenzhen, PRD—Industrial Park • Kunshan—PCBA, SA • Beijing—PCBA, SA • Zhongshan, PRD—PCBA, SA • Several other smaller sites in China—N/A
Flextronics	• Beijing—Software • Hong Kong—Regional office • Doumen—Industrial park: PCBA, SA, PCB, Manuf., Plastics • Shenzhen, PRD—Plastics, PCBA, SA, Des • Dongguan, PRD—Plastics • Guangzhou, PRD—Des • Shanghai—PCBA, SA, Plastics • Changzhou—Sheet metal encl • Nanjing • Qingdao • Taipei, Taiwan—Regional office, PIC
Solectron	• Suzhou—PCBA, SA, Rep • Shenzhen, PRD—PCBA, SA • Shanghai—Des, Rep, PCBA, Encl • Taipei, Taiwan—Sales, NPI
Sanmina—SCI	• Kunshan—PCBA, Encl., Des • Shenzhen, PRD—PCBA, Encl., Des
Celestica	• Hong Kong—Admin., Log • Dongguan, PRD—PCBA, SA • Shanghai—PCBA • Suzhou—PCBA
Jabil	• Shanghai—PCBA, Des • Guangzhou, PRD—PCBA • Wuxi—PCBA • Suzhou—PCBA

Note PRD = Pearl River Delta. Admin. = administration and office work; Des. = design; Encl. = metal enclosures and frames; HQ = headquarters; Log. = logistics; Manuf. = assembly of printed circuit boards, end products, backplanes, cables; NPI = new product introduction; PCBA = printed circuit board assembly; PIC = production and inventory control; Rep. = repair; SA = systems assembly. Company information from (Lüthje, Boy, et. al. 2013)

and a few R&D firms. The "China price" readily available and widely covered in the news and government reports overemphasized low Chinese labor costs.

This account neglects several factors that have helped Shenzhen's manufacturing upgrade. Shenzhen's innovation economy reveals a phenomenon that I call a "Shenzhen grassroots participatory innovation," riffing off cultural studies scholar Henry Jenkins's term "participatory culture." Jenkins (1992/2012) used "participatory culture" in his book *Textual Poachers* to refer to fandom: Fans interpreted fandom as an informal community centered around equality, sociality, diversity, and reciprocity. They had a largely shared understanding of the activities they were participating in and of the outcomes of their participation, for instance, how their production and media content circulation contributed to their shared well-being. Further, he defined participatory culture:

> A participatory culture is a culture with relatively low barriers to artistic expression and civic engagement, strong support for creating and sharing one's creations, and some type of informal mentorship whereby what is known by the most experienced is passed along to novices. A participatory culture is also one in which members believe their contributions matter and feel some degree of social connection with one another (at the least they care what other people think about what they have created). (Jenkins et al., 2015, p. 4)

Borrowing from Jenkins's concept, I suggest that participants in Hua Qiang Bei's electronics manufacturing—namely factory workers, migrant labors, designers, and entrepreneurs—enter with relatively low engineering, design, and business barriers. They show each other support in the manufacturing supply chain and collectively make commercial profits. Skilled and experienced engineers continually learn new skills, allowing flexible volume production, maintenance, and repair work. Unlike manufacturing workers in Malaysia, Chinese workers and production engineers perform most of the repair, maintenance, and programming of production equipment (Lüthje, Boy, et al., 2013). Many production engineers prefer tasks where equipment design is involved. Engineers at Shenzhen electronics manufacturing factories care about their salaries but they care more about improving their engineering skills. Multinational producers of electronic components, such as chips, motherboards, hard disk drives, displays, and other materials, are located in Shenzhen or its environs because the exposure to cutting-edge electronics products and production techniques presents production engineers with major learning opportunities. Unlike top-down models popular in many developed countries in which university research moves to factory innovation, Shenzhen's technological innovation has evolved from its manufacturing-enabled process and product innovation.

An electronics manufacturing company owner who got his start in Shenzhen manufacturing factories said, "We design our own products and manufacture them to sell in markets. This is how we developed a successful brand. It is no longer copycat (Shan Zhai). It is our own brand." He continued, "Apple's business logic is to create commercial competition [by creating a technology and market monopoly], but I really do not like Apple." He strongly advocated for open-source and maker innovation. As someone who once made "Shan Zhai" products, he believes the underlining logic of "maker" is the same as that of "Shan Zhai," which is a grassroots innovation spirit, moving from the bottom to the top.[16]

Grassroots participatory innovation in Shenzhen is linked to the city's original small-scale manufacturing networks. It also reflects Shenzhen city culture: Make your own destiny and future. People who enter the Shan Zhai ecosystem do not usually come from privileged socioeconomic backgrounds which make many of them grassroots entrepreneurs. Many arrive as migrant workers, sometimes through extended families and their local networks, the same hometown, for instance (Wu et al., 2023) (see Chapter 4, City Culture—Experimental and Entrepreneurial DNA). They seize Shenzhen's entrepreneurial spirit and the city's possibilities. Grassroots entrepreneurs are critical participants in Shenzhen's grassroots participatory innovation process. Increasing recognition in academic literature has been given to the role of entrepreneurship can play in the improvement of those people at the bottom of the economic structure or "bottom of the pyramid" (BOP) if both social development and economic advancement goals are set (Ansari et al., 2012; Prahalad, 2012; Prahalad & Hammond, 2002). Grassroots entrepreneurs think of themselves as driven, diligent who devote themselves to making money and improving their standard of living (Lindtner et al., 2015). Often, those grassroots entrepreneurs obtain little formal education or sophisticated technology knowledge, particularly when they just arrived at Shenzhen. But they know their unique advantages in the form of the specific consumer needs of their communities (Gupta & Harris, 2010; Pansera & Sarkar, 2016). An ethnographic interview by Lindtner et al. (2015) depicted the city as follows:

> Shenzhen is working just like this. You can understand it as crowdfunding. It works differently from crowdfunding via online social networking . . . you must be firmly settled in the industry, be recognized, have a good

> personality. . . . Everybody in the industry chain gives you things for free, all the materials, and only when you have sold your product, you do the bills [and pay back]. (p. 8)

People in the Shan Zhai ecosystem build relationships and gain trust as in all other social networks. They participate in informal face-to-face gatherings such as dinners and KTV (Karaoke Television), as well as through online social networking groups, such as on WeChat. All the personal interaction builds on a collective goal: the discovery of business opportunities, the expansion of existing manufacturing factories, and ultimately the generation of additional value (Lindtner et al., 2015). Shenzhen's grassroots participatory innovation reveals an innovation culture that is not dissimilar from Silicon Valley: industrious labors, and people with business acumen and entrepreneurial insights, who form a community that facilitates information sharing and exchange (Saxenian, 1996). But unlike elite networks from Stanford or University of California, Berkeley, in Shenzhen's grassroots participatory innovation, this information sharing and exchange is built on the closely interconnected manufacturing supply chain and human relations among grassroots entrepreneurs who are resilient and creative (Prahalad & Ramaswamy, 2004) since a vast majority of grassroots entrepreneurs are initially motivated by survival needs (Carsrud & Brännback, 2011). Ian Lesnet, from the open-source hardware project Dangerous Prototypes, spoke of the enticement of Shenzhen:

> The wonderful thing about Shenzhen is that we have both horizontal and vertical integration. In Hua Qiang Bei, you can buy components. Go a little bit further out, people sell circuit boards. A little bit further out, there are people who manufacture things and attach components to circuit boards. So, you can actually have something built. And a little further out there are people who make product cases. A little further out you have garages with large-format printers who make labels for your products and a little further out they recycle it back down again. So you can build something, design it entirely, have it manufactured, sell it, and then break down its components and recycle it back into the center of the markets. You have all the skills and all the people who can do that, and they are all in one place.[17]

Ian Lesnet's company, Dangerous Prototypes, forms a partnership with Seeed Studio (mentioned in the first section of this chapter) so that he could sell his original versions of his company's products through Seeed Studio. According to Ian Lesnet, the sales at Seeed studio made it possible to develop both the hardware and firmware to an extent that a much bigger and mature company, SparkFun began to sell a clone of their company's product (Keane & Zhao, 2012). This kind of grassroots participatory innovation, combined with Shenzhen's manufacturing capacity, allowed some low-end manufacturing enterprises and the maker community-oriented organizations to develop into advanced manufacturing companies that are able to compete in domestic and international markets. 3Nod,[18] for instance, a traditional manufacturer of plastic multimedia audio molds, founded in 1996, effected a manufacturing upgrade by increasing investment in industrial design and technological innovation to develop high-end products for Chinese and global markets. 3Nod has evolved into a company that constructs a complete ecological industry chain of smart life using both hardware and software. The company's model of "original planning manufacturing" spans planning, design, supply chain, manufacture, market, and service. Offering products for "smart home," "smart work," and "smart travel," 3Nod uses its audio manufacturing capacity to enhance its products in audio–video entertainment, smart home audio products, and other information technology products. The company emphasizes maker creativity in producing new smart lifestyle products. 3Nod's transition from a low-end manufacturing enterprise to an advanced manufacturing company with independent product design and innovation capacity shows that manufacturing advantage can enhance product advantage and facilitate continued product innovation (Cohen & Zysman, 1987).

Conclusion

The analysis in this chapter starts from the maker movement and the encouragement of maker innovation in Shenzhen and moves to the role of the hardware paradise, Shenzhen's Hua Qiang Bei electronics market, in global electronics contract manufacturing. A key term I coined in this chapter that demonstrates Shenzhen's innovation characteristics is *Shenzhen grassroots participatory innovation.* It is a distinct global innovation phenomenon: Shenzhen grassroots participatory innovation is rooted in local maker culture, and it connects grassroots maker movement with comprehensive hardware manufacturing supply chain in the advantages of global electronics manufacturing networks. In particular, government policies on digital devices changed from the initial lack of regulations on copycat mobile phones and products to the state call for indigenous innovation which facilitated Shenzhen and China's industrial manufacturing upgrading and technological innovation capacity. Moreover, regulations and increasing awareness of intellectual property, most of the time enforced by the government, also help with industrial upgrading and the gradual disappearance of copycat products in domestic markets.

Shenzhen grassroots participatory innovation plays a key role in understanding its innovation because it negates the fundamental misunderstanding of its innovation advantage, which is claimed to be its low-cost manufacturing labor. Similar to how global technology leaders and producers used to view Japan's electronics industry in the 1980s (for Japan, it was U.S. producers), people seem to continue to focus on wage differences between the developing and the developed ones. They worried that Shenzhen's core advantage was low-cost labor, at least until Chinese wages rose. They ignored the significance of manufacturing in Shenzhen's economic development and its technological improvements. Cohen and Zysman (1987) emphasized the significance of manufacturing production and argued that manufacturing production is directly related to the capacity to support innovation. Weak manufacturing will lead to the erosion of a strong product and market position. Thus Shenzhen's comprehensive electronics supply chain and its manufacturing production system enhance its ability to innovate with proper design, technological research, and strong financial support. A government official from the Shenzhen Economic, Trade, and Information Commission stated:

> Traditional manufacturers have been encouraged to develop high-end products, with more efforts being put into the design and brand-building, as well as technological innovation. Developing future industries does not mean traditional manufacturing will be abandoned in Shenzhen. Instead, manufacturers in the traditional industries will be given more support to upgrade their business from simple processors at the lower end of the market to providers of high-end products and services.[19]

The combination of maker innovation and manufacturing of low- and high-end products and services was Shenzhen's technological innovation advantage. Many people in hardware manufacturing industry believe that electronics merchants at Hua Qiang Bei never say no. They appear to respond to any kind of customer request and quickly manufacture electronics products. Shenzhen's abundant electronics resources and the phenomenal low- to high-end manufacturing facilities created a unique technological ecosystem. Hardware startup entrepreneurs claim that efficient electronics purchase, fast prototyping, and the numerous experimental abilities are Shenzhen's unique advantages. Advanced manufacturing is essential in Shenzhen's transition to its next stage of economic development and technological innovation. Figure 7.3 summarizes critical factors and their roles in the contribution to Shenzhen's grassroots participatory innovation.

However, despite Shenzhen's success in entering niche electronics and consumer technology product markets, high tech is not defined only by the nature of the product:

> High tech, however defined, must be understood as intimately tied to manufacturing, and not as a free-floating laboratory activity. It is tied to manufacturing in two distinct and important ways. First, despite the popularity of home computers and burglar alarms, most high-tech products are producer goods, not consumer goods. They are bought to be used either in the products of other industries (like microprocessors in autos) or in the production process (like robots, computers, and lasers across the range of manufacturing and services) or both. . . .
>
> Second, and most important in the overwhelming majority of cases, unless R&D is tightly tied to the manufacturing of the product—and to the permanent process of innovation in production now required for competitiveness in manufacturing—R&D will fall behind the cutting edge of incremental innovation. (Cohen & Zysman, 1987, p. 8)

Many Shenzhen's technological innovations come from the production process, especially in the consumer electronics product industries. However, Taiwan Semiconductor Manufacturing Company's (TSMC) chip ban on Huawei demonstrated Huawei's innovation gap as well as Shenzhen's: the high-end advanced manufacturing field still depends on external advanced manufacturing suppliers (see Chapter 8, Shenzhen R&D Ecosystem). Although two Huawei-branded chips, Qi Lin and HiSilicon, were originally designed by the company, the lack of chip supplies from the world's largest and most advanced contract chipmaker pulls Huawei behind. Similarly, TSMC, Samsung, and SMIC all rely

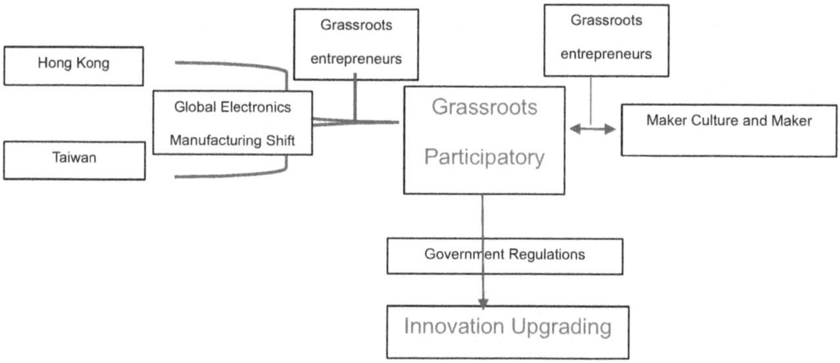

Fig. 7.3 Shenzhen grassroots participatory innovation model (Note Shenzhen Grassroots Participatory Innovation Model created by the author)

heavily on American chip production tools and materials, which will be slow to change.[20]

Conventional wisdom emphasizes the reliance on prestigious research universities and schools to supply skilled workers and engineers which is fundamental in the successful development of advanced contract manufacturing and radical technological innovation. "Shenzhen could be the game changer [in China] if it can bolster up its higher education," said a Chinese American tech investor who returned to China a decade ago post 2008 Beijing Olympics. He thought Shenzhen's tech ecosystem, compared with that of Beijing or Shanghai, is more ready for the next round of technological innovation in China. He made this comment in 2018, long before Shenzhen—Hong Kong—Guangzhou becomes the No.1 global innovation cluster. How does Shenzhen compare in terms of higher education and scientific research? The condemnation of Shenzhen's higher education quality prompted heated discussion, often compared to higher education systems in Beijing and Shanghai. With its open-minded and welcoming city culture, business-supportive city government, ambitious and aggressive entrepreneurs, creative makers, comprehensive electronics supply chain, and the ongoing upgrading of manufacturing, Shenzhen has every ingredient to be the next Silicon Valley—except it lacks a "Shenzhen Stanford University." Is that the case, or will "Shenzhen Stanford University" be the panacea for its final realization to become the next world-class innovation hub? The next chapter describes Shenzhen's R&D ecosystem and unique innovation characteristics by examining its vocational training, enterprises R&D, and its entrepreneurship education.

Notes

1. From Stephen S. Cohen and John Zysman, *Manufacturing Matters*. Basic Books, 1987.
2. Li Keqiang was China's Premier from 2013 to 2023.
3. Interview is retrieved from: https://www.xinhuanet.com/politics/2015-01/11/c_127376994.htm.
4. News article source: https://china.huanqiu.com/article/9CaKrnJGAlV.
5. Information is retrieved from: https://www.thepaper.cn/newsDetail_forward_3071883.
6. Interview information retrieved from the conference article: Designed in Shenzhen: Shanzhai Manufacturing and Maker Entrepreneurs. https://dl.acm.org/doi/10.7146/aahcc.v1i1.21265.
7. Information is retrieved from: https://www.kqed.org/news/11753411/company-behind-popular-maker-faire-closing-down-due-to-financial%20struggles#:~:text=The%20first%20Maker%20Faire%20took,40%20countries%20happening%20each%20year.
8. See the Wired documentary: Shenzhen, The Silicon Valley of Hardware: https://www.youtube.com/watch?v=SGJ5cZnoodY.
9. Phoebe is a pseudonym.
10. Quotation marks indicate a relative understanding of "premium" with respect to electronic components imported from Hong Kong.
11. See the Wired documentary: Shenzhen, The Silicon Valley of Hardware: https://www.youtube.com/watch?v=SGJ5cZnoodY.
12. Article is retrieved from: https://www.chinadaily.com.cn/china/2011-03/11/content_12156650.htm.
13. Interview by Wen Wen, associate professor at Shenzhen University. The material on Hua Qiang Bei evolution is from her unpublished Chinese book (as of 8 January 2020) on maker education. Wen's book is later on published in Mandarin Chinese by Social Science Academic Press.

14. Information is retrieved from China Semiconductor Industry Association: http://old.csia.net.cn/Article/ShowInfo.asp?InfoID=95565.
15. Information is retrieved from China Printed Circuit Association website: http://cpca.org.cn/.
16. See the Wired documentary: Shenzhen, The Silicon Valley of Hardware: https://www.youtube.com/watch?v=SGJ5cZnoodY.
17. Interview information is retrieved from the conference proceeding article: Designed in Shenzhen: Shanzhai Manufacturing and Maker Entrepreneurs: https://dl.acm.org/doi/10.7146/aahcc.v1i1.21265.
18. Company website: https://www.3nod.com.cn/aboutus.html.
19. Information is retrieved from: https://www.chinadaily.com.cn/business/2016-03/24/content_24060329.htm.
20. Information is retrieved from: https://asia.nikkei.com/Spotlight/Huawei-crackdown/TSMC-says-other-clients-can-fill-gap-if-US-ban-hits-Huawei.

CHAPTER 8

Shenzhen R&D Ecosystem

> We need scientists to design new fuels. We need farmers to help grow them. We need engineers to invent new technologies. We need entrepreneurs to sell those technologies. We need workers to operate assembly lines that hum with high-tech, zero-carbon components.
>
> —Barack Obama[1]

Research in Hong Kong, Made in Shenzhen?

Shenzhen has been notorious for its lack of prestigious research universities for quite a long time, particularly when Silicon Valley's innovative reputation has dominated the world stage spanning decades. Companies in Shenzhen understand the importance of self-dependent technological innovation: Research and development are the foundation and the key to any technological activities. Chinese central, provincial, and city government put emphasis on innovation in its next stage of development. As a result, "indigenous innovation" has become a national strategy for driving the development of technological innovation in domestic companies, hoping to own their intellectual property and to realize commercial applications. In 2016, Guangdong provincial government stressed its regional focus on innovation-driven economic development, for instance:

G. Y. Wang, *Dragon Innovation: Shenzhen*, Governing China in the 21st Century, https://doi.org/10.1007/978-981-95-9637-9_8

> Innovation is the first motivation to lead the development. We must put innovation in the core position of the development of our province and allow innovation to run through all the work of party committees and governments so that innovation can become a common practice in the whole society and speed up the process of switching from factor-driven to innovation-driven, from follow-oriented development to lead-oriented development.[2]

Policy directs the focus of economic development and technological innovation. But, what can technology companies in Shenzhen do to achieve their research and development breakthrough without outstanding local scientific research institutions? It is easy to build university buildings and laboratories, but it will take at least four years to have college graduates, and even more years to train advanced doctoral students. Conventional wisdom attributes Shenzhen's technological rise to its physical proximity to Hong Kong. However, the question arises: Why didn't Hong Kong develop into a technological hub utilizing its research institutions and international talent? Capital, talent, free market – it seems that Hong Kong has it all. People often think prestigious universities in Hong Kong, such as Hong Kong University and The Hong Kong University of Science and Technology, fill the research void in Shenzhen's technological development. However, entrepreneurial universities, not universities, facilitate technology transfer and business pursuits. A university cannot claim itself to be entrepreneurial if its faculties and professors do not encourage and support the pursuit of entrepreneurial adventures. Entrepreneurial universities must fulfil three missions, namely teaching, research and entrepreneurship as the universities serve as main drivers within a social system (Jones-Evans et al., 1999). Entrepreneurial universities include the commercialization of science, university technology transfer, and the creation of startups or university spin-offs. Compared to Shenzhen, Hong Kong has better research facilities, infrastructures, and professors who obtained doctoral degrees overseas, especially in the early days. But Hong Kong lacks the application contexts for technological experiments, innovation combination and recombination, as well as massive markets. Several tech companies successfully spun off from universities in Hong Kong are created and founded by students from Chinese Mainland who pursued their graduate studies in Hong Kong. For instance, DJI, the cutting-edge drone manufacturing company, was founded by Frank Wang Tao who was rejected by MIT but accepted into a PhD program at the Hong Kong

University of Science and Technology. Frank Wang Tao's adviser, Li Zexiang, is an internationally known expert on robotics and automation who jointly won the IEEE Robotics and Automation Award with Wang. Bachelor degree in electrical engineering and economics from Carnegie Mellon University, PhD trained in electrical engineering and computer science at UC Berkeley, Li Zexiang once worked as a research scientist at MIT Artificial Intelligence Lab as well as an assistant professor in the Robotics and Manufacturing Lab at New York University. He co-founded Googol Technology Limited in Shenzhen in 1999 with his Berkeley schoolmate before he co-founded DJI as the chairman with his student. "The most important thing is to help DJI look for the right talent and train them," Li Zexiang said. "They are in charge of the company's operation though I am the chairman. When they have questions or run into problems, they come to me and I will give them advice."[3] Frank Wang Tao's interest in consumer drone design and production was his scientific exploration. As Wang's professor, Li saw his interest and supported it. As Li Zexiang commented in an interview that Wang has a great interest and passion for doing something good, and he persevered and did not give up despite various setbacks.[4] It is safe to conclude that Frank Wang Tao's entrepreneurial ambition in turning technological products to commercial uses was encouraged and supported by his adviser Mr. Li.

Li Zexiang is known for his scientific research but also famous for his active participation in connecting university with industries. DJI and Li Zexiang's success indicates the role of star scientist in entrepreneurial business ventures. Li is one of the advocates for XpotPark in Dongguan city. Closest to Shenzhen in Guangdong province, Dongguan has become a rising technology base in recent years thanks to its rich land and less crowded city transportation. 40–50 mins drive to Shenzhen, XpotPark is a startup incubator focused on robotics and smart hardware. It incubated startups across agricultural, industrial, and consumer sectors.[5] Those startups include teams from Chinese universities and foreign ones such as Nanyang Technological University. Those university-based startup teams have an outstanding focus on science, engineering and technology. Besides XpotPark, the widely known robotics and smart hardware incubator, Li Zexiang created Shenzhen innoX in 2021, to explore new approaches and methods to engineering education, with the ultimate goal to cultivate and train innovative and entrepreneurial talents. Shenzhen innoX is considered as a startup incubator, with high-level mentors who have overseas doctoral education and working experience in various industries. Its operational mode is similar to HAX, the hardware incubator written in Chapter 6. It differs from HAX that Shenzhen innoX partners with universities, elementary and middle to high schools to train engineering talents at all levels to reform STEM education in China.

Experts like Li Zexiang offer deep entrepreneurial experience and technical expertise in helping those incubated companies and startup teams. In a TV interview with Phoenix Television, Li Zexiang commented on the supporting role he has served in discovering students with an entrepreneurial quest and then helping them. "Students must love what they do. They pursue entrepreneurial ventures because they love what they do, but not for money." Li emphasized some key qualities which influence his evaluations. Besides pure entrepreneurial intentions, a good understanding of the industrial chains, product creation ability as well as teamwork collectively make a critical difference in Li's assessment. Li's story in influencing Shenzhen and its surrounding cities in scientific research and entrepreneurial adventures is similar to the legendary Stanford professor, Frederick Terman. Often-called *Father of Silicon Valley,* Terman played a critical role in linking university and industry, and he created the Stanford Industrial Park in 1951. Terman utilized his connections, networks, influence, and sometimes his own money to help his students to start electronic firms between 1920 to 1930s (Malone, 1985; Rogers & Larsen, 1984). A famous example is HP, co-founded by Terman's students William Hewlett and David Packard, who got the initial funding of $1538 from Terman in 1938 to start the company. Professors like Terman and Li Zexiang, who helped their students realize their product commercialization, have one thing in common: identify talented and passionate students and facilitate students' scientific discoveries to product commercialization and scaling. In addition, they have industrial insights and vision to utilize resources. When Frank Wang Tao first started DJI and had difficulty securing funding, Li suggested that Wang provide DJI's products to his university as teaching equipment in exchange for money. Meanwhile, Li sought help from his friends in Singapore and Chinese Taiwan for potential investment. DJI CEO Wang's frequent visits to Shenzhen electronics markets and his search for appropriate electronics supplier may also be supported by Li's connections in industries in Shenzhen. Many students' founded startups have one commonality: Their companies are registered in Shenzhen, while key founders are students from Chinese Mainland who study at HUKST. Shenzhen's mature electronics supply chain can be attractive to entrepreneurial students in robotics and hardware. As Li Zexiang commented in the Greater Bay Area Chinese interview: "The world's most complete [electronics] supply chain can realize scientific ideas at the fastest speed and the lowest cost."[6] Another reason for the startup registration in Shenzhen may be the support offered by Shenzhen city government or district government, either through funding or tax deduction. Internet startups such as cross-border medical consulting, another company invested by Li Zexiang at HUKST, aimed to improve medical care quality through cross-border resources. Analyses indicate the important roles Hong Kong has played in one particular talent: Western trained professors (particularly USA graduates in the past) at universities in Hong Kong who happen to have active connections and resources in Shenzhen or other cities in Chinese Mainland play a critical role in both technology transfer and knowledge transfer. Entrepreneurial star scientists, like Li Zexiang, strengthen and amplify HUKST's entrepreneurial university characteristics by connecting it with Shenzhen and Guangdong's industrial competitiveness.

Students from Chinese Mainland who study in Hong Kong are more likely to take advantage of their professors' connections due to their understanding and grasp of fast-changing China market and their interest in doing business in their homeland. Before Covid-19 and the escalating U.S.–China tensions, students from Chinese Mainland were showing a shifting attitude towards Hong Kong and its universities: There is little job opportunity and career advancement within the island while graduates from universities in Hong Kong can hardly compete with those who hold advanced degrees from the USA or the UK. In this respect, Shenzhen seems to provide these students with abundant resources or entrepreneurial opportunities in building their future, particularly in the startup world. Covid-19 and the unpleasant U.S. policies towards international students as well as the increasingly tightening immigration policy, however, seem to alter many students' attitude towards attending universities in Hong Kong: Universities in Hong Kong become a possible destination again. Additionally, with official establishment of the Greater Bay Area since 2019, HUKST has set up GBA Youth Entrepreneur Forum in collaboration with HUKST Guangzhou campus as a closer integration of entrepreneurial and manufacturing resources.

Undeniably, entrepreneurial type of star scientists like Li Zexiang links international talents, research resources in Hong Kong with Shenzhen industrial competitiveness even before the official launch of the Great Bay

Area in 2019. Shenzhen innovation presents a new reality to the study of national system of innovation: Research university is only one format of innovation carrier. With no local Berkeley or Stanford, Shenzhen manages to upgrade itself to a leading technological innovation hub that enjoys a mature world-class supply chain, prominent technology companies, innovative startups that bet on experimenting with new and creative products and services. If American universities, as abundant literature shows, are critical sources of technology transfer and spin-offs, how could Shenzhen incubate its innovation with no classic research universities? Various formats and carriers that encourage scientific research and technological innovation in Shenzhen's evolutionary technology journey shed light on the global exploration of technological innovation in the AI age, particularly to the global south countries: A country or a region does not have to wait to build a prestigious research university like Stanford to embark on its technology entrepreneurship success. This chapter summarizes three outstanding features of Shenzhen R&D and education ecosystem which distinguishes itself from other national system of innovations: vocational education and training, entrepreneurial type of research institutes that focus on applied research and innovation as well as enterprise-led R&D regional innovation.

Gray Collar Worker—Vocational Education and Training

"The founding mission of our school by Shenzhen city government is to serve local economy since 1993." My guide at Shenzhen Polytechnic College proudly introduced the school's origin. In 2019, when I paid my visit to Shenzhen Polytechnic, it was still regarded as a vocational college (大专学院) until in June 2023, the National Ministry of Education approved the establishment of Shenzhen Vocational and Technical University (大学) based on the resource integration of Shenzhen Polytechnic College. Thus, the school has become an undergraduate-level vocational university in the country and implemented the "Standards for the Establishment of Undergraduate Vocational Schools (Trial)" accordingly. Before 2023, as a vocational college initiated and assisted by the municipal government after Shenzhen University, Polytechnic College has been playing an inevitably important role in Shenzhen's economic development and its technological advancement through workforce training. Leveraging the presence of universities for economic development is common, particularly in the United States in the 90s when state policymakers encouraged technology-based economic development. My interest in Shenzhen Polytechnic along with my realization of its significance in local economy came from my interactions with business owners at Hua Qiang Bei electronics market. Several of my informants worked for Huawei before they started their own businesses. My doubt about their eligibility to work for Huawei triggered further investigation since they did not even attend four-year universities. My impression and knowledge of Huawei's strong emphasis on R&D seemed to contradict with their credentials and qualifications.

According to UNESCO's definition, vocational education refers to: "education that is designed for learners to acquire the knowledge, skills and competencies specific to a particular occupation, trade or class of occupations or trades. Vocational education may have work-based components (e.g. apprenticeships). Successful completion of such programs leads to labor-market relevant vocational qualifications acknowledged as occupationally oriented by the relevant national authorities and/or the labor market."[7] Vocational education and training, in short, VET, is indispensable in providing individuals with employment opportunities but also plays a critical role in enhancing the productivity of firms, helping labor mobility and adaptability as well as to improve productive activities of a society in general (Caillods, 1994; Carnoy, 1994). Variant forms, including apprenticeship training, industrial arts, technical education, occupational education, technical and vocational education and training, have been used to depict key elements of VET (Maclean & Lai, 2011). The most popular view regarding the rise of vocational education, according to Agrawal (2013), relates with technological changes produced by the industrial revolution. During the early twentieth century, the main purpose of the expansion of vocational education was to build a loyal and disciplined workforce by integrating lower socio-economic children into the technically proficient labor force (Agrawal, 2013). After the Second Industrial Revolution, three "ideal models" of the vocational system appeared:

> One is a market led system in which a labor market characterized by substantial mobility provides much of the vocational training. Another is a school model where most of the VET takes place in schools. And third is a dual model with the presence of an apprenticeship system. (Nilsson, 2010)

These three models continue to distinguish VET and national systems in various social and cultural contexts. Though translated to English as Shenzhen Polytechnic College, the school does not award comprehensive college degrees at the beginning. It is equivalent to trade school or vocational school in the American context while roots in European polytechnic heritage: focus on applied science, engineering, and a hands-on approach to learning. When Shenzhen Polytechnic was established in 1993, it was one of the only three institutions of higher education in the city, including Shenzhen University, founded in 1983. Shenzhen Polytechnic was founded ten years after the establishment of the first four-year comprehensive university, Shenzhen University. In the Chinese context, this kind of college, 高等职业技术教育, is stereotypically categorized as a destination for "high school students with awful grades who cannot enter formal four-year universities while their families cannot afford to send them abroad for colleges." When Polytechnic was established in 1993, there were 59 enrolled students, and all of them were Shenzhen locals (holding Shenzhen residential permit). The year of its establishment matched well with its founding mission to serve local workforce and economy. Starting 2009, Polytechnic gets permission to recruit students across the country. "The goal of our school is not to train blue collar workers but gray collars. What does "gray collar" mean? Skilled workforce with technical backgrounds who are eligible for management positions. For instance, manufacturing factory managers. Certified nurses who can help train clinical staff." My guide, a middle-aged female administrator came to welcome me during a weekend. Her work ethics and enthusiasm surprised me in a positive way, as I had no experience interacting with a vocational college representative who was so proud of their school and their achievements.

Dean at the School of Electronics and Communication Engineering[8] commented on the standing of the school, "Shenzhen Polytechnic College is viewed as the best one in its genre [in China]. It remains its ranking at No. 6 or No. 7 among all universities and colleges in Guangdong province in recent years. Its popular standing is associated with Shenzhen's location and enterprises in the city. Same as Shenzhen University, Polytechnic gets direct funding from the municipal government. With the financial assistance, schools can invest in purchasing equipment, and other teaching resources to ensure that our graduates master the latest industrial skills and technical knowledge." Shenzhen city government has invested in Shenzhen Polytechnic and set it to train skilled workforce who can be integrated into the local economy since its beginning. Students learn hands-on abilities, obtain industrial certificates, and work at local companies after they graduate. Enterprises in Shenzhen are key benefactors of Polytechnic trained skilled workforce, in the Dean's words, "gray collar workers"; thus they actively invest in collaborations with the school. Huawei is one of them.

In 2011, Huawei cooperated with Shenzhen Polytechnic College in founding its first Huawei Information and Network Academy. In 2014, Huawei ICT industry certificates were first introduced, which were based on its fast-forward company advancement, vertical and horizontal integration into the ICT industry. Dean at the School of Electronics and Communication Engineering compared Cisco's industrial certificates with the Huawei ones: "Back in the 90s, Cisco's industrial certifications were extremely popular. Once you get all the Cisco certifications, you can climb the career ladder very quickly and earn a lot [of money]. Nowadays, our students and industry practitioners prefer to get the Huawei ones rather than Cisco certificates." He further explained to me about the key differences in these two companies' certificates:

> The Huawei certificates cover a comprehensive range of the entire ICT system. They (Huawei) often update and optimize their certifications to ensure that professionals in the ICT industry keep up with the latest technical knowledge and skills. If our students tend to work in the ICT industry, the best qualification is a Huawei certificate but not a Cisco one anymore.
>
> Also, Cisco certifications only comprise two parts: theory and practice (which is experiment test). Huawei one is comprised of theory, practice and in-person interview. We think the interview requirement shows that Huawei not only cares about the industrial professionals' technical background, but also their comprehensive qualities, like interpersonal communication.

The recognition and popularity of the Huawei ICT certificates are associated with Huawei's product market share in China. It makes no sense for college students or industry practitioners to work hard to get Cisco's certificates since not many ICT suppliers are adopting Cisco's products. Huawei has three kinds of certification: Huawei Certified ICT Associate (HCIA), Huawei Certified ICT Professional (HCIP), and Huawei Certified ICT Expert (HCIE). Huawei Career Certification covers three categories in building an ICT talent ecosystem: (1) cloud platform & services (2) basic software & hardware (3) ICT infrastructure. While Huawei certificates cover a wide range from ICT basics to advanced technologies such as AI and cloud, Shenzhen Polytechnic plays its strength in training their students. Dean said, "Since 2011, over 1000 students at Polytechnic obtained Huawei entry level ICT certificates, and about 140 students got the highest-level certificates." Professors at Polytechnic encourage their students to study for Huawei certificates, as explained by the Dean:

> Our school and Huawei get mutual benefits. Polytechnic buys Huawei's equipment to teach students and get them prepared for hands-on industrial products. Huawei makes profit from our purchase. They give our students exam discounts when students register to take the certificates' tests.
> Huawei has grown from an unknown small company to an ICT giant today. It is impossible for it to manage every business sector; therefore, Huawei has many suppliers. Those suppliers manufacture Huawei products (they use Huawei corporate email domain and have Huawei badge, my informant noted). Many of our students work for Huawei suppliers when they graduate with Huawei certificates. As you know, Huawei hires well-known university graduates or overseas returnees to conduct research and development. Our students are trained to do something different. Huawei ICT certificates ensure that our graduates are familiar with Huawei products, know their language, and can guarantee to maintain the reputation of Huawei products and technical services.

Huawei's collaboration with Shenzhen Polytechnic College in equipment purchasing, workforce training, industrial certificates, and employment at Huawei suppliers' enterprises demonstrates a well-developed workforce training system in Shenzhen. "High school graduates with low grades" get trained at Shenzhen Polytechnic and begin their professional career holding highly regarded industry certificates at affiliated companies. This training system supplies Huawei with skilled workers that the company and the industry demands; at the same time, the satisfactory employment rate at Polytechnic satisfies the school and helps maintain its prestige and good reputation in its genre. In recent years, due to fast advancement of ICT technologies, Huawei ICT certificates program has introduced "recertification" which requires the updates of Huawei certification content and the validity of a certificate. Most importantly, the resource allocation displayed in the system reflects one philosophy of state-interference in education and national economy in the Chinese society: the guarantee of social and political stability. To me, it seems like a story of the once widely spread Chinese film 一个都不能少, *Not One Less* in socialist China in comparison to meritocracy in capitalism societies: You are left behind because of individual incapability. Do not blame society. Do not expect the government to help you. The Dean of Educational and Social function at Shenzhen Polytechnic noted:

> There are students of different levels in our society. We cannot expect every student to do well in exams and attend universities. Vocational schools like Shenzhen Polytechnic takes the responsibility in training "less-well graded" students. To be honest, it is not exactly that our students are less intelligent or awful. Maybe some are not good at test-oriented education in high schools. Maybe some are more of a mechanical type of talent, instead of a coding programmer, a software developer or an advanced engineer. You know, it is not easy to get the highest level of Huawei certificates. Our students can pass these exams, which means that they excel at what they are doing.

Shenzhen Polytechnic College's success in training talent for local economy is credited to its close collaboration with companies, at least the local ones in its infancy. In return, enterprises get a chance to experiment with their business models at the same time. For instance, Huawei has replicated its domestic ICT certificates program in Africa, Southeast Asia and Latin America through its overseas Seeds for the Future program, largely thanks to its successful implementations and vocational trainings in Shenzhen and China. Seeds for the Future, first launched in Thailand in 2008, is Huawei's ICT training program to educate technical talents, to promote both technology transfer and knowledge transfer by helping local communities participate in digital economy. One hundred and forty-one countries have joined so far. During my research in South Africa, a marketing director from a local non-profit organization in the field of digital literacy shared with me that Huawei's Seeds for the Future ICT trainings are quite recognized among local employers. Some of their students who completed Huawei's ICT certificates were able to be employed by Huawei offices in Africa. With high unemployment rate in many African countries, the possibility of not attending colleges while being able to join a world-famous technology company seems appealing to many African youths.

Besides Huawei, Shenzhen Polytechnic has close collaboration and talent training programs with other international and domestic industrial leaders. For instance, Amazon, Cisco, Linux, 360, and Tencent. In 2020, Tencent established official collaboration with Shenzhen Polytechnic to jointly explore the training of interdisciplinary internet talent—people who have both technical and creative design background to advance the development of internet industries in China. Meanwhile, Tencent assists Shenzhen Polytechnic with the planning and design of "smart campus" (智慧校园). As Polytechnic required, Tencent will help build smart campus platforms and architecture to create a convenient and intelligent campus life for students, faculties, and staff utilizing data-focused management system. Similar to "Huawei – Polytechnic" collaboration, Tencent could introduce its "smart campus" to other colleges, and universities once it proves to be a successful model. Additionally, Tencent has signed collaboration agreements with Shenzhen Polytechnic with regards to Tencent Cloud, Tencent Education under the broader Greater Bay Area initiative context.[9] In addition to ICT companies, in 2019, Shenzhen Polytechnic jointly built the "BYD Institute of Applied Technology" with BYD company, the internationally known Chinese electric vehicle automaker.

Technical colleges and trade schools are mostly absent in analyses of Silicon Valley's success. Stanford, Berkeley, MIT, and Carnegie Mellon issue entry tickets to entrepreneurial success. Silicon Valley represents a culture of elitism, highly individualism, and aggressive competition (Castells & Hall, 1994). Saxenian (1983) noted community colleges and vocational schools in the valley instituted courses and programs to meet the needs of local economy though. Santa Clara College began to offer classes in semiconductor industry. A study of San Jose junior college system showed that more than half of the job placements were electric technicians (Keller, 1979). Vocational schools in Shenzhen, in the representation of Shenzhen Polytechnic, were born out of the occupational needs of local economy. Its evolving collaboration with local enterprises indicates its success in training skilled workforce that plays a fundamental and supplemental role in Shenzhen's innovation ecosystem, especially in ICT and advanced manufacturing. Tencent has started its training workshops with instructors and professors from China's vocational schools, led by Shenzhen Polytechnic, to upgrade instructors and professors' knowledge, and to learn the talent needs for industrial internet and artificial intelligence. They hope to jointly train the next generation of technical talent, for instance, people who can work with robots in factories. Just as my guide at Shenzhen Polytechnic told me when I was touring their exhibit: "The goal of our college is to train technical talent for local industries and economy to set an example for other vocational colleges in China."

Match between skilled labor trained at vocational schools with local industries has been the primary reason for the success of VET in different national systems. Take Singapore for example. Its education and training system has played significant role in its national economic and educational success. For instance, Singapore introduced training levies to create enterprise interest in training workers for high and semi-technical skilled jobs (ADB, 2004) since education through polytechnic was the backbone of Singapore's industrialization. In the early stage of its economic development in its post-colonial period, Singapore government tried systematic policies to transform and upgrade its educational systems to meet local industrial demands. Similar to the Shenzhen case, polytechnic institutes in Singapore are set to train technical personnel and middle-level professionals who can support local economic and technological development (Mun, 2008). Courses and programs provided at those institutes can lead directly to employment opportunities since the programs are practice-oriented and match well with local industrial needs. Shenzhen Polytechnic University is a classic example which links vocational training and education with local industries as the first of its kind in China. Since its humble beginning in 1993, Shenzhen Polytechnic has grown into a flagship vocational education and training school not only in China but also on the world stage. It has sponsored an international academic journal, *Vocation, Technology and Education*, which publishes peer-reviewed research in English to foster and advance the understanding of technical and vocational education as well as technology and occupations. Other ones, for instance, Shenzhen Institute of Information Technology and Shenzhen Technology University, established in 2002 and 2018 respectively, are also undergraduate level universities with a focus on vocational education and training, founded by Shenzhen municipal government. Regarded as applied undergraduate level universities, they offer similar functions to local enterprises fulfilling Shenzhen and China's industrial developmental needs. For example, Shenzhen Technology University and Tencent jointly established the first "Tencent Security Talent Class" in China. It opened its Fengxue Industrial College of Modern Logistics and Supply Chain College with China's leading logistics company SF Express. Strongly influenced by German style vocational education, both Shenzhen Institute of Information Technology and Shenzhen Technology University partner with German institutes and enterprises in building their advanced manufacturing departments to advance local robotics, drone and industrial internet industries. These schools' curriculum exactly reflects Shenzhen and China's industrial needs at different developmental stages. It may take further investigations and verifications to ensure that the employment rate at these universities reaches 95% level as widely circulated on the internet. But through my interactions with several students on Shenzhen Polytechnic's campus, they seemed to embrace an unusual confidence in their technical skills and career prospects. Not surprisingly, Shenzhen's vibrant information and technology ecosystem, along with its mature manufacturing supply chain, not just provide grassroots entrepreneurs and makers with entrepreneurial opportunities (Chapter 5, Local Governance: Bureaucratic Entrepreneurs and Chapter 6, The Entrepreneurial Ecosystem in Shenzhen). More importantly, on an educational level, Shenzhen's technological ecosystem transforms how education interacts and intertwines with its local industry and economy.

In recent years, conversations around the importance of and the need for vocational education and training programs have been prominent among policymakers in many countries. In my conversations with several UK representatives in a China–UK artificial intelligence expert forum, the UK delegates came to ask me if Chinese students feel inferior to attend vocational education and trainings since many UK youths are reluctant to consider vocational education as a choice over formal comprehensive universities, since they regard graduates from vocational schools less prestigious in social and cultural standing. Undoubtedly, in the traditional cultural sense, both in China and in the UK, people consider four-year comprehensive universities more prestigious. The success of vocational colleges such as Shenzhen Polytechnic is largely credited to the local enterprises' demand for workforces that meet local industrial trends and economic development needs. For instance, local enterprises invest in major digitalization upgrade through their collaborations and partnerships with Shenzhen vocational colleges, in faculty education, software and hardware to ensure teachers can keep up with the pace of industrial upgrading. Only in this way can students constantly learn hands-on and updated practical knowledge. Examples such as Huawei ICT certificates and Shenzhen vocational colleges' partnership with Tencent and BYD exactly reflect the essence of a sustainable and beneficial vocational education model. Success of vocational education is closely intertwined with local industries, enterprises as well as the careful curriculum design within local and national higher education systems which requires governments to play a role in (see Chapter 10, New Innovation Hubs are Possible).

Applied Innovation and Entrepreneurship Institute—Taiwan Influence

Besides flagship vocational education in Shenzhen's innovation success, Taiwan's success in electronics and the information technology industry enlightened Shenzhen's technological development in another way at its initial stage. Shenzhen's idea in creating research institutes that are focused on industrial applications and applied innovation is similar to Taiwan's research-industry collaborative model. To this extent, it indicates the significant role Taiwan played in Shenzhen's development and technological innovation, besides the manufacturing production shift noted in Chapter 6. In conversation about whether Shenzhen initially adopted the developmental model from Taiwan, a city government official said to me that Shenzhen has learned from many cities and countries in deciding its own destiny. It was easier for Shenzhen to learn from Taiwan, one of the Four Asian Tigers, since there is less linguistic, cultural and social difference (see Chapter 2, The Genesis of Shenzhen).

In 1973, Taiwan Industrial Technology Research Institute (台湾工业技术研究院) was established (name in short, ITRI). It pioneered in integrated circuit development, delivered significant R&D discoveries to applied products and services in industries. It also nurtured new tech ventures in Taiwan. ITRI has set up and incubated companies, including internationally known TSMC, UMC, Taiwan Mask Corp., Epistar Corp., Mirle Automation Corp., and Taiwan Biomaterial Co.[10] Taiwan Industrial Technology Research Institute is a historical outcome of Taiwan's economic transition: In the early 1970s, Taiwan was faced with the challenge of transforming its economy from labor-intensive economy to technology-led direction to realize its economic revival. Chinese Taiwan learnt from South Korea to launch its own scientific and technology research institute. Unlike the Korea Advanced Institute of Science and Technology (KAIST) established in 1971, ITRI was established in 1973 and is not a comprehensive research university. It is positioned as an applied technology research institute that aims to drive Taiwan's industrial development and to create economic values through technology transfers since its founding. It has served as a macro-incubator and has established close collaboration with companies and their R&D divisions to reduce corporate R&D risks, hoping to nurture new startup ventures and to improve startup survival rate.

Figure 8.2 shows ITRI's overall function in Taiwan's technological innovation system. Researchers and scientists do not conduct basic research at ITRI, instead, they focus on application-focused basic research (应用型基础研究), application research and innovation (应用型研究和创新), product and process development (产品与工艺开发), and quantitative trial production (量化生产). Big corporations, as displayed in purple in Fig. 8.2, do not conduct application-focused basic research like ITRI does, and they have two service functions which are commercial production (商业化生产) and marketing and service (营销与服务). It is worthwhile mentioning that the well-known Taiwan industrial park, Hsinchu Science Park, another product of Chinese Taiwan's developmental planning that started operations in 1980. A key factor for the choice of the location of Hsinchu Science Park seems to have been the presence of ITRI in Hsinchu County. Taiwan government offers job training programs for young engineers working at firms located in the park, provides tax incentives for the firms, low-cost rental benefits, and a variety of other services. Physical proximity between ITRI and firms in Hsinchu Science Park has facilitated technology spillovers. One of sub-organizations at ITRI, ERSO (Electronics Research and Service Organization), has played a significant role in spin-offs from ERSO to the private sector. One director from ERSO thought the technological spin-offs to private firms influence the upgrading of technological level in Taiwan (Castells & Hall, 1994).

Similar to ITRI and Taiwan innovation system, research institutes in Shenzhen at its early times enjoy some unusual characteristics that distinguish its local innovation system from the ones in Beijing. First, research institutes in Shenzhen are neither state-owned companies, nor government agencies. Instead, they register as private non-corporate institutions and operate in a market-oriented approach. In Chinese, they are positioned as "以企业化形式运营的事业单位." They are not for profit; thus, they are not operating under financial pressure. Due to high investment, risk and knowledge spillover, city government has offered necessary administrative and financial assistance to the research institutes at their initial stage. These two features demonstrate those research institute's

Fig. 8.1 Shenzhen Polytechnic (*Note* Photo taken by the author in 2019, before it became Shenzhen Polytechnic University)

identity: public institution, in Chinese, shi ye dan wei (事业单位).[12] Second, research institutes build a scientific research system and manage the system like operating enterprises. Their innovations and institutes are market oriented. Third, research institutes focus on Shenzhen industrial development, applied innovations and product development, linking all key economic nodes in technology industries. Last, research institutes introduce capital to their innovation system early on to create a comprehensive "capital – research – enterprises – market – capital (profit)" system.

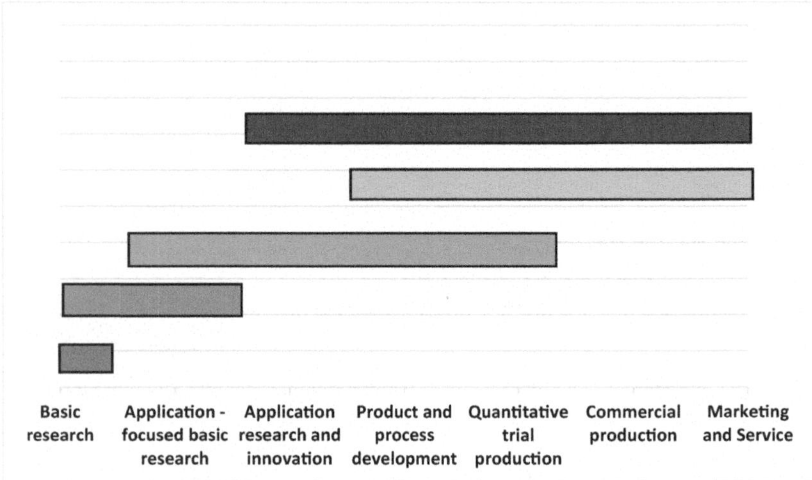

Fig. 8.2 Taiwan Industrial Technology Research Institute innovation system (*Note* Blue chunk: Taiwan Academia Sinica; Orange: Comprehensive universities; Green: ITRI; Yellow: Taiwan Hsinchu science park and mid-small size enterprises there; Purple: Big corporations)[11]

Model One: Research Institute of Tsinghua University in Shenzhen (RITS)

Learning from Taiwan ITRI's model, Shenzhen city government and Tsinghua University co-founded Research Institute of Tsinghua University in Shenzhen (in short, RITS; 深圳清华大学研究院) in 1996. In its official Chinese name, Shenzhen leads the institute's name in the title because the institute is co-founded by the Shenzhen city government and Tsinghua University in Beijing though it is hard to identify the feature in its English name. Each of the two parties holds 50% of its shares and the entity operates in an enterprise management style. RITS served two missions: realize social and economic development of Shenzhen and facilitate Tsinghua University's scientific achievements and technology transfer. The missions revealed that the advancement of Shenzhen's technological innovation and scientific research was not the priority at that historical point. Shenzhen wanted to create economic values through technology transfer and knowledge spin-offs of Tsinghua's science and engineering

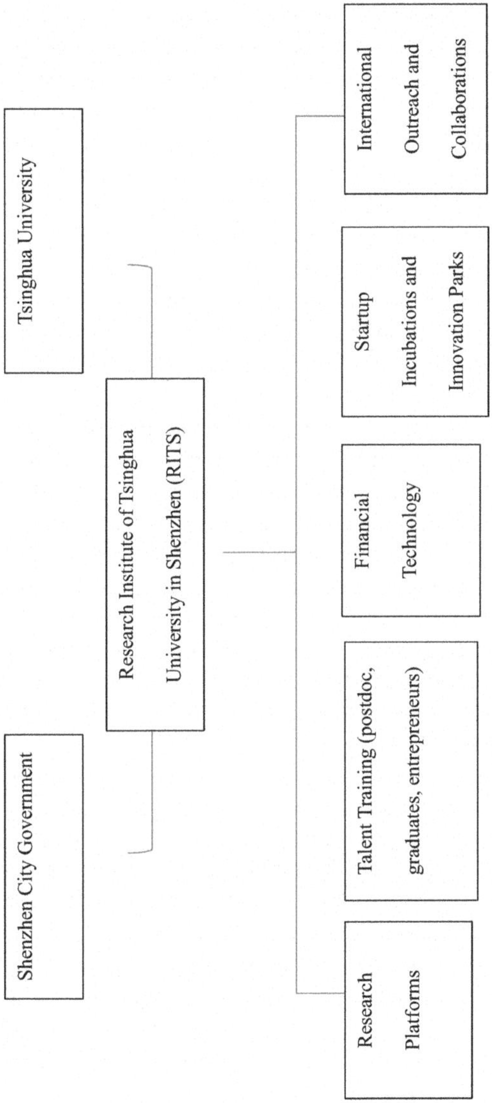

Fig. 8.3 Research Institute of Tsinghua University structure

research. Economic development was essential. Four proposed key development goals: (1) to promote a series of market-oriented technology achievements with independent intellectual property; (2) to speed up technology transfer; (3) to incubate high tech startups; (4) to cultivate high-level talents. RITS has created "Four Characteristics" theory[13]: an university with different culture from the traditional universities; a research institute with different R&D focus from the regular research institutions; an enterprise with different purpose from the pure profit-driven enterprises; and a public organization with a different operational mode from the non-profit organizations.[14] Technology transfer and accomplishments with financial gains are main focuses of RITS. Similar to Taiwan's ITRI, Research Institute of Tsinghua University in Shenzhen is designed to be an innovation incubator and an investment platform that is open to both China and abroad, in order to cultivate emerging technological industries in the long term.

RITS's establishment meets historical developmental needs of both Shenzhen city goverment and Tsinghua University. RITS was said to be the first research institute in China that is co-established by a city (Shenzhen) and a university (Tsinghua), which was praised as another innovation in Shenzhen—institutional innovation. Tsinghua University in Beijing is known as the best university in China, especially in science and engineering. Shenzhen lacked advanced research institutions and universities, but it has had a growing market and developmental potential in electronic industry in the early 90s. Markets provide scientists and engineers with real testing settings for applied research and development as well as product commercialization.

In 1999, RITS founded a high-tech venture capital firm, Shenzhen Leaguer Venture Capital Corporation (力合创投).[15] This firm mainly engaged in technology transfer projects investment at RITS and trained many venture capital talents. In 2019, Leaguer Venture Capital Corporation and the listed company Tong Chan Li Xing (002243) completed their reorganization which led to Leaguer's successful entry to the capital market. Leaguer defines itself as a "technology innovation service platform company" instead of a venture capital firm.[16] Venture capital investment is one of its four main functions. Its service also includes application R&D, talent training, and innovation parks. In 2002, RITS established its Department of Overseas Cooperation (DOC) to further international technology transfer and investment. The directors of DOC are foreign-trained engineers or scientists who have both technical and commercial experiences in their host countries. It seems like a strategic move to link Shenzhen applied innovation and ventures to the overseas markets after China's entry to the WTO in 2000.

RITS replicated Taiwan ITRI's operational model, however, none of the well-known global level tech companies in Shenzhen such as Huawei, DJI, Tencent, are incubated at RITS. According to its official website by August 2025, RITS has incubated over 3000 companies, invested in over 400 enterprises and cultivated over 30 publicly listed corporations.[17] Compared to Taiwan's ITRI, Shenzhen RITS's achievements may appear less notable since, Taiwan's ITRI and Hsinchu Science Park have successfully incubated famous Taiwan tech companies, such as Taiwan Semiconductor Manufacturing Company (TSMC), United Microelectronics Corporation (UMC), and Winbond. One possible explanation might be the lack of world-class brain circulation to Shenzhen in the 90s since Beijing, where is known for its prestigious research universities, was more likely to attract overseas returnees at that time. Morris Chang, founder of TSMC, initially was recruited back to Taiwan as the President of ITRI. Mr. Chang worked as the manager of semiconductor at Texas Instruments for decades and then joined General Instrument as COO in New York. His undergraduate and graduate studies at MIT and Stanford, along with his professional experiences caught the attention of officials in Taiwan. Mr. Chang shared his return to Taiwan:

> At that time ITRI was a very important institution in Taiwan. It was the largest and the only significant industrial technology research institute in Taiwan. The Premier [of Taiwan] who appoints the president of ITRI told me that he particularly wanted to use my ability to transfer technology from just research results to economic benefits for Taiwan industry.
> [......] It was part of the Premier's appeal—that he wanted me to use my abilities to transfer research results into economic gains for Taiwan industry—that really appealed to me because I had not been a purely research or technical person for a long time when I took the job in ITRI. But I had always, at Texas Instruments and later for a short while in General Instrument, I always thought of my job as one of transferring R&D results to economic gains for the company. So I felt as if I could do this ITRI job also.[18]

Chang took the job offer at a reduced salary level (as income level lagged the United States). He went back to Taiwan for excitement and novelty, and he did not go back to Taiwan for the salary: "This was a completely new kind of a job for me, and also the environment would be completely different: a Taiwanese environment as opposed to the U.S. environment. The kind of people that I would work with would also be different. So it was the newness that appealed to me." Later he founded TSMC in Hsinchu Science Park. Chang's experience back then is quite similar to some chief scientists at AI companies in Shenzhen nowadays who returned from major U.S. tech giants to create their own robotics or AI enterprises. New environment and unknown but exciting opportunities thrill entrepreneurial scientists.

Taiwan started to make its entry to the semiconductor industry by licensing technology from RCA. Political leaders who aimed to develop and advance Taiwan's semiconductor industry took the credit for the successful licensing, though the then technology gotten from RCA was a generation behind the USA. Afterwards, ITRI sent a group of engineers to RCA for extensive learning for several months, and they continued to work on the technology at a small scale when they returned to Taiwan in a laboratory until later, they spun off a company.

Key factors in Taiwan's research and development supported by ITRI were missed in the case of Shenzhen's RITS. There is no key industry leader like Morris Chang guiding critical research and taking on leadership position to develop local electronics and semiconductor industry, who happened to possess abundant educational experiences and U.S. professional networks. The first President at RITS came down to Shenzhen from Tsinghua University in Beijing. He had no overseas educational experience but was a researcher with a background in precision instruction and mechanics who had short-term academic visit in Germany.[19] It is likely that he did not hold significant overseas connections both in academia and industries like Morris Chang did in the American semiconductor industry. Second, as shown in Fig. 8.2, different institutions and organizations took on specific industrial and marketing divisions in Taiwan, which reduced the waste of resources. Taiwan's brain circulation, particularly the ones back from the U.S., was probably good at the western style marketing in introducing and advertising their electronics products to the global markets. Shenzhen's RITS's evolutional development in the 90s is more like exploration with existing resources Shenzhen was able to utilize. The discussion of Morris Chang and Taiwan's ITRI here makes two points. Taiwan's industrial development and applied technology innovation most likely influenced Shenzhen municipal government's decision to build applied technology-oriented research institute since this kind of innovation partnership can produce economic values by advancing industrial development. Furthermore, brain circulation in Taiwan in the 70s, such as Morris Chang, demonstrates the value of critical talents in building an industry from scratch as well as the role those talents can play in connecting high-quality research with industries. On this note, both Morris Chang and Li Zexiang play similar roles in their respective fields as star scientists. Shenzhen's early experiences in founding RITS have offered local officials valuable lessons in crafting its high-level overseas talent attraction policy at its later developmental stage (see Chapter 10, Human Capital and National Competitiveness).

RITS is an exemplary in Shenzhen's innovation ecosystem which is still evolving nowadays. "Many mid-level management personnels attend our programs and it is relatively easy for them to obtain a joint management degree from both Tsinghua University and the UK universities." In addition to RITS's emphasis on applied research and innovation, it has offered advanced management degrees to local enterprise personnel. An overseas returnee from the UK who once worked at RITS told me that she facilitated the joint program partnerships between RITS and many UK universities in granting business owners, entrepreneurs and local government officials with advanced management degrees like MBA. "You know, RITS is not a traditional university. Its existence at that time did help boost the educational levels of local enterprises management personnel. Tina (the overseas returnee from the UK) was surprised when I enthusiastically asked about her past work experience over a decade ago at Shenzhen Virtual University Park, where RITS was initially located at. Shenzhen Virtual University Park, established in 1999, can be seen as an innovative initiative which is co-sponsored by Shenzhen municipal government and universities across China to promote high-tech applied research and innovation as well as local entrepreneurship. In today's educational language, it is no exaggeration to regard Shenzhen Virtual University Park as some format of Harvard Extension School. In essence, the model integrates domestic and international resources in higher education, research and industry when leading scientific research universities are absent, another format of "Shenzhen-Inland collaboration model" mentioned in Chapter 5, Local Governance: Bureaucratic Entrepreneurs.

Model Two—Shenzhen Institutes of Advanced Technology Chinese Academy of Sciences

Differing from RITS, the Shenzhen Institutes of Advanced Technology (SIAT) of the Chinese Academy of Science (CAS) presents another type of research-industry partnership in building Shenzhen's R&D and innovation ecosystem. SIAT was jointly established by Shenzhen city government, the Chinese Academy of Science headquartered in Beijing, and the Chinese University of Hong Kong in 2006, thirteen years before the Greater Bay Area initiative. Since its founding, it is said that SITA is committed to building China's world-class science and technology research institute. It integrates four elements in creating its micro innovation ecosystem: scientific research, education, industry, and capital, where research is at its core. SIAT's two scientific and industrial focuses are information technology and biological engineering, namely IBT. SIAT appears to have research segments that focus on advanced scientific research. For instance, Shenzhen Institute of Advanced Integration Technology, Institute of Biomedical and Health Engineering and Frontier Science and Technology Research Center. In 2017, SIAT recruited its part-time graduates for the first time, and the cohort graduated in 2020. Among the first batch of 179 graduates in 2020, 61% entered local high-tech enterprises such as Huawei and Tencent, 14% went to work at public institutions like SIAT, government agencies, and financial organizations. Thirty-six chose to continue their studies at well-known universities including MIT, the University of Tokyo, and Tsinghua University.[20] Rewarding salary might be possible explanation for the higher percentage of graduates who chose to work in high-tech enterprises. Graduates from SIAT get paid more working in tech companies than being employed at public institutions and universities. Reasons for a relatively high percentage of graduates furthering their studies may be explained by SIAT's students training objective which emphasizes basic research more than applied technology as it evolves. In fact, in 2019, 1461 papers were published by faculties and researchers at SIAT, of which 668 are international collaborations which demonstrates an increasing trend of papers published by researchers at SIAT and its international counterparts, as shown in Table 8.1 Publishing academic research papers is a distinctive indicator that differs SIAT from RITS. By the time of March 2025, SIAT published over 20,000 academic papers. Besides academic publications, as shown in Table 8.2, SIAT's PCT application increased from 4 in 2008 to 366 in 2019, and has achieved over 3000 in 2025 as displayed on its website.[21]

Table 8.1 SIAT's number of internationally collaborative published papers

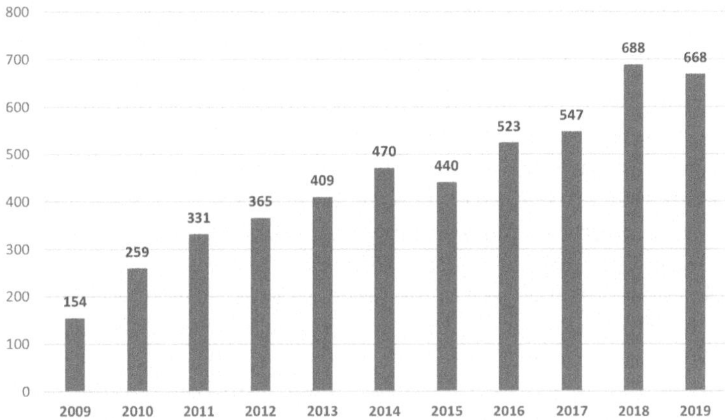

Note 2019 SIAT annual report

Table 8.2 SIAT's number of PCT application

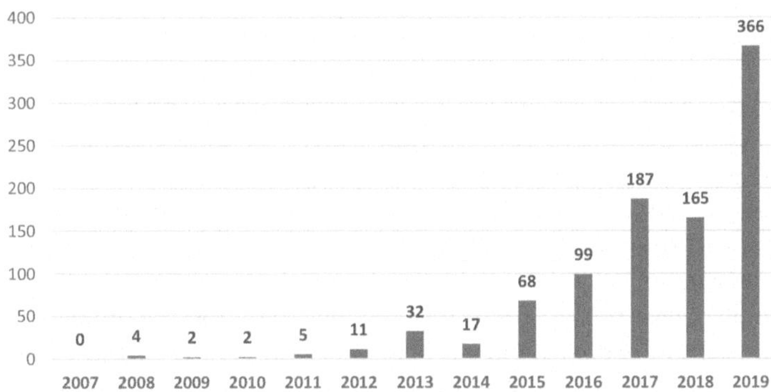

Note 2019 SIAT annual report

Four 90%—Key R&D Player: Shenzhen Enterprises

Though the Shenzhen Institutes of Advanced Technology (SIAT) of the Chinese Academy of Science has started to produce basic scientific research since its establishment in 2006, local enterprises such as Huawei relies heavily on collaborations with leading international scientists for Huawei's corporate development. Huawei's CEO, Ren Zhengfei repeatedly expressed the view in public and said during our in-person interview in 2019: "Huawei's 5G breakthrough originates from a scientific research paper published by a Turkish professor. Everyone has access to that academic paper." Ren Zhengfei was implicitly responding to the accusations that Huawei stole U.S. technologies.[22] He referred to Erdal Arikan, a receiver of Shannon Award in 2018. His paper titled *Polar codes: A pipelined implementation* inspired Huawei's development of 5G technology. Huawei believes in the power of polar code which can be realized with a small-scale chip and more suitable for 5G small base stations. Commercialized hardware of polar coding method is relatively cheaper and competitive in markets. Huawei's long-term collaboration with Dr. Arikan and investment in his lab in Turkey helped the company along the way in its 5G technology innovation. Huawei's rotating chairman Guo Ping in 2019 emphasized on R&D: "Our determination on research and development will not waver, no matter what happens". In fact, more than 10% of Huawei's annual revenues is invested in its R&D, which makes it the only Chinese company enter the top 5 global R&D expenses companies in the world. According to 2019 EU Industrial R&D Investment Scoreboard, Huawei ranked as No.5 world's total R&D investment in 2019, in the amount of over 12,000 Euro million, following Alphabet U.S., Samsung Electronics, Microsoft U.S., Volkswagen Germany.[23]

Vocational education and applied innovation-oriented colleges such as Research Institute of Tsinghua University in Shenzhen complement Shenzhen's shortcomings in world-class scientific research universities which successfully carve out an innovation model that closely connects manufacturing supply chains, applied research and development as well as technological innovations. Most importantly, enterprise-led innovation highlights the distinguishing characteristic of Shenzhen R&D ecosystem. It exactly reflects the motto in Shenzhen's development path since its establishment as a special economic zone: *Enterprises as the main body, market as the basis, and government as the backing support*. Those autonomies can be understood from various perspectives. First, compared to other municipal governments in China, Shenzhen city government invests tremendously in research and development in terms of government funding, the percentage of R&D personnel as well as research equipment purchase. City government works closely with local firms to advance technological development and innovation. Table 8.3 shows R&D expenses in Shenzhen from 2010 to 2018, in comparison to Guangzhou's, which indicates a substantial difference in regional R&D expenditure and a predicable increasing gap in their cities' R&D spending. Shenzhen's escalating R&D expenses are also reflected in its percentage of annual GDP, from 3.48% in 2010 to 4.8% in 2018 with a gradual increasing amount every year (see Table 8.4). Second, city government understands the symbiotic relationship between regional innovation, economic growth and local enterprises' innovation capacity and success. Companies' achievement and corporate breakthroughs can be seen as Shenzhen's accomplishment, which is associated with local governance. For instance, relatively free from government interventions in daily corporate operations. There are "Four 90%" in Shenzhen's R&D: More than 90% of the city's research and development institutions are affiliated with local enterprises; More than 90% of scientific researchers come from companies; More than 90% of R&D funding comes from enterprises; More than 90% of patents are applied and filed by enterprises.[24] Table 8.5 shows the enterprise R&D expenditure compared to government spending on R&D in Shenzhen. Enterprises R&D has been the leading R&D investment since 2011 though funding from both government funds and corporate R&D has been increasing. R&D expenses are classified into three categories: basic scientific research, applied research, and experimental development (see Table 8.6). Huawei's collaboration with international star scientists may indicate that Shenzhen lacks behind breakthrough basic scientific research so that local enterprises like Huawei need to seek outside. The allocation of R&D expending explains the reasons. Table 8.7 identified the percentage of R&D expenses from 2009 to 2016. Experimental development expense in 2009 accounted for 98.7% of the total R&D investment, while applied research and basic scientific research only accounted for 1.1% and 0.2% respectively. Enterprises led R&D focus more on product innovation and development rather than basic scientific discoveries. Experimental development and R&D investment satisfy companies that seek financial benefits as they need to constantly update their products to meet the market demands. In 2016, the percentage of basic scientific research has increased to 2.9% from 0.2% in 2009, whereas investment in experimental research has decreased to 87.3 in 2016 from 98.7% in 2009 (see Table 8.7). This change may be partially explained by the increased percentage of R&D investment from scientific research and technology development institutions as well as those from four-year full-time universities and colleges (see Table 8.8). It also reflects Shenzhen's innovation path does not originate from basic scientific research. Regardless of the R&D investment increase from other sources, industry and enterprises R&D investment keeps its lead substantially. Among all the enterprises, Huawei remains its top position in research and development spending in Shenzhen. Table 8.9 shows a comparison between Huawei's R&D investment and Cisco's, which is an American telecommunications equipment, hardware, and software product provider. As shown in the table, Huawei's R&D expenditure has surpassed 100 billion RMB in 2018 while Cisco's R&D remained roughly the same from 2014 – 2020, around $6.00 billion. Huawei's aggressive R&D investment indicates its technological ambition but also sets an example for other companies in Shenzhen: It is possible for a Chinese company to realize its technological breakthrough. Unlike companies which merely focus on product development, Huawei has employed approximately 15,000 employees working on basic scientific research. Among them, 700 PhDs specialize in mathematics, over 200 PhDs have expertise at physics and chemistry, and more than 5000 PhDs specialize in engineering.[25]

Table 8.3 R&D expenses comparison between Shenzhen and Guangzhou from 2010–2018 (10,000 Yuan)

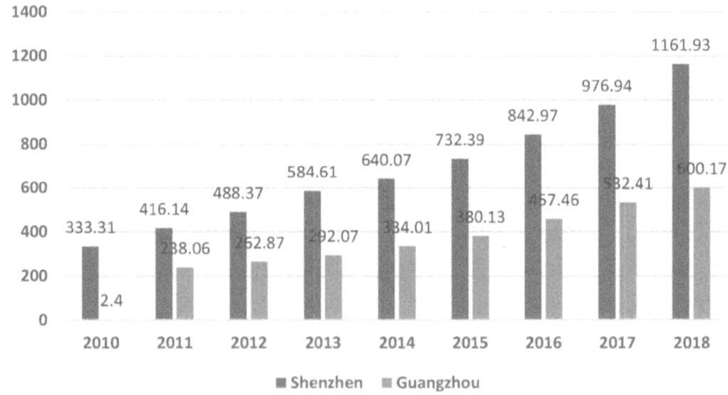

Note Information organized from Shenzhen Statistic Bureau.

Table 8.4 Shenzhen R&D in GDP percentage from 2010 to 2018

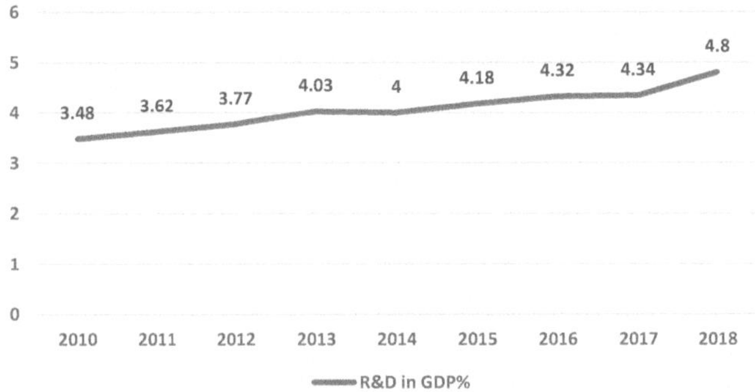

Note Information retrieved from 2018 Shenzhen Statistical Yearbook

Table 8.5 R&D expenses in Shenzhen government vs enterprises (10,000 Yuan)

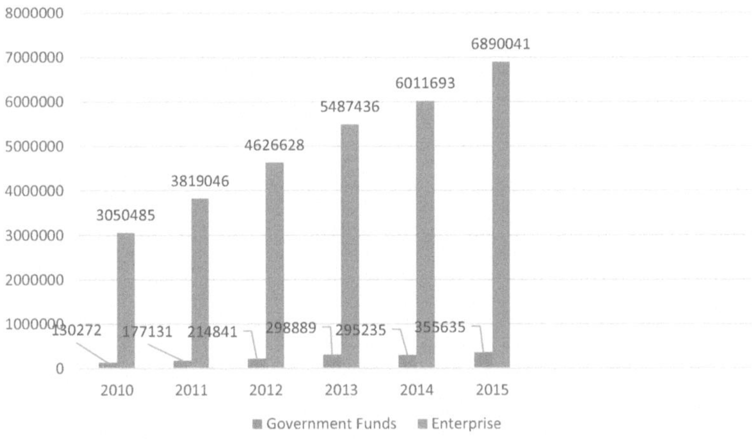

Note Information retrieved from 2016 Shenzhen Statistical Yearbook

The then-rotating chairman, Guo Ping, emphasized the significance of R&D in Huawei's development in an in-person interview in 2019: "As the old Chinese saying, the longer you live, the more you eat."[26] Huawei's innovation strategy includes Innovation 1.0 and Innovation 2.0, which demonstrate the company's practical development needs. At stage one, it focuses on the innovation of products, technologies, engineering,

Table 8.6 Shenzhen R&D expenses in three categories from 2009 to 2016

Year	*Three categories R&D expenses*			
	Basic scientific research	*Applied research*	*Experimental development*	*Total expense*
2009	0.68	2.94	276.08	279.71
2010	0.67	4.27	328.37	333.31
2011	2.48	10.32	403.34	416.14
2012	2.33	42.97	443.07	488.37
2013	5.18	55.28	524.15	584.61
2014	5.76	73.33	560.99	640.07
2015	6.73	92.51	633.14	732.39
2016	24.33	82.89	735.75	842.97

Note Shenzhen Research and Development Spending Report, 深圳R&D投入结构报告, p. 35

Table 8.7 2009–2016 R&D expense percentage in basic scientific research, applied research, and experimental development

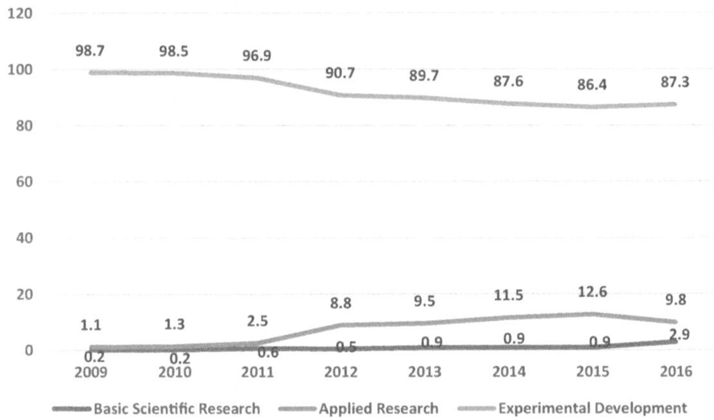

Note Information organized from Shenzhen Statistic Bureau

and solutions to meet its clients' and customers' needs in order to help reduce corporate costs and stay competitive in the market. At stage two, Huawei aims to break the theoretical bottlenecks that hinder the development of the ICT industry. Toward this goal, they invest in university research for theoretical advancement.

Table 8.8 Scientific research institutes, four-year universities, and industries and enterprises R&D spending

Year	*Scientific research and technology development institutions*		*Four-year full-time universities and colleges*		*Industries and enterprises*	
	Absolute value	*Percentage (%)*	*Absolute value*	*Percentage (%)*	*Absolute value*	*Percentage (%)*
2009	1.58	0.6	1.83	0.7	259.00	92.6
2010	0.80	0.2	1.42	0.4	313.79	94.1
2011	8.60	2.1	1.35	0.3	388.89	93.5
2012	7.45	1.5	1.76	0.4	461.87	94.6
2013	17.22	2.9	2.45	0.4	562.75	96.3
2014	15.04	2.4	2.76	0.4	618.16	96.6
2015	20.38	2.8	8.17	1.1	702.46	95.9
2016	10.97	1.3	10.56	1.3	820.06	97.3

Note Shenzhen R&D Investment Structure and Effect Analysis Research, pp. 27–28

Table 8.9 Annual R&D expense comparison between Huawei and Cisco from 2014 to 2020

	Huawei annual R&D expense (Million Yuan)	*Cisco annual R&D expense (billion U.S. dollars)*
2020	141,893	$6.3
2019	131,659	$6.6
2018	101,509	$6.3
2017	89,690	$6.1
2016	76,391	$6.3
2015	59,607	$6.2
2014	40,845	$6.3

Note Both Huawei's and Cisco's Annual R&D information is from their annual reports from 2014 to 2020

Huawei's leading position in R&D investment and its accomplishment set an example for other companies in Shenzhen, in terms of technological development and entrepreneurial ambitions. "To build the next Huawei" seems to be a goal among budding tech entrepreneurs in Shenzhen. Established tech firms compete fiercely for resources, talents and market shares. CEO of Tencent, Pony Ma Huateng, asked the first question "What other companies did you visit?" right after he entered the conference room to join the research interview. Since Tencent, Huawei, and health-tech global insurance company Ping An, are all developing their cloud systems, Pony Ma Huateng's inquiry implicitly indicated the invisible fierce competition among tech giants in Shenzhen and in China overall. Enterprises understand the significance of innovation, therefore, they support it on an organizational and institutional level. Take Tencent as an example. To promote innovation culture and product development, the company sets up a micro-innovation prize that is awarded weekly, monthly, or quarterly, as stated by Tencent's management team at an in-person meeting:

> Consistent with our CEO Pony's constant repetition of "user-centric, continuous innovation", Tencent values talent and regards human capital as the most valuable asset. As a Chinese saying goes, "Jiang Lai Cai You Jiang Lai"[27] (General brings the future, 将来才有将来), Tencent supports innovation from an organizational level. We have a team called "direct team" (直管部门) which does not belong to any other corporate division. This team is in direct charge of product innovation at Tencent and has the freedom to utilize resources within the company to support major innovation development. For instance, leaders in that team can relocate individuals from one division to another if necessary.
>
> The annual top innovation prize winner at Tencent is granted up to 1 million RMB. For example, the team that developed WeChat Pay once got this annual award since, at that time, it was a new product in mobile pay industry, and it remains so nowadays.

Tencent classifies innovation into three categories: innovation 0–1 like QR code; breakthrough product innovation like WeChat Pay; and incremental product innovation like WeChat Mini program. Tencent Mini program is an open-source internet platform that allows developers to create and develop their own applications on Tencent WeChat platform. With an increasing number of student developers creating their apps on WeChat Mini program, in 2018, Tencent announced its collaboration with the Chinese National Ministry of Education. Tencent plans to support forty teaching content and curriculum projects utilizing WeChat public platforms like Mini program and its application development technology. At the first phase, Tencent is said to plan to provide more than 2 million RMB in total to fund curriculum reform projects, as well as to offer official technical support, guidance, and technological platform like Tencent Cloud. This collaboration is built on the goal that new WeChat application development will be developed or transformed based on real application cases and internet product developmental models.[28]

Tencent's utilization of university resources in China is a win–win. On one hand, universities and educators at those schools can adopt innovative technologies and services to assist with their teaching and college students' learning. On the other hand, Tencent is able to cultivate the talented developers or product designers who are students in colleges and hire them to Tencent right after their graduation. In this way, Tencent is incubating its talent pool for its corporate's future. In addition, educational cases in real life settings provide this tech giant with immediate feedback to refine its products to keep Tencent on the top of competition. Just as Tencent's Head of Human Resources shared during our conversations: "We, as a company, need to constantly challenge ourselves. The key to doing that is to motivate our teams and employees to innovate. If we do not innovate internally (at Tencent), other people will go to do it. If that happens, we are beaten up."

The urgency of survival, development and innovation is common among companies in Shenzhen, including those well-established ones. Peter Ma, CEO and founder of Ping An, used "walking on thin ice" (如履薄冰) to describe his journey in founding and managing this corporate giant. On the company's website, Ping An is described as a for-profit organization that aims to grow itself into an internationally known financial life service provider. Founded as a private insurance company in Shekou, one of Shenzhen's open window districts to Hong Kong in early 80s, Ping An seems to have inherited the reform spirit embedded in Shenzhen special economic zone. This enterprise is recognized for its institutional reform and support for innovation. CEO Peter Ma repeatedly addressed his employees that "Tomorrow will never come. We either change or die."[29] As a pioneer in China's quasi-market economy, Peter Ma believes that the vitality of a market economy lies in its incentives for innovation and creativity, as well as its punishment for lack of innovation and creativity.

As part of Ping An's organizational innovation, its Head of Public Relations[30] described to me while touring its AI lab: "In many divisions at Ping An, we use AI-enabled robots to conduct the first round of interviews." Born as a traditional financial company in China's insurance sector, Ping An has transformed itself to a key player in China's tech industry. It targets technology enterprises as their main competitors rather than the conventional insurance companies. Ping An's strategic realignment in 2013 officially occurred when CEO Peter Ma returned to Shenzhen upon his business trip from the United States. Ping An's focuses then turned to resolve the integration of technology to transform traditional financial industry. Instead of adopting technological tools and solutions from other tech companies, Ping An creates innovative tools and financial platforms utilizing their own commercial applications and products. It wants to catch the first-mover advantage in the technology-led financial industry in China, just as when it entered China's insurance sector as a private enterprise over four decades ago. Ultimately, they aim to integrate conventional non-financial industries and markets to the fast-growing digital world, to form and establish new market rules and orders in the digital economy sector in China.[31] Ping An's fin-tech ambition attracts overseas scientists and engineers back to Shenzhen. In the words of its chief scientist in 2019:

> Artificial Intelligence is a complementary technology. It does not exist in isolation. It is the perfect time now for AI to enter traditional industries, such as health and education. However, those traditional sectors in the United States are too stagnant and established. Shenzhen, or China, offers a different experimental context. It is an experimental playground for innovation.

Ping An's fin-tech ecosystem includes consumer to consumer and business to business settings. For instance, *Ping An Good Doctor*, officially launched in 2014–2015, is the first medical application platform in China to provide online medical consulting service and to create customized personal medical records in association with patients' insurance histories. Furthermore, this app recommends health management and nutritional advice based on customers' medical data. Two years after its launch, it received its pre-IPO (01833.HK) investment from Soft Bank, in the amount of 4 billion dollars. As of the end of June 2019, the number of registered users of this app reached 289 million, and the number of monthly active users was 62.7 million.[32]

Similar successful product and service innovation like Ping An Good Doctor is largely credited to Chinese consumers' willingness to adopt and to try out new services and products in a fast-changing world. The market for technological experiments is responsive and vibrant. In spite of the acknowledgment of Silicon Valley being the origin of technological innovation in the world, in 2019, Ping An's chief scientist, at the time of our interview, differentiated Shenzhen and Silicon Valley's respective strength in innovation:

> One of my PhD research tracks was knowledge graph which was the initial research on artificial intelligence. At that time, wherever I went to international conferences, most often, I was the only Chinese. To me, it is striking to see that AI along with other technologies are advancing so rapidly in China. Shenzhen takes the lead in applied AI technologies, but not in basic research. Most of our overseas returnees who hold PhDs are great, but the most talented ones are staying in the U.S. It takes time (to advance basic scientific research).

Fast changing markets as well as domestic and international competition force Chinese technology companies to adjust to market needs quickly, to constantly upgrade their technological products, and to enhance their management styles. *Enterprises as the main body, market as the basis, and government as the backing support,* is encouraged, implemented, and worked out. Local autonomies along with product experiments in real application settings have enabled those companies to develop and innovate despite the lack of advanced scientific institutions and well-known research universities. Analysis on Research Institute of Tsinghua University in Shenzhen (RITS) has shown Shenzhen's efforts in filling out its void in scientific research in its nascency. Shenzhen has abundant overseas returnees working in tech, however, most top leaders at RITS and SIAT are not senior overseas returnees, at least for now. One Chinese chief scientist who returned to Shenzhen from the U.S. commented:

> A lot of overseas talent come back to work at tech companies in Shenzhen. Enterprises are driven by profits and revenues, but not scientific discoveries and R&D. Shenzhen has a very mature industrial supply chain, which attracts many human capitals. However, most of them are relatively young at a junior level. Among all the PhD overseas returnees in my company, we hardly find any veterans. Further, in my observations, those junior scientists lack proper mentorship. As a result, their career growth is stagnant or slow.

His comment on the lack of mentorship for junior scientists is consistent with the fact that there is a lack of mentorship for budding tech entrepreneurs in Shenzhen, compared to Silicon Valley (see Chapter 6, The Entrepreneurial Ecosystem in Shenzhen). This phenomenon is, in fact, reflects a distinctive trait of Shenzhen's innovation ecosystem. Shenzhen has a diverse educational and R&D innovation ecosystem that centers around local enterprises, supplemented by technical colleges as well as universities in Shenzhen and Hong Kong. Local enterprises are at the core of Shenzhen's technological innovation activities, driven by corporate efforts to maximize profits and to ensure their own organizational growth. The critical element of Shenzhen's education and R&D is enterprise, and many R&D initiatives are either enterprise-led or enterprise-collaborated. Business fosters economic growth and creates long-term productivity by investing in R&D and education. Enterprises-led innovation focuses more on applied innovation, though companies like Huawei and BGI invest in long-term scientific research by establishing their own research institutes. Huawei's efforts in solving theoretical bottlenecks in the ICT field were briefly described in this chapter. Its global hunt for leading researchers will be discussed in "Chapter 9, Human Capital and National Competitiveness." BGI Genomics (in short, BGI), formerly Beijing Genomics Institute, is similar to Huawei, in terms of its investment in groundbreaking scientific research. BGI has its own comprehensive bioengineering and genocide research ecosystem. Established in 1999 in Beijing and moved down to Shenzhen in 2007, BGI followed human genetics scientific discovery path, the HGP, founded its own research institute and created its scientific journal *GigaScience*. GigaScience publishes BGI's scientific research and makes some BGI's data accessible for accumulative scientific discoveries and research. At the same time, BGI research personnel publish research articles in journals like *Science* and *Nature* to be involved in world-class scientific community. Like many companies in Shenzhen which value technological applications, BGI has a division named BGI Medical, with an aim to turn its biological research to medical clinical trial.[33]

Companies like Huawei and BGI are a special category of corporations in Shenzhen as they engage in R&D and scientific publications at a high-intensity level. Their existence, evolution and development reaffirm a key argument in this book: University is just one form of knowledge and innovation carrier. In terms of the reasons that motivate firms to produce scientific publications, Hicks (1995) argued in his study that scientific publishing enables firms to build their scientific credibility in the academic research community, to recruit and maintain leading researchers, and to meet regulatory demands in certain industries. More recently, D Rotolo et al. (2022) proposed a conceptual framework after a systematic analysis based on a total sample of 164 studies, and conclude that there are five major reasons for firms' engagement in scientific publishing: (1) access external knowledge and resources; (2) attract and retain researchers; (3) support IP strategies; (4) build the firm's reputation; (5) support commercialization strategies. As catchup players on the global stage, Huawei and BGI's motivations for academic publishing and creating their own scientific ecosystem match with the exact five reasons for scientific publishing. The number of Huawei's global PCT filing is an indicator that the company pays close attention to its corporate intellectual property. Huawei's investment in prestigious research universities on the global stage reflects its intention to access advanced external knowledge (see Chapter 9, Human Capital and National Competitiveness). Like Huawei, BGI has expanded its global research and corporate outreach in countries including Australia, Denmark, Thailand, and Saudi Arabia. Interestingly, BGI has started to publish its research early on. Academic journal, Giga-Science, initially published by GigaScience Press, the open access and open data publishing division of BGI, now has become a flagship open science journal. GigaScience's publishing work now is carried out by international publishers and infrastructure providers, including BioMed Central, Oxford University Press, ORCID, and CrossRef.[34] Huawei and BGI, as global leaders in their respective industries, demonstrate a subcategory of R&D ecosystem in Shenzhen.

Conclusion

The analysis in this chapter highlights distinctive characteristics that contribute to the understanding of the role of local education in Shen-zhen' R&D ecosystem and its technological development. This chapter details the reasons for Shenzhen's innovation success and industrial upgrading when Shenzhen Stanford and Shenzhen Berkeley were missing. These characteristics, for instance, vocational education and training, supplement the existing discourse on the success of western tech-nology centers by adding the significant role vocational training play in connecting education and industries in building successful innovation clusters. Shenzhen's success in training "gray collar" workers who possess both technical and management skills further explains the connections between successful grassroots entrepreneurs and Shenzhen innovation, as discussed in Chapter 6. Research institutes, like RITS and SIAT, demonstrate Shenzhen's evolutionary innovation path in longitudinal lens. Table 8.10 shows Shenzhen's demand for labor forces as well as its changes for talents as local industries grow and evolve. Shenzhen Polytechnic established in 1993 justifies Shenzhen's industrial development stage and its labor-intensive driven industries in the early days. The founding of RITS in 1994 reflects Shenzhen's shift from low-cost traditional manufacturing to high-tech industries and advanced manufacturing. As shown in the table, at this stage, applied technology and capital were required to advance industrial development and local economies while the need for technological innovation was not striking, until stage three started in 2006 when SIAT was founded. From Shenzhen Polytechnic to SIAT, these explorations in Shenzhen's education sector, prove from another perspective that "cross the river while feeling the stone" was the historical reality Shenzhen has been faced with.

Betting on education is equally risky and difficult as betting on innovation. At the core of Shenzhen's innovation success lies in local enterprises' R&D investment. "At the early stage of Huawei, especially during our

Table 8.10 Shenzhen talent/labor developmental stages and talents demand for city environment at different stages

Developmental stages	*Leading industries*	*Growth-driven factors*	*Talent/labor demands*	*Talents demands for city environment*
1980–1994	Labor-intensive industries dominated by traditional manufacturing	Labor and capital	Large demand for blue collar workers	Low
1995–2005	High-tech industries and advanced manufacturing	Technology, capital	Shift from blue collar workers to skilled and highly skilled technical workers	Relatively high
Since 2006	High-tech industries, strategic new industries, modern service industries	Technology, capital and innovation	Huge demand for management personnel, advanced high-tech talents, experts in needed disciplines and their research teams	Very high, comprehensive city facilities

Note Source from Shenzhen Talent Research Report, 2013

fastest corporate developmental stage, the company was deeply indebted with a 60–70% asset liability ratio every year. However, we did not pay much attention to short-term financial gains. We care more about the long-term healthy business operation," the then-rotating chairman, Guo Ping noted in our conversations. A London School of Economics graduate, a British citizen, who was vice president of Huawei's Public Affairs and Communication during one of my Huawei tours, stated, "We have 16 global research centers all over the world, and we are a truly global company."[35] Though enterprise-led R&D is a key feature of Shenzhen's innovation experiences, Huawei not only partners with vocational colleges like Shenzhen Polytechnic but also invests in domestic and overseas research centers through its partnerships. Is this just a corporate strategy? Can't Shenzhen's local talents meet Huawei's research and development objective? What kind of obstacles is Shenzhen or China currently faced with in scientific research and industrial upgrading? Next chapter delves into Shenzhen talent attraction policy and analyzes its talent circumstances.

Notes

1. 44th U.S. President Barack Obama spoke at the UC Irvine commencement ceremony on June 14, 2014 in Anaheim, California.
2. 2016 Guangdong Province 13th Five-Year Plan Outline. Retrieved from http://www.zktw.com/LiangHuiZhuanTi/467346.html.
3. Information is retrieved from: https://tech.qq.com/a/20160906/006360.htm.
4. Information is retrieved from: https://www.hkcd.com/content/2021-04/20/content_1263242.html.
5. Company official website: http://www.xbotpark.com/?lang=en#story/5.
6. This interview is retrieved from the Chinese documentary: https://www.youtube.com/watch?v=Wm-D4JYp9Io.
7. Information is retrieved from: https://uis.unesco.org/en/glossary-term/vocational-education.
8. In 2019, my interviewee served as the dean of the School of Electronics and Communication Engineering.
9. Information is retrieved from: https://www.geekpark.net/news/260195.

10. Information is retrieved from: https://www.itri.org.tw/english/ListStyle.aspx?DisplayStyle=20&SiteID=1&MmmID=617731521661672477.
11. Information is retrieved from a published Mandarin Chinese article: 《公立产业技术研究院与新兴工业化经济体技术能力跃迁—来自台湾工业技术研究院地经验》.
12. The general definition of Chinese public institution (事业单位): Public institutions are social service organizations established by the state for public welfare purposes, run by state agencies or other organizations using state-owned assets, and engaged in activities such as education, science and technology, culture, health, and sports. They have public welfare attributes but are not government agencies, and their staff have different statuses from civil servants.
13. In Chinese, it is called: 四不像: 既是大学又不完全像大学, 既是科研机构又不完全像科研院所, 既是企业又不完全像企业, 既是事业单位又不完全像事业单位。I used "four characteristics" here since the essence of the Chinese describes four features of ITRI.
14. Official website: https://www.tsinghua-sz.org/.
15. Information is retrieved from: https://www.crunchbase.com/organization/shenzhen-leaguer-venture-capital.
16. Information is retrieved from: https://www.leaguer.com.cn/about/index/1.
17. Information is retrieved from: https://www.tsinghua-sz.edu.cn/about#s1.
18. Interview is retrieved from: https://www.semi.org/en/Oral-History-Interview-Morris-Chang. Excerpt in the paragraph is from the interview. Further information can also be found from Morris Chang's Chinese memoir.
19. Information is retrieved from: https://www.sohu.com/a/304577383_594383.
20. Information is retrieved from: http://www.siat.cas.cn/yjsjy2016/jygk2016/.
21. Information is retrieved from: https://www.siat.ac.cn/jggl/tjsj/.
22. Information is retrieved from: https://www.justice.gov/archives/opa/pr/chinese-telecommunications-device-manufacturer-and-its-us-affiliate-indicted-theft-trade.

23. The 2019 EU Industrial R&D Investment Scoreboard. Document retrieved from: https://op.europa.eu/en/publication-detail/-/publication/bcbeb233-216c-11ea-95ab-01aa75ed71a1/language-en.
24. Information obtained from Shenzhen Social Science Report:《深圳R&D 投入结构与成效分析研究》(Shenzhen R&D Investment Structure and Effect Analysis Research).
25. Information is retrieved from: https://www.huawei.com/us/corporate-information/research-development.
26. This metaphor, in his original Chinese wording, "活得越久, 吃得越多 ", emphasizes on the importance of having a long-term vision and strategy instead of focusing merely on the short-term benefits. In this context, Guo meant that Huawei invested much on R&D in spite of the lack of financial gains in a very long period. Also see the article, How Chinese culture led Huawei from surviving to thriving, https://blogs.lse.ac.uk/businessreview/2023/10/04/how-chinese-culture-led-huawei-from-surviving-to-thriving/.
27. In Mandarin Chinese, Jiang means "talent, general." In this sentence, the first "Jiang Lai" means "Generals come", while the second "Jiang Lai" means "future."
28. Information retrieved from: https://edu.qq.com/a/20180510/022479.htm.
29. From the book in Mandarin Chinese: 无止之境, 中国平安, p. 287.
30. The Head of Public Relations is no longer at Ping An upon the finalization of this book.
31. From the book in Mandarin Chinese: 无止之境, 平安中安, p. 272.
32. Information is retrieved from: https://www.pagd.net/allPage/aboutUs/37?lang=ZH_CN.
33. BGI Genomics, 华大基因website: https://en.genomics.cn/.
34. Information is retrieved from: https://en.genomics.cn/en-periodical-1818.html.
35. There is a change of the number of Huawei's overseas research center as some were shutdown. This person noted that there were 16 at the time of our conversation.

CHAPTER 9

Human Capital and National Competitiveness

What is important for growth is integration not into an economy with a large number of people, but rather into one with a large amount of human capital.

Paul Romer, Nobel Laureate.

The acquisition of... talents during... education, study, or apprenticeship, costs a real expense, which is capital in [a] person. Those talents [are] part of his fortune [and] likewise that of society.

Adam Smith, Author of *The Wealth of Nations*.

Goodwill Hunting

Huawei, as a Chinese company expanding globally, is faced with its dilemma in the midst of international geopolitical competition. Slapped with unexpected sanctions from the United States and its allies, Huawei had to close many of its research centers and terminate its international scientific collaborations. In early 2019, the University of California at Berkeley (hereto UC Berkeley) suspended a research partnership with Huawei, despite it being one of the school's largest corporate donors, having provided about $9 million to the university from 2011 to 2019. Randy Katz, UC Berkeley's vice chancellor for research, nevertheless

G. Y. Wang, *Dragon Innovation: Shenzhen*, Governing China in the 21st Century, https://doi.org/10.1007/978-981-95-9637-9_9

described Huawei as a "responsible corporate partner" and made a statement that UC Berkeley values high quality international scientific research collaboration and said that none of Huawei's existing grants to Berkeley involved sensitive technological secrets.[1] In fact, as a corporate donor, Huawei followed the same donation rules and regulations like other companies do. UC Berkeley's corporate donors on artificial intelligence research include Huawei, Intel, and Google— none of which have exclusive rights to scientific results. Despite so, Stanford University followed UC Berkeley and announced a moratorium on new engagement, gifts, affiliated membership fees and other support from Huawei.[2] The University of California at San Diego and University of Illinois took similar steps.

Huawei's vision and ambition in its global scientific research and business partnerships is stifled by geopolitical chaos. As of early September 2020, Huawei was forced to close its U.S. research centers in San Jose, California, and Texas. The University of Oxford also terminated its research ties with Huawei because of the U.S. ban. Huawei also withdrew its 5G installation in Australia, claiming that it had lost confidence in R&D and other collaborations due to volatile uncertainties and political sanctions imposed by the Australian government.[3] The disconnection with top U.S. research institutions extinguished Huawei's idealism in global scientific research, especially in the United States. Although the freeze by top research universities is unlikely to negatively impact Huawei's current 5G technology, long-term damage could occur if Huawei's scientific advance slows down. The U.S. chip ban on Huawei's suppliers is already having a devastating influence on the company, and the manufacturing of advanced chips largely depends on foreign equipment such as lithography.

"The chip ban certainly affects Huawei's business negatively, initially on its smart phone sectors in 2019," said a reasoned Chinese internet entrepreneur and a university professor in China who authored several books on Huawei's Harmony OS system in 2025. U.S. chip ban on Huawei reveals that the company, and China in general, are lacking top talent in the semiconductor industry. To compensate for problems in its advanced chip supply chain, China has turned to Taiwan's manufacturing company, TSMC, for chip imports. TSMC is the world's supply leader, outperforming Intel in market capitalization, hitting $168.4 billion in 2017, compared to Intel's at $165.7 billion.[4] Taiwanese chips were flowing to Chinese Mainland, motivated by generous cash incentives. China was also systematically importing Taiwanese semiconductor production talent since 2019. More than 3,000 semiconductor engineers and executives have left Taiwan for positions at mainland companies that offer more than twice the salary and pay for private education of their children. One senior Taiwan engineer said, "It is a natural decision to go to mainland semiconductor companies."[5] In fact, according to The China Semiconductor Association, China's semiconductor industry faces a shortage of skilled workers, roughly about 220,000 labor as of the end of 2020. However, with the increasing geopolitical tensions between the U.S. and China, Taiwan's Labor Ministry issued a notice to ban recruitment and headhunting from helping or representing companies hire talents to work in Chinese Mainland in 2021. It is said that if the recruitment involves semiconductor and integrated circuits industries, headhunters will face a higher fine if they violate the regulation.[6]

The disruption of the global semiconductor supply chain was not a huge surprise for Huawei, said Guo Ping, who was the rotating chairman at Huawei in 2019:

> Huawei always has a plan B. It is not because we want to stop business and trade with America (though we never truly enter the U.S. market). In 1949, the United States initiated the Coordinating Committee for Export to Communist Countries. The purpose of that committee is to restrict its member states from exporting strategic materials and advanced technologies to socialist countries. There are tens of thousands of products listed in the sanctions, including cutting-edge technology products. And Huawei does not want to seek approval for licenses on the international stage. In order to maintain our competitiveness in the industry, we need to set our standards.

Huawei's preparation for the "worst-case scenario" is embedded in its well-established survival mode. Guo Ping, the third person to join Huawei, in 1988, said that the company recognized the importance of self-dependence very early on. After the 1989 Tiananmen Square incident, Huawei's Hong Kong private branch exchange (PBX) supplier stopped their supply, leaving the company with no products to sell. Huawei realized that to stay competitive, it needed to develop and sell its own products. In a 2019 interview with Guo, the then PBX development manager appointed by Huawei's founder Ren Zhengfei, he recalled, "At that time, I even did not make several phone calls myself, not to mention how to make telephones. I was simply encouraged to do whatever I can do, to take whatever risks on research and development". The culture of innovation at Huawei was, in short, "take risks, tolerate failure, and allow waste [on R&D]." This approach helped the fledgling Chinese telecommunications company play catch-up with western giants and finally become a global ICT leader. Huawei's attention to and success in R&D are attributed to its risk-taking culture of innovation, diligent employees and Shenzhen's local autonomy (see Chapter 5 , Local Governance: Bureaucratic Entrepreneurs). Its state-of-the-art technological innovation breakthroughs are contributed to its investment in research and development.

The abrupt termination of research partnerships with top-notched U.S. universities propels Huawei to cultivate and expand scientific research collaborations with domestic universities. Huawei's CEO Ren Zhengfei visited several prestigious Chinese universities—Fudan, Shanghai Jiao Tong, Southeast, and Nanjing—with his top-level executive team in the summer of 2020. Ren and his team sent a clear signal to the outside: Huawei needs to strengthen its research-industrial collaborations with Chinese universities, particularly with leading scientific and engineering research universities in China. In recent years, Huawei established scientific research cooperation in all areas related to artificial intelligence and telecommunications. Nanjing University, in particular, jointly established seven labs with Huawei for research closely relevant to the company's semiconductor display, acoustic technology, and software engineering enterprises.[7] During Ren's university tours, he made the following remarks at each institution:

> We should give more freedom to scientific research and more tolerance for failure given the uncertainty of the future and the difficulty of understanding and coping with it. The determination to deal with future uncertainty can start from children's education. China's future and revitalization depend on children, and the future of children only relies on education.[8]

Ren's call for scientific research autonomy and "tolerance for failure" in scientific explorations and innovation is critical to Huawei's future development as well as for educational advancement in China in general. In 2019, Huawei's rotating chairman Guo Ping said regarding the company's university-corporate collaboration:

> Huawei supports many universities' research, but intellectual property is owned by those universities. There are two categories of our university-corporate collaboration: know and own (知道和拥有). Huawei, as a pioneering telecommunications company, we want to know the advancement of basic scientific theories. For instance, neither Moore's Law nor Shannon Theory can lead ICT [information and communications technology] development to move forward and to break through 6G. Huawei invests and supports scientific research for this kind of human advancement.

As a matter of fact, in 2019, Huawei invested $18.65 billion in R&D, accounting for 15.3% of their annual revenue, making Huawei one of the largest R&D spenders worldwide, on the level of Samsung, Alphabet, and Microsoft.[9] As of 2020, Huawei was one of the world's largest patent holders, with 85,000 patents in total, over 90% of which are inventive ones.[10] Table 9.1 shows the holdings of the number of effectively granted patents in four kinds: Huawei, China, countries except for China, and European countries and the United States, of which Huawei topped first with 85,000 patents at the end of 2019.

Huawei's investment in R&D is not limited to research funding though. It has invested tremendously in its physical facilities, scientific environment and a sense of belongings for its staff and employees. In 2019, I was accompanied by a young female Huawei employee in touring

Table 9.1 Number of effectively granted patents by the end of 2019

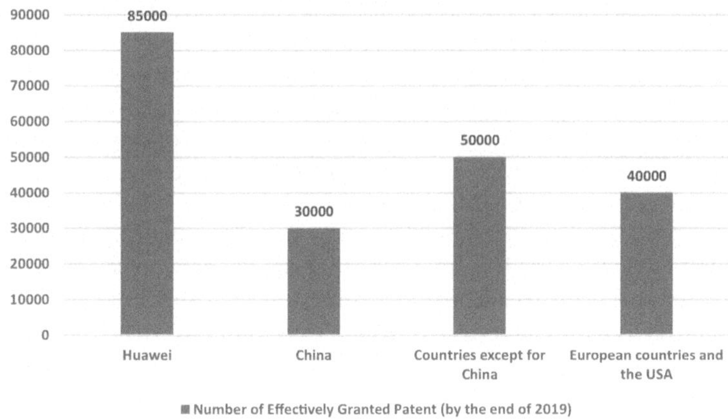

Note Source from 2019 Huawei Annual Report

Huawei Dongguang Songshan Lake campus which is the headquarter of the company's R&D, located in Dongguan Songshan Lake Science and Technology Industrial Park. The campus is famous for its European style architecture, thus, it is widely known as Huawei's "European Town", where visitors and employees can take trains on campus commuting between office buildings. My guide, a young woman who joined Huawei in a relatively short time, spent almost five hours taking me to different "European cities" on campus and checked in several cafeterias characterized by Japanese, French, Italian and Chinese cuisine. "Let me get you a cup of coffee," she offered when we were in a Huawei café where the counters were filled with Chinese books such as *Will Huawei be the Next One that Falls (下一个倒下的会不会是华为)*. I thanked her for her hospitality and took the coffee cup with Ms. Meng Wanzhou's image on. Ms. Meng, the daughter of Huawei's founder Ren Zhengfei, was arrested in Canada in 2018 when she was on a stopover from Hong Kong en route to several Latin American countries. "This is good coffee," I told my guide, though not sure if she knew about the Italian brand Illy. Shunning away from the sensitive Meng Wanzhou incident, I asked her why I saw several men holding small equipment walking around the campus. She burst into laughter and proudly told me that those men whom we passed by are "elites of elites" at Huawei and they were probably testing new sample equipment. Many R&D staff reside in Dongguan R&D center, where Huawei corporate subsidies on housing. Delicate cuisine at multiple cafeterias, world-class coffee, British style commuting trains on campus, office buildings and sceneries replicating Bologna, Burgundy, Luxembourg and many other European celebrity spots, are all efforts made to ensure that Huawei R&D staff and employees can concentrate on scientific discoveries and research without external concerns for personal matters. "Mr. Ren is very charismatic. A sense of strength. I enjoy working at Huawei." Staring at her shining eyes, I was convinced that she was not overestimating her content or broadcasting corporate public relations. With no college degree, she was hired by Huawei to start her career from scratch as a corporate receptionist. It is no doubt that she devotes herself to working for Huawei and plans to advance her career there. "Maybe I can also find a husband at Huawei Dongguan. Many examples like that." I was hesitant to ask her if she had already eyed on any "elite of elite." I understood her marriage wish with a Huawei colleague since the professional connection would provide her, a young migrant worker in Dongguan, with a sense of reliability that reduces the chance of being tricked. Her corporate loyalty, at that moment, seemed to have nothing to do nationalism. Instead, it is a migrant woman's longing for safety and belonging (see Chapter 11, Research Note: Emerging Sensitive Research).

My day at Huawei's European Town helped me understand Huawei's R&D in a fresh way. When western studies abound in attracting high-tech and creative talents via urban clusters and night clubs alike, Huawei built its R&D headquarter in Dongguan Songshan, hoping to provide its researchers with a peace of mind and comprehensive working facilities, particularly when those R&D employees are from across China or even abroad. Ren's tour of Chinese universities demonstrated its need for "self-dependence," meaning Huawei's dependence on itself and its reliance on China's scientific research. In spite of Huawei's headquarter in Shenzhen, none of the universities mentioned above were in Shenzhen. The lack of advanced ICT talent remains a local problem. Its talent pool could not match Huawei's or other tech companies' demand for breakthrough or basic scientific research development since it has been focused on applied innovation and experimental development for a long period (see Chapter 8 , Shenzhen R&D Ecosystem). The manufacturing and innovation upgrading of Shenzhen local industries and China's innovation capacity, requires both enterprises and universities to perform at world-class level scientific research to advance the whole innovation ecosystem.

A Shenzhen city government official I talked to during his executive training in the United States before Covid-19 reinforced this idea. According to him, the establishment and development of an excellent scientific research university in Shenzhen would take time, although Shenzhen local government has actively sought Chinese heritage scientists to return to Shenzhen:

> The current Peacock Talents program in Shenzhen has focused on the brain circulation of accomplished and established scientists. However, their decision to relocate to Shenzhen involves too many family matters, for instance, where their kids can go to school, where their partners can continue with their careers, if the whole family leaves for Shenzhen.

"Peacock Talents" was frequently mentioned to me by both advocates and opponents of this policy program. One city government official who opposes heavy financial incentives of the program said to me:

> Do you think people who are incentivized by money really hold the dream to develop Shenzhen? We should create an environment that naturally attracts those innovators and scientists to come to Shenzhen. Does Silicon Valley spend millions of dollars luring world-renowned scientists to the Bay Area?

Indeed, his comments on Shenzhen's strategy to attract global talents reveal the differences of innovation synergy and competitive attractiveness among global tech clusters. More importantly, those differences pose the questions and challenges, for Shenzhen government, other municipal government in China, or even governments in other countries: What role does state interference can really play in attracting talents when human capital can determine their career development, their lifestyle and freedom to choose at their own will? Though international news media cover widely on the U.S.—China tech rivalry as well as the decline of Chinese students studying in the U.S., statistics show that in 2018/19–2023/24 academic calendars, the percentage of international students from Chinese Mainland who major in Math and Computer Science has been increasing steadily, as shown in Table 9.2. Percentage in Math and Computer Science implicitly demonstrates the AI talent war between the United States and China, as per 2025 Stanford AI Index Report noted that, until 2023, not so many university programs in the U.S. specify artificial intelligence in their program names. Therefore, the report counted existing computer science programs that contain AI courses in their document. Except for Math and Computer Science, Table 9.2 shows that the percentage in Physical/ Life science as well as in Engineering both has seen a steady increase trend from 2018/19 to 2023/24. These figures explain several key phenomena behind the rising U.S.—China geopolitical tensions. First, U.S.—China trade tensions and technological competition has likely had a negative impact on Chinese students enrolling in U.S. Ph.D. programs which probably are more subject to scrutiny and university censorship. Second, those figures in Table 9.2 do not differentiate bachelor, master and doctoral degrees, and they reflect that U.S. remains a top destination for Chinese students who study Math/Computer Science, Engineering and Life Science over a longitudinal period, which is part of U.S.'s national competitiveness.

Clearly, Huawei's Chinese university tours came at a critical time and sounded the alarm. Only when higher education becomes a national asset, can domestic universities retain Chinese students as well as attract talented

Table 9.2 Percentage of international students from Chinese Mainland in math/computer science, physical/life sciences and engineering from 2018/19 to 2023/24

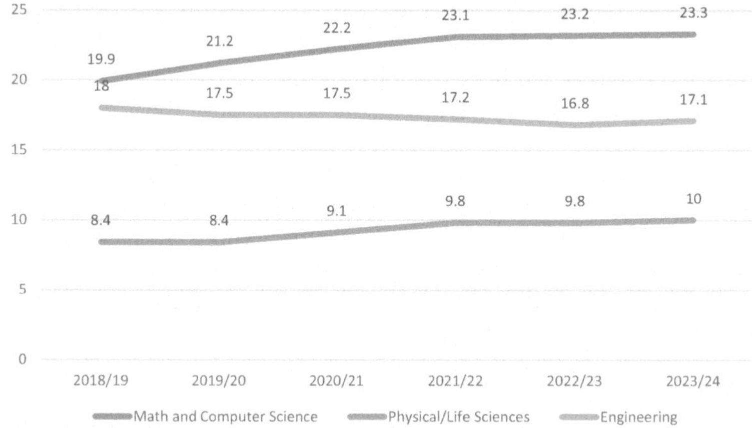

Note Source from: Open Doors Data: https://opendoorsdata.org/data/international-students/fields-of-study-by-place-of-origin/

overseas human capital effortlessly. Given Shenzhen's technological development and China's economic transition, more and more people oppose the idea of attracting talent back to China with financial incentives. They worry that people are motivated only by money and funding rather than be driven by advancing Shenzhen's technological innovation. The debate on how Shenzhen (or China) should attract top talent will require more investigation of the Peacock Talents Policy program.

Shenzhen Talents[1]

Peacock Talents Program

Shenzhen Talent Park in Shenzhen Bay is one of the most desirable and most expensive locations in the city. A peacock statue struts in a park on one side of the lake, symbolizing an ancient Chinese poem: "The

[1] Wang, G.Y. Talent Migration in Knowledge Economy: The Case of China's Silicon Valley, Shenzhen. Int. Migration & Integration 23, 1175–1196 (2022). Copyright 2022 Springer Nature.

peacock flies toward the Southeast." (孔雀东南飞) The "peacock" of Shenzhen's overseas talent policy reflects ancient Chinese Yin and Yang philosophy. Southeast is the direction toward which a peacock flies to die and be reborn. In my interpretation, local government names this policy program "Peacock Talents" with the possible hope that the talents back to Shenzhen could be "reborn" to bring values to the city.

In 1978, when China launched the Open and Reform policy to advance its economic modernization, it also renewed its national policy of sending students and scholars overseas. Deng Xiaoping wanted China to catch up with the western developed countries and to learn from their advanced technologies and management methods. In Deng's famous speech *Emancipate the mind, Seek truth from facts, Unite and Look forward*, he emphasized the importance of economic development with Chinese characteristics, which sent a clear economic development message (also see Chapter 2 , The Genesis of Shenzhen):

> We must learn to manage the economy following the economic and scientific methods. If we do not understand it, we should learn from people who know it, and learn from advanced foreign management methods. New enterprises must use advanced methods, existing enterprises must also adapt new, advanced methods.[11]

Chinese nationals who studied abroad were expected to return to China with new information, technologies, and management methods. In 1992, during his southern trip, Deng emphasized that the Chinese government did not care about overseas students' political attitudes toward the 1989 Tiananmen incident. He warranted that all those people could return and would be taken care of (Zweig et al., 2004). Positioned as a leading global innovation hub in China, Shenzhen has made great efforts to attract both domestic human capital and overseas returnees to develop cutting-edge technologies that are "Created and Made in China" as well as to advance its basic scientific research and radical innovation.

Established in 2011, the Peacock Talents Policy program is designed to attract talented human capital, both Chinese nationals and foreign citizens from abroad. Many Peacock Talents statues on display at Shenzhen Talent Park seem to concentrate on middle-aged men who are experts in science and engineering, that is, mostly accomplished scientists and businessmen. My guide, a middle-aged man noted, "This one is a fellow at the Academy of Science of the Royal Society of Canada. This one is from

Hong Kong. This one is an American." When my guide asked me about my expertise, he could not understand my area of study but commented that my expertise was not what they currently needed.[12]

The Peacock Talents Policy program started in 2011 is a high-level overseas talents initiative led by the municipal government to attract talents who help fulfill Shenzhen's fast-changing developmental needs at the international level. It is reported that on September 1st, 2021, applications for Shenzhen's high-level talent (including "high-level professional talent recognition", "overseas high-level talent confirmation", and "academic training allowance") were suspended.[13] According to its 2020 application requirements,[14] the demand for Peacock Talents falls into

Fig. 9.1 Peacock statue in Shenzhen Talent Park (*Note* Photo taken by the author)

three categories: The first is A Talents, superstars who received international awards such as the Nobel Prize and Turing Award. Money incentives up to 3 million RMB are available for these applicants. CEOs from fortune global 500 companies are also considered A Talents, and so are Olympic gold medalists. The statues that stand on Shenzhen Talent Park are of A Talents, and their contributions to Shenzhen's technological innovation and development make them akin to "city ambassadors." For instance, Yan Ning, a female structural biologist, who was a Tsinghua professor before she resigned from her position at Princeton and returned to China to become the inaugural dean of the Shenzhen Medical Academy of Research and Translation can be regarded as an A talent though it is unsure if she went through this route. B and C Talents are more popular and accessible appointments. For instance, anyone who served as a full or associate professor at a world-renowned university for more than five years qualifies as a B Talent, while assistant professors from these universities can apply as C Talents. The initial funding from the Peacock Talents Policy program was 2 million RMB and 1.6 million RMB,[15] respectively. One research dean at a collaborative international institution, considered as a B Talent, for example, would come to Shenzhen every summer for research and guide students for two to three months. He would then spend the rest of his time in the United States. It is unclear to me during the in-person conversation with him how much he knew about Shenzhen's technological and scientific research landscape and if his short-term presence in Shenzhen really benefits the school. Despite the fame and international reputation of some research lab supervisors, young Chinese researchers and scientists receive limited guidance from Peacock Talents professors. The lack of mentorship for junior scientists is briefly mentioned by a chief scientist at a Shenzhen tech firm, as documented in Chapter Eight (see Chapter 8, Shenzhen R&D Ecosystem). Full-time local advisors are much more involved. The research dean I spoke to acknowledged that some of his students chose to be at his lab with the hope of eventually transferring to his counterpart lab in the United States.

The reasons Chinese returnee scientists opt not to relocate permanently to Shenzhen vary. A study on the cultural analysis of academic returnees explains why some Chinese academics and scientists who held academic positions in Canada, for example, chose not to return to China. In Fu's (2014) research interview, one Chinese scientific professor mentioned the excess workloads and tight schedules of his Chinese counterparts, which he observed during his trip to Beijing. Busy with the hustle and bustle, he did not think it would be possible to conduct quality research and teaching in China since he felt academic research takes time and a calm mind to focus (Fu, 2014). Moreover, some held the view that the Chinese *guanxi* (connections) culture has a tremendous influence on finding and attaining research grants, since Chinese academics, compared to their western counterparts, focus more on maintaining social relationships to get promoted and obtain those grants than wholeheartedly conduct academic research. The prevalent guanxi culture in society and within China's scientific community makes it difficult for academics to advance based on fairness and equity. As Shi and Rao (2010) observed, in China's science academic community, connections with bureaucrats and powerful experts are critical and essential for their career advancement.

Criticisms of China's scientific education system and Peacock Talent Policy do exist. Some opponents believe that it is all about money. The city government provides subsidies to attract people to create businesses and conduct basic scientific research in Shenzhen, while some people take advantage of it though they did not really make any serious contributions. This phenomenon is not unique to Shenzhen but prevalent in China's talent attraction strategies overall. In order to attract high-quality talents, Shenzhen government officials also go overseas to attract international talents to spur innovation to advance the development of Shenzhen innovation cluster. For instance, some Shenzhen local government officials serve as "city ambassadors" and introduce Peacock Talents Policy program to some possible candidates during their executive training programs in the United States (see Chapter 5, Local Governance: Bureaucratic Entrepreneurs). Some top scientists and engineers are attracted to Shenzhen and want to collaborate with local institutions on applied scientific innovations because they are scientific entrepreneurs. Many of them hold foreign passports but are of Chinese descent. When they move to Shenzhen, some end up working at large corporations as chief scientists or owning technology firms. They also serve as practical advisors at research institutions or universities, including institutions not located in Shenzhen. One chief scientist who came to Shenzhen under the "Thousand Talents" initiative[16] said:

> I feel very comfortable coming back [to China]. I was born and grew up here until my doctoral pursuit in the U.S. I do not even have to adjust. I can get whatever I need here, at both the personal and professional level.

He served as a practical advisor for one of the highest-ranked science and engineering universities in northern China and worked as the chief scientist at a famous fin-tech company in Shenzhen. A 2013 Shenzhen Talent Research Report showed that the top two reasons that Peacock Talents choose to work and settle in Shenzhen are career interests (50%) and societal acknowledgment (47.26%).[17] Peacock Talents who return to Shenzhen from overseas tend to care most about their personal and professional satisfaction. They choose Shenzhen over other Chinese cities because it can fulfill their ambitions to further their careers. A and B Talents from overseas are already established leaders. They recognize what Shenzhen offers them and what it does not: well-developed manufacturing supply chains, rapid applied innovation, and supportive entrepreneurship policy, but not top-ranked research universities. Chinese news and government reports often note that Peacock Talents publish frequently in the journals such as *Nature* and *Science*, while they usually come to visit rather than stay in Shenzhen. Shenzhen city, or the research institutes that those Peacock Talents are associated with, enjoy the prestige of having researchers published in top journals. However, based on my research interviews, some are not contributing much to mentoring and educating the next generation of Chinese scientific researchers. The real scientific research exploration and knowledge creation process comes from the constant exchange of ideas, timely feedback, and repeated experiments. Young researchers require their adviser's or principal investigator's sustained guidance over time.

Unlike a journal publication or immediate technology transfer in Shenzhen, the education process takes longer, with no immediate outcomes. One survey sponsored by the city's Social Science Committee, *Research on Shenzhen Talent Development Environment*, included in the 2013 Shenzhen Talent Research Report, found that more than 60% of the survey participants thought Shenzhen's higher education system and academic environment is "average or dissatisfying."[18] Only 27% believed that living and working in Shenzhen helped advance their academic career opportunities, while more than 60% complained that Shenzhen was an "average or unpleasant place" to pursue academic career because their academic and intellectual pursuits were hampered and academic exchange opportunities with foreign counterparts were limited. No specific reasons were given for the lack of academic exchange opportunities reported in the survey. Shenzhen's lack of a nurturing educational environment may be a key factor in its failure to build top-notch scientific institutions and universities. Overseas returnees who have the ambition to advance science and innovation are lured not by benefits such as a spacious house but by a healthy environment and a positive atmosphere for their professional development (Ni, 2005). According to Simon and Cao (2009), the absence of a nurturing academic environment in Shenzhen, or in China, is what has persuaded some scientists to keep their academic positions abroad. Moreover, my conversations with some overseas PhD graduates during 2023–2025 reflect a kind of mismatch between young ambitious academics in social science with the current higher-education landscape in China. A doctoral graduate from a renowned European university said to me that she wanted to be a pioneer in building a new field in China upon her return. She holds an EU certified license in her field with working experiences in the EU. However, not many universities in China currently have that major and she was often mistaken as a physical sports teacher during job applications in Chinese Mainland.

One drawback of the Peacock Talents Policy program, survey participants reported, is the overemphasis on technical and high-level talents. The study found that 38.24% of the survey participants thought Shenzhen city government put too much emphasis on high-level talents, and 13.26% agreed that it overemphasized attracting technical human capital. That is, the search for talent is a "demand–supply" design set to meet current needs, instead of a long-term cultivation of local academia. Predictably, Shenzhen city and its district governments seek technical talents to fulfill their developmental needs. Shenzhen's tech competitors, such as Chongqing and Chengdu in Southwest China, are increasingly gaining recognition in recent years and are also trying to attract national and international innovators to enhance their own developmental efforts. Compared to Silicon Valley, Shenzhen has a smaller but growing global talent pool. One program director at an international startup incubator viewed native Chinese professionals as good at mechanical engineering design but not at industrial design:

> Design is a form of art creation. The more you have seen, the more open-minded you are, the more creative your designs are. Native Chinese are still

> lacking that training in their school education. But the situation is getting better with more *haigui* or sea turtles [overseas students who return to China] with degrees and training in art and design.

The interviewee observed that Huawei opened its global aesthetic design center in Paris in 2015 for this reason. Huawei aims to enhance its interior and exterior product design by building on Paris's long-standing reputation in art and design. Huawei's "seeking out" strategy reflects the talents shortage in the design field in Shenzhen. Technology startups in Shenzhen that value the aesthetics of their products also seek international partners in art & product design. Despite the talents shortage, the 2020 Peacock Talents application instructions set a high criterion to match the design talent demand needed for the B Talent recipients: a product design award from the German-based iF international industrial design award.[19] It is extremely unlikely that an iF award winner would work at a local startup incubator to help unknown budding tech entrepreneurs with their product design. Shenzhen's local government is aware of the "take money with no concrete contributions" issue in the implementation of the Peacock Talents Policy program. The average age of science academics is 74. Some of the first batch of Peacock Talents were later disqualified due to their part-time positions; more than 1,500 of them held 9,000 part-time jobs and did not reside in Shenzhen. Some officials have sought to reform the program by restricting the location option to avoid wasting funding resources, in the hope of providing more concrete support to attract senior technicians to Shenzhen. New *haigui*, or new sea turtles (the young generation of overseas Chinese students) are the proposed talent targets.[20]

Brain Circulation: Overseas Returnees

Brain drain, as a form of migration, refers to talented young people moving from poor developing countries to advanced countries in pursuit of education at universities and research institutions or work in areas where employment opportunities are limited in their home countries. Countries and regions, such as India, Chinese Taiwan, and Chinese Mainland have all experienced a tremendous loss of human resources to developed countries at different developmental stages. These countries and regions worry about their brain drain and its consequential economic loss—human capital was the last resource they wanted to lose in their national advantages and the world competition for talent (Todaro, 1985; Saxenian, 2005). In the past decades, migration of skilled talent from developing countries to advanced countries has mainly involved migration from India and China to the United States. For instance, between 1998 and 1999, 10.4% of all international students who enrolled in U.S. universities were from Chinese Mainland (51,000, not including Hong Kong) and 7.6% were from India (37,482) (Todd, 2000). Further, between 1990 and 1996, 16,749 Chinese students and 8, 211 Indian students received their Ph.D.s in science and engineering from U.S. universities (Johnson, 1998). With Silicon Valley's rapid growth from the 1970s through the 1990s, skilled technical immigrants from developing countries who came to the U.S. for science and engineering education found jobs in companies in the Bay Area. By 2000, 53% of Silicon Valley's scientists and engineers were foreign born, with Indian and Chinese nationals accounting for over one quarter of its total personnel (estimated at 20,000 Indians, 5,000 Taiwanese, and 1,500 mainland-born Chinese) (Saxenian, 2005). Notable Chinese who came to the United States for their PhDs in science and engineering degrees during this period include Founder and CEO of Zoom Video Communications Eric Yuan, Co-founder and CEO of Baidu.com Robin Li Yanhong (who later dropped out of his Ph.D. program), though their later life choices differ as Robin Li returned to China as brain circulation.

In contrast to brain drain, brain circulation happens when skilled overseas population return to their home countries after years of learning, living, and working abroad. Those who return to start a business through their established overseas business links are called transnational entrepreneurs. Transnational entrepreneurs spread international knowledge about the global markets and, at the same time, link economic opportunities between their home countries and host countries (Liu, 2017; Saxenian, 2005). Other returnees go back to teach at universities or work for multinational companies (Beaverstock, 2002; Cyranoski, 2002; Varshney, 2013; Zweig et al., 2004). Brain circulation, or brain gain, usually generates positive outcomes for home countries because of the skills, capital, knowledge, or business connections people bring back with them (Stark et al., 1998). The brain circulation of transnational engineers and entrepreneurs to their home countries is not new. U.S. educated and trained talents return home to create and take advantage of promising economic opportunities, like Baidu.com's CEO Robin

Li. He returned to Beijing to establish this Chinese technology multinational (i.e., Baidu.com) in 2000 while his family stayed in Silicon Valley. AnneLee Saxenian (2002) wrote extensively on brain circulation from Silicon Valley to Chinese Taiwan, India, and Chinese Mainland, especially in the 1990s. She explored how policymakers and representatives in Chinese Mainland visited Silicon Valley repeatedly to recruit Chinese technical professionals to go back home. Early on, most representatives were from Beijing and Shanghai. Chinese cities like Beijing established "returning students venture parks" exclusively designed for enterprises established or run by overseas returnees, and municipal governments offered infrastructure and financial benefits such as housing, tax benefits, and education for their children (Saxenian, 2002). Zhongguancun in Beijing's Haidian district was known as a famous "returning students venture park." In 1995, Shanghai municipal government launched its first talent attraction policy to attract and cultivate talents in service sectors such as insurance, international law, finance, and foreign trade. Additionally, Shanghai's Talent Highland Initiative also included strategies to attract technical talents to enhance Shanghai's R&D and innovation capabilities (Froy et al., 2009). Chinese Mainland's efforts to attract talents back with policies and incentives resembled Chinese Taiwan's policies of the 1970s and 1980s (Saxenian, 2002). It is interesting to note that, by 2000, when representatives from Beijing flew to Silicon Valley to lure back talent to turn Beijing to "China's Silicon Valley," Shenzhen was transitioning from a labor-intensive export economy to an "electronic-focused, and innovation-oriented" (see Chapter 3, China, the New Development) direction led by the local government. As a new city in a catch-up mode, Shenzhen's Peacock Talent Policy program is nothing new, but it differs from Beijing or Shanghai's efforts of the early 1990s. Today's robust internet industries, advanced manufacturing and AI-driven technological companies in Shenzhen enable it to attract significant overseas talent which symbolizes Shenzhen's "soft power" as a technological ecosystem nowadays.

In recent years, more Chinese nationals completing their studies overseas have chosen to return to China. Shenzhen is one of their top choices, particularly for knowledge workers in the technology industry. In 2019, Tencent, the internet giant headquartered in Shenzhen, is the most attractive employer among overseas returnees. Alibaba Group, founded by Jack Ma, comes second and Huawei fourth. ByteDance, TikTok's parent company, is 14th. Table 9.3 shows that the top 15 employers attracting overseas returnees in the country are all Chinese companies, many of them technology enterprises. Headquarters of Tencent, Huawei and Ping An are located in Shenzhen. Differing from overseas returnees previous employment choices such as Microsoft, PwC and Amazon, this ranking showcases the successful growth of Chinese technology sector in the past decades. Table 9.4 shows the 2024 number of priority positions for overseas returnees, Beijing, Shanghai and Shenzhen rank top three, with a respective percentage of 16%, 8.7% and 8.4%. Opportunities and career positions for overseas returnees are closely related to regional development. "Shenzhen city government wants to attract high-level foreign enterprises," said Tina, head of South China at the China Britian Business Council. In fact, with the high-quality development and investment initiative in China, cities and regions are competing for foreign investment in many ways. Chengdu, as shown in the table, ranks No. 4 in overseas returnees placement, partially because the city's increase in demand for overseas talents. According to Chengdu Municipal Bureau of Statistics, in 2023, foreign direct investment totaled 2.29 billion U.S. dollars and two new foreign-invested enterprises were added on average every day.[21] Table 9.5 shows the percentage of different industries in hiring overseas returnees, with internet industry continuing to top the position, in the percentage of 8.4%.

Haigui's increasing return is intertwined with uncertain geopolitical tensions faced by China overseas. As of October 2020, during the Covid-19 pandemic, about two thirds of Chinese students who studied in the United States, United Kingdom, or Australia had returned to China.

Table 9.3 2019 Top 15 most attractive employers among overseas returnees

1	*Tencent*	*9*	*Ping An*
2	Alibaba Group	10	China Construction Bank
3	Bank of China	11	DiDi
4	Huawei	12	CITIC Securities
5	XDF.cn	13	JD.com
6	NetEase	14	ByteDance
7	Industrial and Commercial Bank of China	15	Meituan
8	Baidu		

Note Information obtained from report released by Boss Career Science Lab, *2019 Overseas returnee students' employment trend report*

Table 9.4 Number of priority positions for overseas returnees in 2024 across Chinese cities

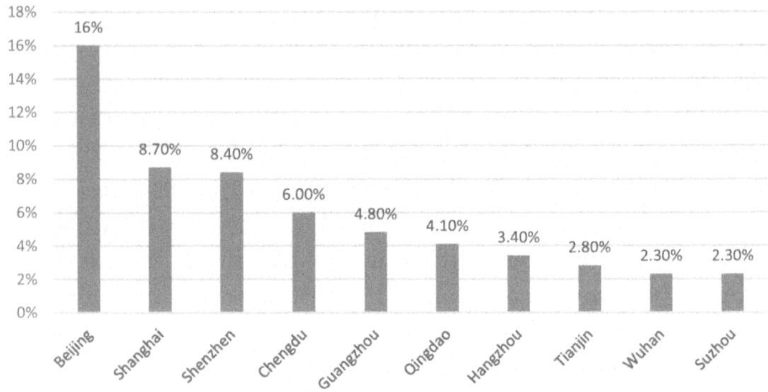

Note Survey Report on Employment of Returnees from Overseas Chinese. Information retrieved from: https://www.hrssit.cn/info/3600.html

Table 9.5 Top ten industries that overseas returnees hired in 2024

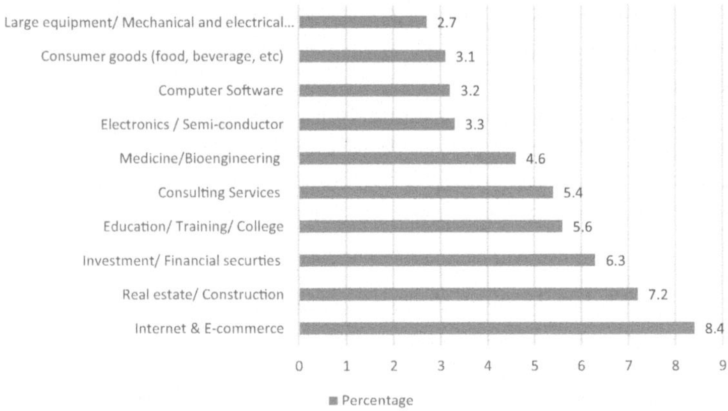

Note Survey Report on Employment of Returnees from Overseas Chinese. Information retrieved from: https://www.hrssit.cn/info/3600.html

Three-fifths of them hold at least a master's degree.[22] UniCareer, the online career development platform, found a 70% increase of haigui returns in 2019, and identified the Covid-19 pandemic and tightening immigration and employment rules overseas as major reasons for this development. For example, the Trump administration threatened to suspend the U.S. Optional Practical Training (i.e., OPT) program, a post-graduation work permit that allows international students to legally work after they complete their study. Faced with these unpredictable circumstances, some Chinese students opted for returning to China immediately after finishing their studies. They did not want to miss the job recruitment cycle in China. Meanwhile, during the Biden administration, U.S. consular officers were still denying Chinese student visas, based on the Chinese universities they attended as a continuation of presidential proclamation 10,043 on the "suspension of entry as nonimmigrants of certain students and researchers from the People's Republic of China" issued during the Trump administration.[23] This policy continuation, to some extent, is pushing away highly educated Chinese nationals in the United States who pursued and completed their studies in artificial intelligence, machine learning and other disciplines which will benefit the U.S. economy and its national innovation capacity. For instance, according to the finding of a National Foundation for American Policy, every 1,000 doctoral students blocked from attending U.S. universities costs the national economy about $210 billion in the expected value of patents produced at universities in a decade. Additionally, preventing highly productive scientists and engineers from working in the United States will create economic costs from losing patents or innovations produced outside of universities.[24] Table 9.6 indicates that geopolitical tensions have an overall negative impact on Chinese students enrolled in the US from 2018 to 2024, though factors such as financial constraint caused by the slowdown of the global economy and post-covid 19 effect may contribute to the decline of the number of Chinese students. The slight decline of international students from East Asia as a region might also be explained by the anti-Asian attacks as well as global economic slowdowns.

Similarly, the H-1B program was destabilized during the first Trump administration. By definition, H-1B refers to:

> The H-1B program applies to employers seeking to hire nonimmigrant aliens as workers in specialty occupations or as fashion models of distinguished merit and ability. A specialty occupation is one that requires the application of a body of highly specialized knowledge and the attainment of at least a bachelor's degree or its equivalent.[25]

Table 9.6 Chinese students enrolled in the U.S. from 2018/19 to 2023/24

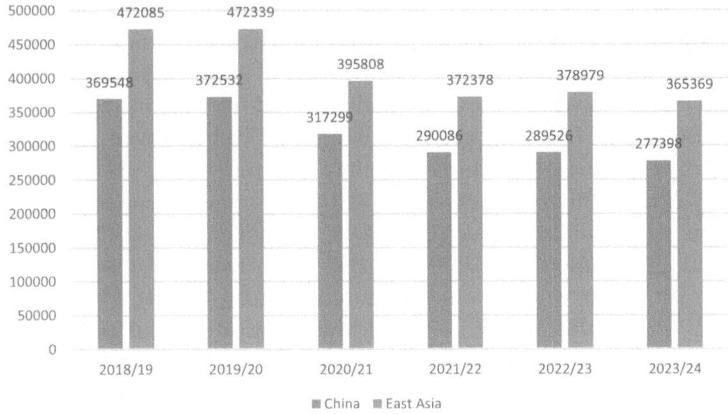

Note Sources 2024 Open Doors International Students Data: https://opendoorsdata.org/data/international-students/all-places-of-origin/

The majority of Chinese students in the United States hold a bachelor's degree or above. They tend to seek employment opportunities in the U.S., no matter if they plan to permanently return to China or not. Before they go into U.S. lottery for work permit, foreign students need to apply for OPT excluding individuals with extraordinary abilities who can apply for green cards direclty. Table 9.7 shows the number of international students with Chinese origin at undergraduate and graduate levels from 2018/19 – 2023/24. The number of OPT applicants, as shown, has greatly decreased overall. Table 9.8 shows that the denial rate for H-1B visas petition increased from 6% in 2015 to 29% in 2020. The H-1B denial indicates how hard it was for foreigners overall to seek further training or pursue careers in the United States during a critical time. The difficulties and uncertainties of winning the H-1B visas may be the reasons for the decline of OPT applications among Chinese students.

The number of Chinese students returning to China after graduation increased, as it became more difficult to obtain post-graduation work permits and H-1B sponsorship in the United States. Safety issue has become a reason, that many Chinese students chose to leave the United States, largely caused by anti-Asian incidents during the Covid-19 period.[26] An extremely popular sentiment among entrepreneurial overseas returnees is that "there are many more opportunities in China," at

Table 9.7 Academic level and places of origin (P.R China) from 2018–2024

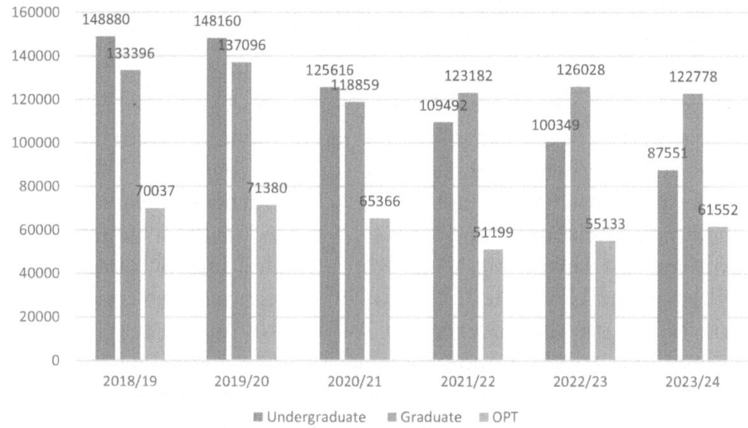

Note Sources 2024 Open Doors International Students Data: https://opendoorsdata.org/data/international-students/academic-level-and-places-of-origin/

Table 9.8 Denial rate of H-1B petitions in the U.S., 2015–2020

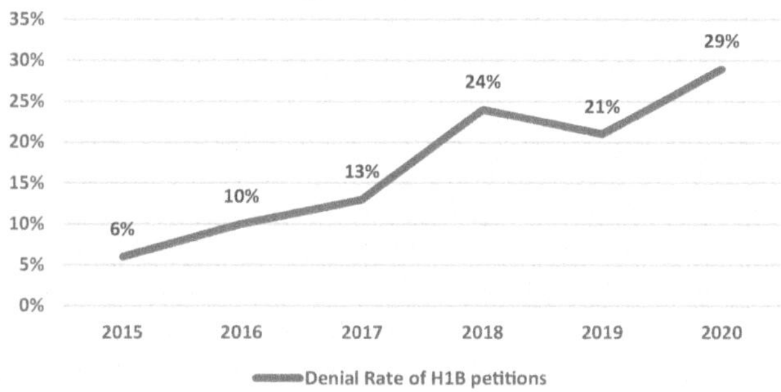

Note Source from U.S. Citizenship and Immigration Services website; 2015–end of the quarter in 2020

least before Covid-19. There are two categories of overseas returnees: those seeking work with employers in China and those focusing on creating businesses in China built on their international experience and the potential of a massive Chinese market. Shenzhen city was ranked third in 2019 as a top destination city among overseas returnees (see Table 9.9). To welcome new business and talents, the city's government subsidizes overseas returnee entrepreneurs in the amount of 500,000 RMB (74,117.30 U.S. dollars), 250,000 RMB (37,058.65 U.S. dollars), and 150,000 RMB (22,235.22 U.S. dollars), based on their educational attainments. Preferred industries for funding include information technologies, new material engineering, new energies, biomedical engineering, advanced manufacturing and equipment, modern agriculture, clean-tech, and professional services such as logistics.[27] The startup funding awarded to entrepreneurial overseas returnees, however, is far less than the financial resources and housing awarded to Peacock Talents. One entrepreneur at a coworking space who attended high school in the UK and college in the U.S. stated, "Shenzhen government is very supportive. It is possible to use the government startup funding to purchase several office computers to get a company started." Once considered as a "rich second generation" (Fuerdai), he seems to have reintegrated into a unique Chinese business environment, which requires him to "play it well with the government" by reinforcing the positive role government plays. Unlike overseas talents or transnational entrepreneurs lured back by the city's government, he took the initiative to quit his job in finance in Shanghai before pursuing his entrepreneurial ambitions in Shenzhen. His major motivation was to make more money than what he was paid for working for others. He also wanted to prove to his parents that he could make his own fortune. In a follow-up phone interview, he expressed his frustrations at not understanding why U.S. employers did not hire him. "Maybe because of the language, cultural barriers, GPA, or unwillingness to sponsor foreigners. Who knows? No employer explained to me why they did not hire me." As a "rich second generation," he did not lack connections and financial support from his family in China, though, personal freedom and lack of constraint seemed to be his top reasons for wanting to stay in the U.S.. His comments on U.S. employers' unwillingness to sponsor foreigners is worth pointing out as it has been reported by several people as a main barrier for foreigners to find a job in the United States.

Overseas returnee entrepreneurs who hold advanced degrees like a Ph.D. tell a different story. Three overseas returnees were optimistic and positive about their startup's growth and development after founding a medical data startup in Shenzhen in 2019. One of them shared in an interview:

> My other two cofounders are all male and received their PhDs in biomedical engineering and statistics from renowned American universities. It is easy for them to get jobs in the United States in relevant industries. But is it boring to just live a middle-class American life when you have the chance to be a first-mover startup founder in your field in China?

A female entrepreneur shared her entrepreneurial journey and enthusiasm with me. "In just two years our startup has started to make promising revenues. We did not go through venture capital, instead, we simply applied for 2 million RMB Peacock Talent government money to establish our company two years ago." However, it is not easy for all top-notch overseas returnees to achieve business success. A key obstacle some face is counter-cultural shock. The female entrepreneur further shared:

> To be honest, some overseas returnees are too arrogant and proud of themselves. They consider themselves as elites who hold state-of-the-art technology, patent, and knowledge that they obtain from their PhD training. But in Chinese business culture, most of the time it is not necessarily your technology but your personality, your character, and your connections that gain you the first business deal.

Table 9.9 2019 top five overseas returnee student (Haigui) destination cities in China

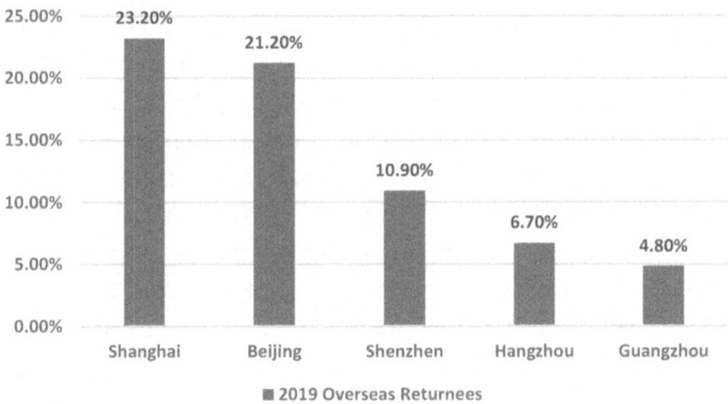

Note Information obtained from report released by Boss Career Science Lab, *2019 Overseas returnee students' employment trend report*

Interestingly, I was told by another returnee to Shenzhen from the UK that the manager at her first company commented that her working attitude was too western. "The head of human resource told me that they did not like to work with some overseas returnees in corporations because they are too full of themselves and individualistic." The UK returnee left that corporation and joined another technology company in Shenzhen later, saying that her supervisor at her new firm is a British national, whom she feels more comfortable working with. My interviewees' reflection demonstrates an intensifying cultural battle between young generation overseas returnees and many domestic Chinese employers, including corporate and higher-education ones. "Hard to manage" seems to be a popular excuse that some employers incline not to hire overseas returnees for corporate positions.

Talent Dilemma—Need for Internationalized Higher Education

Young overseas Chinese returnees share their unique views on their motivations and experiences when they return. How long they spent in foreign countries, especially in North America, the UK, and other European countries, affects their adjustment to Chinese culture and life in different ways. Sometimes, their foreign experiences influence their decisions on which city they prefer to live and work in. Despite Shenzhen city government's efforts to attract overseas talent, many overseas Chinese returnees prefer Shanghai or Beijing. One major complaint is Shenzhen's lack of fine museums, theaters, or entertainment channels. Cultural facilities are a weak indicator in Shenzhen's overall city attractiveness. The city's percentage of "highly educated people among permanent residents" also counts as a disadvantage for returnees compared to the percentages in Beijing or Shanghai. Shenzhen's University Town (Xi Li College Town, 西丽镇大学城) on the subdistrict is located on the edge of the city and county areas. Some overseas returnees who become professors in Shenzhen's universities complain that schools for their children are substandard; they want international-level, not county-level, schools. According to Fu (2014), children's education has been a critical factor in overseas returnees' decision-making about relocating to China. One of my informants with a wealthier family background expressed her frustration about the lack of artistic interior design in many high-end apartments in Shenzhen: "Also, I have never seen one tasteful art exhibition since I am back to Shenzhen from London", she expressed her frustration.

Similarly, several interviewees who are hardcore music fans told me that they often commute to Guangzhou for entertainment events. Shenzhen's lack of cultural opportunities and facilities for people with fine taste and its shortage of top-flight schools indicate its current barriers to attracting talent. Even though not every foreigner or overseas returnee cares the most about cultural facilities when choosing where to settle or to work, internationalization is a key indicator of competitiveness among metropolitan cities and regions when more and more overseas organizations are exploring to expand in China. The role of amenities matters not only to individuals but also to firms' and industries' perceived attractiveness. As urban scholar Florida noted:

> Quality of place is a critical factor in regional competitiveness . . . To compete in the age of talent, regions must make the quality-of-place and the amenities of the new economy central elements of their strategies to attract knowledge workers and build high-technology economies. Regions must seamlessly link their amenities strategies to ongoing economic development and competitiveness efforts. (Florida, 2000, pp. 47–48)

What Shenzhen lacks in cultural facilities and amenities, it makes up for with its welcoming, tolerant culture. This especially attracts young Chinese professionals who dislike dealing with "guan xi maintenance," according to my many informants. Survey results from the *Research on Shenzhen Talent Development Environment* (2019) show that among both overseas and domestic talents, 62.44% rated "Shenzhen city tolerance" (i.e., *深圳城市包容度*, it refers to the open and welcoming environment of a city) as the top reason it attracts talent. Career opportunities was second at 40.37%. Local government policy toward talents ranks seventh (see Table 9.10). Survey participants benefited from either Peacock overseas talents or domestic talents programs, although no differentiation was made between overseas and domestic participants' responses. Some of my interviewees did not hold overseas degrees but had overseas exchange study experience and degrees from local Chinese universities. They reported the government talent policy played a significant role in their decisions. One male interviewee in his early 30 s said:

> Among the first-tier cities in China, namely Beijing, Shanghai, Guangzhou, and Shenzhen, the welcoming and tolerant culture in Shenzhen is unbeatable. I happen to hold a doctoral degree that is in demand in the city.

> Therefore, I was assessed as a "high-talented reserved talent," and I receive 320,000 RMB exempt tax from the city government every year. I am scheduled to receive this amount in a maximum of five years as a "reserved talent."

Like many other young migrant professionals, he also praised the timely professional information exchange in Shenzhen's fast-changing environment. "I probably cannot even adjust to a slow-paced work and lifestyle if I go to a third-tier city. And more than Shenzhen's lifestyle keeps me in the city." He works at a technical company and serves as an advisor to a local think tank, occasionally giving lectures on supply chain management. City dynamism and various job-hopping opportunities excite him. "I am just doing this for fun" was his catchphrase during our conversations, which suggested he could change jobs easily in Shenzhen thanks to his expertise. He holds a PhD degree but acknowledged "Shenzhen's talent dilemma: Local universities do not steward basic scientific research. Some renowned Chinese and foreign universities have set up outposts in Shenzhen, but they do not bring their best professors in relevant disciplines. Sometimes students on Shenzhen campuses need to commute to Beijing or other cities to meet with their advisors and research peers. "You know why there are so many postdoctoral fellows in Shenzhen? Because being a postdoctoral fellow increases your chances to secure national scientific research projects, so you would be qualified as a domestic high talent in Shenzhen." A similar opinion was expressed by a

Table 9.10 Factors that attract talents to Shenzhen

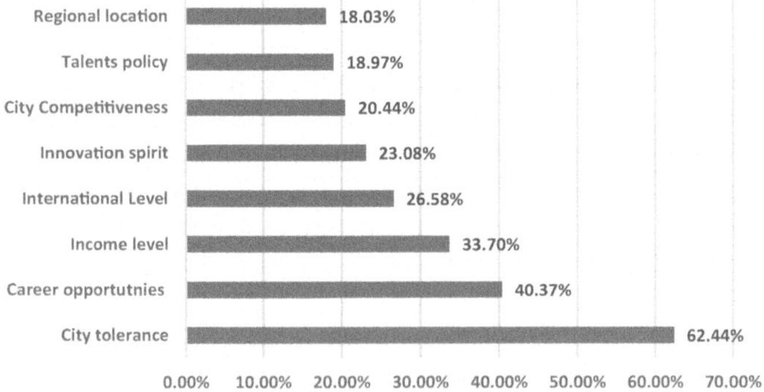

Note Information is from *Research on Shenzhen Talent Development Environment*, p. 69

full professor at a prestigious university in Beijing to further explain why Shenzhen lacks top-notch research universities:

> To some extent, it is not Shenzhen's problem that it does not have advanced scientific research institutions or good comprehensive universities. The National Ministry of Education assigns quotas to each university regarding the disciplines and subjects it allows them to have.

Shenzhen's talent dilemma reflects its research and education drawbacks and highlights the overall dilemma of Chinese higher education. A professor from a renowned Chinese university commented on the stagnant progress of Southern University of Science and Technology, established in Shenzhen in 2010:

> The goal they set for Southern University of Science and Technology at that time was unreachable. It did not match with the overall social and political environment in China. The initial wish is good: Let intellectuals but not bureaucrats be in charge of the university. But where does the university get funding from? They wanted to follow the American style to organize a board and raise money from private enterprises or individuals. However, in the end, governments are back in charge.

This professor's comment on "governments are back in charge" seems to contradict with the private enterprises and entrepreneurial success in Shenzhen, as documented in various chapters in this book from different perspectives. "Enterprise as the main focus, government as the backing support" since Shenzhen's establishment as a special economic zone provides a relatively friendly environment for private enterprises in Shenzhen, with local government being a facilitator and platform. The establishment of Southern University of Science and Technology since 2010, is said to undertake the mission of higher-education reform in China. In 2007, Shenzhen local government officially issued the announcement that *Shenzhen City's Plan for the Establishment of Southern University of Science and Technology*《深圳市筹建南方科技大学办学方案》was submitted to Guangdong provincial government, which would report to National Ministry of Education.[28] The initiative to establish this university was not approved until 2012 by National Ministry of Education,[29] which required Guangdong and Shenzhen governments to resolve fundings needed for university development without national government's financial support. But, the setting of university curriculum and majors should be in accordance with the regulations of the National Ministry of Education. It is reported that several professors from The Hong Kong University of Science and Technology excitedly wanted to get involved with the establishment of this university in Shenzhen at the initial stage. In recent years, especially after the central government's Greater Bay Area initiative in 2019, many Hong Kong universities start to expand and strengthen their partnerships with Shenzhen and other cities in Guangdong by setting up their Shenzhen or Great Bay Area campuses. For instance, The Chinese University of Hong Kong – Shenzhen (CUHK - Shenzhen) is one of them. I was told by my interviewees that The Chinese University of Hong Kong - Shenzhen operates independently from The Chinese University of Hong Kong as an entity, while most courses taught at CUHK - Shenzhen need to be approved by the administrators from CUHK. This information is reaffirmed when I saw General Education textbooks displayed at coffee shops and bookstore at CUHK - Shenzhen during my campus visit in 2025. Will a more balanced approach to education that combines Chinese ideals and western contents, as shown in many of CUHK's General Education courses, make up for some educational shortcomings in Shenzhen? This remains a question that deserves long-term observations as the Greater Bay Area initiative proceeds.

Scolded by the disadvantage in the higher education sector for such a long time, Shenzhen has thrived in its technological innovation and regional entrepreneurship. Built on Chapter Eight's examination on Shenzhen's innovation and R&D with its distinctive characteristics, Chapter Nine continues the investigation of human capital and higher education in Shenzhen. Huawei Dongguan Songshan lake campus in this chapter demonstrates that enterprises enjoy a degree of freedom by allocating its organizational R&D and building its corporate campus. In spite of Shenzhen government's autonomy as a special economic zone, local bureaucrats are constrained in certain areas, for instance, higher-education reform. Local enterprises, for instance, are free to choose whether they want to donate to universities such as Southern University of Science and Technology, however, local government cannot enforce corporate wills. Therefore, the "stagnant progress" the professor at the renowned Chinese university described in his comment reveals partial obstacles Shenzhen local government has faced with in its regional development and innovation. To continue to develop and maintain its regional innovation competitiveness, Shenzhen has to upgrade its top-notched scientific capacity, both at the enterprise and the university level. While Shenzhen is overcoming its shortcomings to transform its innovation capability, is it possible for other cities and regions in China to replace its standing? Next Chapter, "New Innovation Hubs are Possible," summarizes key elements that contribute to Shenzhen's development and innovation success, aiming to provide lessons for other cities, regions and nations that hope to build its own innovation cluster.

Notes

1. Information is retrieved from: https://www.latimes.com/business/la-na-pol-universities-ban-huawei-funding-donations-20190321-story.html
2. Information is retrieved from: https://stanforddaily.com/2019/02/05/stanford-halts-research-ties-with-huawei-amid-surveillance-controversy/
3. Information is retrieved from: https://www.reuters.com/article/australia-china-huawei-sports-idINKBN25R0KH.
4. Bloomberg news, *Chipzilla Got Toppled*, retrieved from: https://www.bloomberg.com/opinion/articles/2017-03-22/chipzilla-intel-toppled-by-taiwan-s-supplier-to-the-stars
5. News article, *Taiwan loses 3,000 chip engineers to 'Made in China 2025'*, retrieved from: https://asia.nikkei.com/Business/China-tech/Taiwan-loses-3-000-chip-engineers-to-Made-in-China-2025.
6. Information is retrieved from: https://asia.nikkei.com/business/tech/semiconductors/taiwan-bans-recruitment-for-jobs-in-china-to-combat-brain-drain.
7. Information is retrieved from: https://www.sohu.com/a/410975520_465270
8. Ren's speech in Mandarin Chinese can be retrieved from: https://new.qq.com/omn/20200829/20200829A090OC00.html.
9. Information is retrieved from Bloomberg news, *No Pay, No Gain: Huawei Outspends Apple on R&D for a 5G Edge*, retrieved from: https://www.bloomberg.com/news/articles/2019-04-25/huawei-s-r-d-spending-balloons-as-u-s-tensions-flare-over-5g
10. Information is retrieved from 2019 Huawei Annual Report: https://www.huawei.com/en/annual-report/2019
11. Speech by Deng Xiaoping at the closing ceremony of the Work Conference of the CCP Central Committee on December 13,

1978. The original Chinese translation of his speech is named: 解放思想,实事求是,团结一致向前看。

12. I was invited to a Chinese podcast to talk about Shenzhen talent policy in July 2021. In my podcast interview, I pointed that Shenzhen's current talent policy is too limited on attracting technical talents while neglecting the significance of recruiting social scientists with international trainings. After the release of the interview, several Shenzhen local government officials I once interviewed or interacted with told me that they agreed with me.
13. Information is retrieved from: https://www.sohu.com/a/710444682_699502
14. 2021年深圳市海外高层次海外留学人才(孔雀计划)认定办法, translated into English: 2021 Shenzhen Overseas High-talents (Peacock Talents Program) Evaluation and Application Requirements. This talent policy updates annually.
15. 2 million RMB = 293690.00 U.S. dollars, 1.6 million RMB = 234952.00 U.S. dollars, in the currency exchange of 6.81, last updated in May, 2026.
16. Thousand Talents Policy, 千人计划, is a program initiated by China's central government to recruit experts in science and technology from abroad, principally but not exclusively from overseas Chinese communities.
17. Original report in Mandarin Chinese: 深圳人才研究报告, Shenzhen Talent Research Report, 2013.
18. This survey is included in 2013 Shenzhen Talent Research Report, 深圳人才研究报告.
19. Detailed information about this design award: https://ifdesign.com/en/
20. Information obtained from the complied documents released by Shenzhen People's Political Consultative Conference. Original mandarin Chinese document, 关于落实海归人才政策,避免人才流失的提案及答复, translated into English, *Proposals and Answers on the Implementation of Policy on Overseas Returning Talents to Avoid Brain Drain*. http://www1.szzx.gov.cn/content/2017-01/09/content_14765282.htm
21. Information is retrieved from: https://www.hrssit.cn/info/3600.html

22. *China's overseas graduates return in record numbers into already crowded domestic job market*, article retrieved from: https://www.scmp.com/economy/china-economy/article/3102384/chinas-overseas-graduates-return-record-numbers-already
23. Information is retrieved from: https://www.forbes.com/sites/stuartanderson/2023/04/11/chinesestudents-still-denied-visas-under-trump-immigration-order/?sh=a605db150956
24. Information can be retrieved from: https://nfap.com/wp-content/uploads/2022/03/Analysis-of-International-Student-Data.NFAP-Policy-Brief.March-2022.pdf
25. Information is retrieved from, U.S. Department of Labor, https://www.dol.gov/agencies/whd/immigration/h1b
26. Information is retrieved from: https://www.aapihatecrimes.org/facts
27. Shenzhen Overseas Chinese Returnees Association: http://szhaigui.com/Home/Content/show/type/policy/id/423.html.
28. Information is retrieved from: https://web.archive.org/web/20150214101725/http://paper.sznews.com/tqb/20070907/ca2768165.htm.
29. Information is retrieved from: https://news.sciencenet.cn/htmlnews/2012/4/263140.shtm.

CHAPTER 10

New Innovation Hubs are Possible

Shenzhen Development and Innovation: Meaning for China and the World

In early 2025, the whole world turned its spotlight on Hangzhou, located in Zhejiang province. The emergency of DeepSeek, China's artificial intelligence chatpot suddenly has shifted the global debate for over a decade: Which city is China's Silicon Valley? Is it Shenzhen, China's first special economic zone? Shanghai, China's international financial center? Or Beijing, the political and cultural epicenter? In fact, Hangzhou is no newcomer to the tech world since it is home to the world-known Alibaba Group. But, flooding discussion on the international stage seems to demonstrate that global investors and venture capitalists are no longer satisfied with China having only one "Silicon Valley." "It's wise to pay close attention to Zhejiang University graduates," says Edith Yeung, partner at a Silicon Valley VC fund that invests in global artificial intelligence startups.[1] Competition among existing and rising innovation hubs in China is an indication of its national strength, technological development and innovation capabilities overall. Healthy competition is an effective incentive which serves as the source of regional innovation and entrepreneurship. The rise of new innovation hubs in China does not diminish Shenzhen's standing as a leading global innovation cluster, in the present and in the future.

G. Y. Wang, *Dragon Innovation: Shenzhen*, Governing China in the 21st Century, https://doi.org/10.1007/978-981-95-9637-9_10

This book examines Shenzhen development and innovation from historical, cultural, political, institutional, and social perspectives. There is a multidimensional and culturally diverse development and innovation experience in the 21st information society in addition to Silicon Valley, Finnish experience, Singapore model, and Japanese success. Innovation clusters are critical drivers of economic growth connecting businesses, institutions, suppliers and cultures in geographically concentrated areas. Shenzhen innovation cluster, as an important global innovation hub, is the first and foremost significant innovation cluster that originated from the global south. This book challenges the conventional wisdom about China's innovation success that the Chinese central government has done everything everywhere all the same. The detailed examination of Shenzhen's economic development trajectory and technological innovation success refutes the idea that government backed funding has supported and helped to realize Shenzhen's R&D and innovation, the one and the only panacea for China's innovation. Breakdowns of Shenzhen experimental and entrepreneurial cultures, bureaucratic entrepreneurs, grassroots participatory innovations, manufacturing networks, vocational trainings, entrepreneurship education and enterprises led R&D, offer lessons to regions and countries that differ from China's political system. Only in this way, countries that are aspiring to revive their national innovation systems or to develop and build their innovation clusters could learn from Shenzhen and China's successful experiences. In this way, countries that are facing stagnant economic challenges, failed in government policy implementations, and those are left behind in the low-value end of the global manufacturing supply chains, could begin a reflective internal examination of their entrepreneurial cultures, diversity of educational platforms, governance structures as well as the role of state and institutions in development and innovation. Most importantly, when regional competition within China and technological innovation across the globe become unprecedented, Shenzhen, as a global innovation cluster, must learn to maintain its competitiveness, clearly identify and upgrade its advantages, and to establish and build various networks with rising innovation clusters. The AI revolution is formidable and is facilitating budding innovation clusters in regions such as Southeast Asia and Africa. The need for building AI-driven innovation clusters requires closer technical collaborations between nation-state and technology corporations. During the ASEAN AI Malaysia Summit, Malaysia's Digital Minister Gobind Singh Deo, addressed at the Huawei Cloud AI Ecosystem Summit APAC

2025, that "AI-driven productivity must benefit every Malaysian, with no one left behind, and we must be inclusive and work together." In fact, Huawei has entered a new phase to help Malaysia to train 30,000 local professionals to build its local AI ecosystem.[2] Malaysia's race to build a homegrown AI workforce and innovation cluster is common among global south countries. Many African research institutions are undertaking a significant amount of research to represent African voices on the global stage, of which the work is funded by international agencies. For example, Makerere University, active in Uganda's AI ecosystem, has established and characterized itself as an AI knowledge and research incubator, trying to develop new AI solutions to tackle African challenges. Entrepreneurial enthusiasm and community eagerness play a critical part in the building of successful innovation clusters, shown from Shenzhen and Silicon Valley experiences. As Celina Lee, Founder and CEO at Zindi put it: "What is incredible for Africa is that there's no such thing as someone with ten years of experience in generative AI or large language models. Anyone who has one year of experience at this point is competitive even globally. So I think there's a huge opportunity. Young people in Africa are digital natives, they're connected, they're educated."[3]

Looking forward, global innovation clusters will center around AI technologies, transforming existing innovation ecosystems to AI innovation ecosystems that rely on a diverse talent pool that requires a different skill set from the factory manufacturers documented in "Chapter 7, Shenzhen Grassroots Participatory Innovation." AI innovation ecosystems require highly trained people to drive research and development, skilled professionals to create socially and culturally tailored AI algorithms, which not only demand technical knowledge in data science and machine learning, but also require deep social and philosophical understanding of cultures and human cognitions. Thus, Shenzhen's trajectory offers aspiring innovation clusters a fundamental lesson: A comprehensive understanding of the local cultures, institutions, contexts, challenges and opportunities can enable and support the development of technological solutions and the building of innovation clusters that meet the local and national needs.

Key Lessons from Shenzhen Development and Innovation

National Identity: Cultural and Historical Heritage

Shenzhen's ability to leapfrog in forty years to become China's technology hub and to advance its domestic and global economic competitiveness lies in its strong national identity. Though often portraited as an economic miracle in international media, Shenzhen's achievement and success is the outcome of ingenious human efforts. As stressed in "Chapter 1, China Innovation Myth," the examination of Shenzhen development offers some lessons and hopes for countries and regions that are still low-income national economy in the global south as well as advanced economies currently in stagnant growth rate. Before Open and Reform policy in China in 1979, China was a poor country. As written in "Chapter 3, China, the New Development," Shenzhen started as an agricultural base and fishing village with rare industrial development. In 2019, Shenzhen ranked first among all Chinese cities with the strongest GDP per capita, reaching $29,498 (Shanghai, $22,800; Beijing, $23,800; Guangzhou, $22,700).[4] National rejuvenation and strong motives of realizing China's modernization appear to be an important incentive to fully understand Shenzhen's economic development and its technological innovation. The first special economic zone has undertaken China's national mission to experiment, in institutional reforms, economic decentralization as well as technological innovations. Like the Finnish model, national identity is critical in priding Chinese in its economic success and innovation accomplishment. In other words, reviving Middle Kingdom's historical glory and establishing a strong new China with advanced technological capacity is embedded in Shenzhen and China's economic leapfrog and its technological ambition. Importantly, it is not just Chinese government's or Chinese Communist Party's aspiration; it is the Chinese people who want to alleviate themselves out of poverty (see Chapter 4, City Culture—Experimental and Entrepreneurial DNA) and be treated respectfully on the international stage which depends on China's overall strength and national competitiveness. This collective sentiment is apparent among Chinese business leaders. National identity adds value to business executives, entrepreneurs, and innovators from Shenzhen in their interaction with global players in business and technology. Many of my interviewees highlighted "made and created in

China" when introducing their companies and technological products at international exhibitions. It is easy to understand their disappointment when foreign business partners acknowledged the creative features and quality of their products but were reluctant to accept that they were "created in China", an anecdote I earlier referenced on maker culture and grassroots participatory innovation (see Chapter 7, Shenzhen Grassroots Participatory Innovation: Let the People Make).

As part of national identity, cultural pride and ethnic heritage play a role in Shenzhen's development and innovation. Chinese business leaders and politicians like to cite masterpiece *The Art of Wars*, written by Sun Tzu, the ancient Chinese military strategist and philosopher. They adopt military strategies and lessons from that book in conducting businesses, forming strategies. Many people are proud of the ancient wisdom they could absorb as Chinese. Huawei's CEO, Ren Zhengfei, is known for his published essays and sharing on Huawei corporate online forum, Xin Sheng (心声). He quoted abundant Chinese historical stories to motivate his employees in hardship to be resilient, to endure difficulties and to overcome challenges. Cultural pride and ethnic heritage seem to play an invisible role in motivating Chinese to advance global business and scientific research race. This phenomenon is striking in the analysis of cultural fabric and China's technological advancement. Chinese were portrayed as "sick man of Asia", a word first appeared in a British-run newspaper, *North China Daily News,* in Shanghai in 1896. The phrase needs not refer to "physical sickness" of Chinese. United Kingdom, Germany, Greek were once called "sick man of Europe" at different historical time points[5] due to their economic meltdown and governmental problems. The key point here is that the utilization of national identity and cultural heritage to achieve technological modernization has worked in Shenzhen and in China. Economic development and technological innovation without the loss of the state control, learned from the Singaporean model, as discussed in "Chapter 2, The Genesis of Shenzhen," satisfy the majority of Chinese people thanks to China's economic leapfrog.

Commercial success in service and product innovations among Chinese technology companies in recent years continue to indicate the role of cultural pride and national identity in domestic technological development. This cultivation of brand loyalty to domestic electronics may lead Chinese technology companies to successful possibilities that beyond imagination. "My smart watch is a Huawei brand", a 2015 year born kid in China once proudly showed me off his kid version smart watch.

This phenomenon is not credited to one particular Chinese leader's political strategies, as some analysts claimed. "Technological nationalism" is a gradual developmental product embedded in domestic customers' perceptions. Tencent's initiative on "building Chinese seniors' digital lives" is an example of Chinese technology companies' reaction to the Covid-19 in 2020. How to integrate Chinese elders to digital lives, invite them to be WeChat wallet users, and potentially turn them into a group of consumers, particularly in digital health sector, is an opportunity for Tencent and other domestic players. Unless global electronics and internet players (not limited to electronics) realize the evolving attitude and mindset of Chinese consumers, and update their marketing strategies, branding, and product customizations to meet with Chinese consumers' habits and fast-changing tastes, they risk losing the China market even before they fully enter.

Regional Openness

Not only does Shenzhen inherit Chinese cultural advantages, it also is unique in its tolerant and welcoming city atmosphere. "Chapter 4, City Culture—Experimental and Entrepreneurial DNA" details tolerant and open-minded city culture which leads to less or no regional discrimination. Scholars once concluded that cultural and social diversity facilitates innovation and entrepreneurship, particularly in the case of Silicon Valley, whose innovation and economy is relied on immigration and multiculturalism (Castells & Himanen, 2002; Florida, 2002; Saxenian, 1996;). In Shenzhen, migrant workers and migrant professionals rather than foreigners are considered as "immigrants". They are unconcerned about "discrimination" because of their accent, dialects, or lack of local connections. In cities like Shanghai, people immediately know you are not local if you do not speak the Shanghai dialect. My observation is that people in Shanghai are proud to be "international" as they parallel their city to New York. Local Beijingers understand what power symbolizes as residents in the core political center of China. Shenzhen maintains its pragmatic and adventurous city culture to a large extent. Scholars find it hard to exactly define "innovation synergy" but commonly acknowledge that it refers to a city or region's cultural, institutional, and social features. Shenzhen innovation experience makes a point about synergy: It can be created and cultivated by human efforts; in return, it will influence innovation and entrepreneurial activities in that locality. Shenzhen bureaucratic entrepreneurs' pragmatic and service-oriented government mindset, its migrant city culture, tolerance of failure, encouragement on self-achievement, down-to-earth market economy spirit, all contribute to Shenzhen's formation and success as a leading global technology hub.

China's technological rising and international recognition, represented by industrial tech giants in Shenzhen, strengthens Shenzhen's city pride. A former senior engineer at SAP Shanghai who quit his job and moved to Shenzhen for his startup, opined: "Seriously, there are a group of crazy entrepreneurs in Shenzhen. Someone talked about his business idea with me for almost four hours till 3 a.m. on the first day I flew from Shanghai." In contrast to state-owned companies conventionally known for their inefficient and hierarchical management styles, private enterprises in Shenzhen share a strong sense of market competition. This implies that those companies have grown, evolved, and developed in a market-oriented environment in Shenzhen. My research suggests that global competitiveness of companies from Shenzhen, for instance, Huawei, Tencent, Ping An, DJI, and Oppo largely comes from their standing of market testing to fully achieve customers' satisfaction. A university professor and an ICT insider who has written several books on Huawei, shared with me, "many private companies that enjoyed state subsides, tax and land benefits did not succeed in China. Those that are successful indeed withstand domestic customers' and markets' testing." Technological advances and competitiveness in Shenzhen rely on competition as well as cooperation among companies that offer similar services and products. Healthy competition strengthens the dynamism of Shenzhen's regional competitiveness, industrial system and its innovation ecosystem. Welcoming culture, accompanied by the centrality of work and aggression continues to make a city attractive to migrants and entrepreneurs, which highlights the significance of regional socio-economy as well as the informal institutions that support regional development and innovation.

Grassroots Maker Culture—Chinese Hackerism

Grassroots participatory spirit and maker movement are major sources of one kind of Shenzhen's technological innovation, which I coined as "Shenzhen grassroots participatory innovation" (see Chapters 6 and 7). Developed out of mature manufacturing supply chain and influenced by maker culture movement, participation in technological innovation has thrived in Shenzhen, which earns its name, "City of Makers."

Differing from hackerism, which is prevalent in western innovation experience, Shenzhen grassroots participatory innovation is not connected to research universities to obtain the cutting-edge research in information society. Instead, it comes from manufacturing experiences, prototyping, product combination and recombination. The underlying spirit of "hacker" and "maker" is the same: rebellion and passion. As Himanen (2001) noted, "hackers program because programming challenges are of intrinsic interest to them" (Kindle version, 2001, p. 3). Makers in Shenzhen enjoy products assembling because of the doing action (like those hardware enthusiasts at HAX incubator). Their difference lies in the fact that hackerism derives from freedom and spirit to think, while makerism lays emphasis on the capacity to produce. More specifically, the ability to produce and turn a product into a profitable commodity excites makers. The threshold and standard for those "maker products" vary. Underprivileged migrant workers in Chinese metropolitan cities cannot afford iPhone, but what about a "maker iPhone" that enables you to enjoy smart phone features within your affordability? This book suggests that the combination of grassroots participatory innovation with Shenzhen's manufacturing supply chain facilitates product experimentations and cultivates innovative spirits.

Local Governance

Shenzhen's networking power in connecting "old, established" nodes to its city depends on its locational advantage, but more importantly, this book suggests that the role state can play in facilitating a city or region's connecting power. Shenzhen local government utilized 1999 Hi-tech Fair to promote Shenzhen's economic development direction to attract foreign investment (for example, Tencent's venture capital investment), domestic and international research collaborations (at the first Hi-tech fair, Wuhan University established research ties with Shenzhen),[6] and the establishment of manufacturing factories (see Chapter 5, Local Governance: Bureaucratic Entrepreneurs). Efforts made by Shenzhen local government add to the understanding of the relationship between state and innovation: The success does not lie in an economy's capitalism or "non-capitalism" nature, but the flexibility and autonomy the local government can have.

Constrained Autonomy

As written in "Chapter 2, The Genesis of Shenzhen," I argued that it is too simplified to examine China's economic development and innovation in one single lens though its one-party political system appears to make many people think that the central state decides everything. The examination of China's first and by far one of the most successful special economic zones in human history, reveals two facts. First, Shenzhen is a special economic zone which enjoys special economic policies and autonomy to conduct experimental institutional reforms that can benefit economic advancement. Examples mainly illustrated in "Chapter 3, China, The New Development" and "Chapter 5 Local Governance: The Bureaucratic Entrepreneurs," demonstrated Shenzhen's ground-breaking roles in economic experiments, such as 1998 Document, 1999 Document and 2023 Private Economy Regulation before the official launch of China's Private Economy Promotional Law in 2025. With regards to artificial intelligence, in early 2023, Shenzhen launched China's first legislation specifically for the artificial intelligence industry, "*Shenzhen Special Economic Zone Artificial Intelligence Industry Promotion Regulations*,"《深圳经济特区人工智能产业促进条例》。Both the private economy regulation and artificial intelligence regulation confirm Shenzhen's role in continuing to pioneer in institutional reforms in China as well as its leadership position in China's technological arena. Second, differing from the United States' federal and state government systems, Shenzhen local autonomy and governance is constrained in aspects such as higher-education reform, an example presented in "Chapter 9, Human Capital and National Competitiveness." Similarly, when I brought up the inconvenience caused by indirect flights from Shenzhen to major international cities, a local government official explained that Shenzhen had to balance social and political relationships with cities such as Hong Kong even in terms of airline routes to ensure Hong Kong's strategic position as an international trade and financial center. This insider information offers critical understanding of the relationship between Hong Kong and Shenzhen as well as the ongoing Greater Bay Area development. Hong Kong, as a Special Administrative Region, shares a symbiotic relationship with its neighboring cities, and is indirectly benefited from the adjacent regions' supportive functions. Shenzhen and Guangdong's support to Hong Kong can be traced back to 1963 when Dong Shen Water Supply to Hong Kong (东深供水工程) was initiated.[7] (see Chapter 2, The Genesis of

Shenzhen) How can Hong Kong realize its development potentials under the Greater Bay Area initiative will also be reliant on its own economic governance as a SAR. Thus, the Greater Bay Area initiative is worthy of longitudinal analysis and observation.

Government Efficiency

In spite of governing challenges in balancing regional development, Shenzhen city and district government officials embrace and facilitate an open and welcoming culture in the form of their civil services. Thus, a symbiotic healthy relationship between local bureaucrats and businesspeople is established. Many entrepreneurs commented on the drastic difference between Shenzhen local government officials and their counterparts from other cities in China, particularly in government efficiency. Businesspeople require efficient enterprise registration and procedures to successfully enter the market, to conquer their market shares and to compete for, for instance, human capital. As documented in "Chapter 5, Local Governance: Bureaucratic Entrepreneurs," foreign citizens graduated from Chinese universities who want to work in China expect faster process of their working permits. Shenzhen government efficiency in processing working permits and visas for foreigners can ensure the attraction of talents and workforce to fulfil Shenzhen's evolving development. In this way, "government as the backing support" becomes a reality to serve local public and private institutions in attracting and retaining competent human capital. Other cities and regions can learn from Shenzhen government efficiency to attract foreign talents at a time when China introduced the K visa in 2025, a type of visa that allows foreign professionals in STEM to enjoy more flexibility to enter and stay in China, without the sponsorship from a local Chinese employer.

In addition to government efficiency, Shenzhen local government usually does not intervene local businesses except to provide assistance as needed which reflects the spirit of "government as the backing support" in another way. Local government officials care about local business operations and get ready to help them get rid of hurdles when necessary (also because the success of local enterprises can be seen as their administrative accomplishments). The adaptability of Shenzhen local government is in contrast with stereotypical portrait of Chinese politicians, which is often seen as an obstacle in business operation due to its state control. One informant with close government connections noted in personal exchanges: "In China, a country that government influence is penetrated to almost all aspects of life, if city government does not intervene and interfere with business operation, that already grants local businesses a great deal of freedom and opportunities."

Policy Consistency

Shenzhen development and innovation experience sheds light on the understanding of the relationship between Chinese central state and local government. Specifically, central government leads national economic planning, while Shenzhen local government adjusts its economic goals and directions accordingly. We should not interpret "planning" as a rigid, planned economic development approach. It is important to note that, in official Chinese documents nowadays, China's five-year plan is called "*五年规划*" rather than "*五年计划*," though both wordings are translated to English as "planning." "Planning" is a direction and a map rather than an unaltered checklist. As argued in this book, Shenzhen experience demonstrates the exploratory nature of its development and innovation (see Chapter 1, China Innovation Path and Chapter 3, China, The New Development). Shenzhen experience displays a combination of adaptability to market environment, policy flexibility, international geopolitics as well as national and local economic planning.

Despite criticisms of China's ruling system on the global stage, policy consistency maintains a critical feature in Shenzhen and China's economic success and technological development. Chinese state's advantage in terms of policy consistency ensures Shenzhen economic development and innovation. South Korea, nevertheless, elects new administration every five year which causes the inconsistency of policy since new administration restructures innovation efforts and policy from the past (Cowhey & Aronson, 2017). In addition to innovation policy inconsistency, immigration policy varies in many countries under different administrations. An evident case is the U.S. administration's H1-B visa restriction and OPT application regarding international students' post-graduation work. More recently, the termination of USAID in granting financial and humane assistance to international development has negatively affected many developing countries that have already signed grant contracts with the USAID for their domestic projects. Frequent policy change due to domestic political issues causes uncertainty among talent's migration choices as well as entrepreneurs' and investors' business decisions. On this note, in contrary, Shenzhen local government, with the support from Beijing, is consistent in promoting different genres of policies that advance economic development and innovation. The debate on government regulation, in various national contexts, originates from its own administrative system's advantages and weaknesses. As Castells and Himanen noted (2002), the Finnish state acts as an effective state, which combines with market deregulation, jointly provide and facilitate public infrastructure, like power, energy, telecommunications networks. Efficient and updated public infrastructure offers basis for economic stimulation and growth in Finland. Shenzhen's economic development and technological innovation benefits from telecommunications and network infrastructure initiatives led by the government. Hong's (2017) book shows that Guangdong provincial telecommunications infrastructure pioneered in China in the early 90 s, which contributes to its success in attracting foreign investment and developing regional economy. In contrast, power supply crisis in California in 2001, due to market deregulation of California's energy industry in the 1990s, threatened the state economic landscape caused by the disruption of its IT infrastructure.[8]

Networks

Innovative milieu, as Castells and Hall (1994) documented, in early times, has been in the heart of metropolitan cities around the world, such as London, Paris, New York, and Los Angeles. "You do not have to be young to be innovative" is their empirical conclusion (Castells & Hall, 1994, p. 225). On the opposite of "you don't have to be young to be innovative", is that: You can be young enough to be innovative, meanwhile, getting connected to the right established node(s). Silicon Valley is a good example of this interpretation. Silicon Valley's connection with old industrial cluster like Boston mainly comes from its MIT graduates in science and engineering. For instance, the Father of Silicon Valley, Frederick Terman was an MIT graduate and was a faculty at MIT before he moved back to Stanford. Terman's return to Silicon Valley was not a state initiative like the Shenzhen Peacock Talent (see Chapter 9, Human Capital and National Competitiveness) but his voluntary decision (some writings explained that the warm weather in sunny Palo Alto was good for Terman's health). Taiwan Hsinchu Science Park, when it was first established, was connected to the United States' innovation resources through brain circulation to Taiwan in the semiconductor industry, as well as resources embedded within those talents in their overseas research, business and investment networks. These examples, in the simplest language, reveal one thing: Connection matters in innovation. Successful development and innovation in a city or region is sometimes derived from the connection with the "right" nodes. For instance, overseas Chinese diaspora networks connected Shenzhen (or Guangdong province in general) with foreign capital and investment (Hsing, 1998). (see Chapter 5, Local Governance: Bureaucratic Entrepreneurs) Among all the networks, two are playing critical roles: Shenzhen – Hong Kong and Shenzhen—Taiwan networks.

Shenzhen—Hong Kong

Shenzhen's technological innovation is intertwined with the shift of global production networks. Spatial clustering and network enterprises in the manufacturing industries initially have been critical forces of Shenzhen's industrial productivity, which is credited to local, regional and central government's policy in China's integration to the global economy. In particular, regional policy serves as a catalyst to facilitate network-based industrial systems in the South of China. As discussed in "Chapter 7, Shenzhen Grassroots Participatory Innovation: Let the People Make," small-to-mid sized Hong Kong manufacturing production businesses in textiles, shoes, garments, and consumer products (Lin, 1984) started to relocate to Guangdong province, after the conclusion of the 1984 Sino-British agreement on the transfer of sovereignty to China in 1997. Hong Kong took advantage of its post-colonial flexible financial regulations, language strength (i.e., English as official working language), business infrastructure, law system, and international and regional networks of connections to strengthen its role as an international business hub and financial center. Taiwan began to relocate electronics manufacturing factories to Shenzhen in the early 90 s. Thus, Shenzhen's local economies are mobilized into a techno-economic and informational paradigm which is supported by city government, amplified by the local government and elevated by China's official entry to WTO in December 2001. Low labor cost, export-oriented economy in global manufacturing networks in Shenzhen and Guangdong province contributed to its economic growth. Most importantly, it enabled Shenzhen to focus on "electronics-based" industry which planted the seed for the rising of technology private enterprises' as an electronics industrial cluster. Unlike inefficient state enterprises, electronics manufacturing factories (some are formed based on family, friends, and *tongxiang*[9] networks) and companies flourished in Shenzhen and its neighbors such as Dongguang due to its structural and organizational flexibility (see Chapters 6 and 7). Similar to Silicon Vally's network-based industrial system, grassroots participatory innovation and its manufacturing supply chain system in Shenzhen encourage and promote collaboration among local producers. The informal networks formed among civic entrepreneurs, electronics makers, and hardware sellers, are decentralized though they rely on intuitional support that can transcend the interests of individual sellers, makers and firms.

Shenzhen's geographical proximity to Hong Kong plays an important role at the early stage of its technological development, particularly in terms of information exchange and venture capital investment networks. But, it is critical to assess Hong Kong's role in Shenzhen's development and its linking to Shenzhen in an objective and evolutionary way. In terms of its role in Shenzhen's rise, timely information and international business trends from Hong Kong spread quickly in early days when people cannot access to the internet for information. People in Shenzhen with business acumen seized opportunities, for instance, Huawei's phone switcher supply from Hong Kong consumer electronics market. Venture capital investment on Tencent circulated from Hong Kong in 1999 is another example. However, with the deepening of Open and Reform policy in Shenzhen and other cities in Chinese Mainland, Hong Kong's economic linking role has gradually diminished. A Co-founder in a bio-medical startup in Shenzhen noted, "our company does not have any business connections with Hong Kong. We are in bio-medical field, a weak industry in Hong Kong." Similar views were expressed, for instance, "we do not really need to go to Hong Kong for venture capital nowadays. They are in Shenzhen, Shanghai, and Beijing" during my interviews with Chinese entrepreneurs. In fact, before the Greater Bay Area initiative started in 2019, Tencent's CEO, Pony Ma Huateng, in 2017, submitted his proposal, *Suggestions on leveraging the advantages of collaborative innovation to build a world-class technology bay area in Guangdong, Hong Kong and Macao,* to call for expansion of economic and digital integration in Guangdong, Hong Kong and Macao to deepen regional collaboration.[10] As mentioned earlier, how can Hong Kong maintain its international competitiveness require a close examination of Hong Kong's economic governance and its current financial advantages.

Shenzhen—Taiwan

Besides Shenzhen—Hong Kong network, this study reveals that Taiwan played an influential role in Shenzhen's electronics and technological innovation. Taiwan's influence on Shenzhen can be summarized in two aspects: (1) manufacturing production shift to Shenzhen in the 1990s, "Made in China by Taiwan" as a collaborative model (see Chapter 7, Shenzhen Grassroots Participatory Innovation: Let the People Make); (2) Shenzhen imitated Taiwan in establishing its own research institutes (see Chapter 8, Shenzhen R&D Ecosystem). Similarities between Taiwan Industrial Technology Research Institute founded in 1973, and the Research Institute of Tsinghua University in Shenzhen (RITS) and Shenzhen Institutes of Advanced Technology Chinese Academy of Sciences demonstrate the importance of Taiwan lessons. They are institutions with a distinct focus on technology transfer. Taiwan Industrial Technology Research Institute model met Shenzhen's historical developmental needs: Applied technology innovation incubated at a research institute that can be commercialized at a fast speed to generate revenues.

Global Knowledge Networks

Enterprise R&D investment is a key feature in Shenzhen's innovation ecosystem which demonstrates the importance of R&D diversity in developing new innovation hubs in both developing and developed countries. Corporations have the capacity to organize cutting-edge scientific research through their collaborations, in the form of university-industry partnership or corporate investment in prestigious research universities or scientific labs. Global research and knowledge networks, in the classic example of Huawei and BGI Genomics, make it possible for private technology enterprises to grow and thrive when there was no top-ranked research university in Shenzhen (see Chapter 8, Shenzhen R&D Ecosystem). The utilization of global research networks that are not based on physical proximity between firms and universities can be an applicable and generalizable corporate development strategy. A lesson can be distilled from Huawei's talent dilemma is that sustainable and long-term development in cutting-edge indigenous innovation depends on a nation's high-quality talent. Talent mobility is enabled by their physical migration as well as knowledge networks facilitated by communication technologies. In other words, "brain" can move either physically or virtually. Innovation talent does not need to reside in research universities. Huawei experience suggests that corporations can focus on basic scientific research that will benefit enterprises' future innovation and development. R&D talent needs an "incubator" to freely think, experiment, and thrive. The key is the type of support and autonomy an "incubator" can provide scientists with, but not the genre of "incubator." Research universities, national research labs, corporations all can be potential scientific discovery "incubators." In addition, GigaScience, BGI Genomics's flagship academic journal, has shown the significance of gathering a scientific and knowledge community that serves business as well as human advancement. Huawei and BGI Genomics' knowledge investment has provided global universities and publishers a fresh perspective to integrate business with education and research, particularly when working with partners from the global south countries.

Vocational Education and Training Programs

Vocational colleges' partnership with Shenzhen local enterprises indicates an important network-based training that can be applicable to many countries in the global south to increase local economic productivity as well as to resolve local workforce challenges. Successful implementation of vocational education and training programs depends on respective national education systems. With China's economic transition and technological transformation, significance of vocational education has been emphasized in recent years. In January 2019, the State Council issued the "*Implementation Plan for the Reform of National Vocational Education*" 《国家职业教育改革实施方案》which has consistently prioritized vocational education as a breakthrough point for comprehensive education reform. On the national level, this document officially clarifies that vocational education is a type of education, not a level of education. It is crucial for the Chinese society to appropriately position vocational education and technical talents to leverage its role to serve China's societal development as well as to realize individual ambitions (i.e., many students who attend vocational colleges and schools are from rural China). Moreover, vocational education and trainings, have been put in a position to serve China's national strategies. In modern manufacturing, strategic emerging industries and modern service industries, more than 70% of the frontline workers are graduates of vocational education and training programs. In 2016, "*Manufacturing Talent Development Plan Guidelines*" *《制造业人才发展规划指南》* was published to accelerate the training of highly demanded talents in the manufacturing industry. In 2025, in China's Fifteenth's Five-Year Plan, "*Fifteenth's Five-Year Plan Vocational Education Development Plan 2026–2030*" *《"十五五"职业教育发展规划(2026–2030年)》* was published to deepen education—industry collaboration and integration to further China's industrial upgrading. Local enterprises are called to participate in partnering with vocational colleges and schools to achieve the goals of joint talent cultivation.

As written in Chapter 8, the success of vocational education and training in Shenzhen is largely credited to the close partnership between vocational colleges and local enterprises. Employer employment plays a key role in the success of vocational education, in terms of financial support, facilities, curriculum, professional development and employment. China's push for vocational education and trainings in its Fifteenth's Five-Year Plan reflects its national needs for "gray collar workers" in the era of artificial intelligence (see Chapter 8, Shenzhen R&D Ecosystem). Those "gray collar workers" may not be trained to manage real human beings anymore, instead, they are trained to operate and manage robotics. China's advancement in artificial intelligence, not only requires domestic educational institutions to adjust their curriculum to constantly be aligned with the changing demands, but also poses challenges for its international partners in relevant supply chains: How can other countries train and enhance their skilled workforce to maintain their competitiveness in the supply chains?

Cities and regions are critical agents of economic development, as Goodman puts it, the last entrepreneurs (1979). In the case of Shenzhen, local government not only implements national economic policy but also creates and designs its own economy and innovation policy within their degree of autonomy. Cities' and regions' flexibility in adapting to the changing conditions of markets, culture, technology, and their own developmental needs is greatly shown in innovative milieux including Shenzhen. Cities aim to create unique conditions to attract talent, companies, wealth, and resources to their own place to enhance their regional advantages. If we draw a comparison of different states in the United States with cities or provinces in China, there are some underlying similarities: Despite national political system differences, there is fierce competition among cities, provinces, or states in competing for talents, capital, resources, markets, and technology. As Castells and Hall noted (1994):

> In this process of generating new growth, they compete with each other; but, more often than not, such competition becomes a source of innovation, of efficiency, of a collective effort to create a better place to live and a more effective place to do business. (Castells & Hall, 1994, p. 7)

Competition in innovation and talent among Chinese cities is increasing in recent years. Local government in different provinces issues housing, residential benefits, and tax breaks to attract talent and investment. Shenzhen is facing much competition. However, as discussed in Chapters 1 and 5, "Shenzhen – Inland collaboration model" was adopted at the beginning of Open and Reform policy. Cities and regions in inland China provided Shenzhen with raw materials (for instance, cotton), talents, and resources, while Shenzhen attracted investment to establish manufacturing factories to process those raw materials to be exported products. This book suggests that cities and regions in China enjoy a flexible collaborative and/or competitive relationship depending on China's developmental stage and needs. In the early days, cities such as Wuhan, Nanjing, and Xi'an supplied Shenzhen with human capital in science and engineering, thanks to their domestically top-ranked research institutions with a focus on STEM. Take Huawei for example. Many of its early employees came from Wuhan, graduating from Huazhong University of Science and Technology (华中科技大学). Take Shenzhen University for another example. In 1999, Shenzhen University recruited a renowned Chinese physicist from Xi'an, Niu Hanben, along with18 researchers from his research lab. Shenzhen, at that time, attracted ambitious and entrepreneurial scientists with a patriotic tone like Niu, to explore their professional possibilities.[11] This resource complementary development strategy helped and facilitated Shenzhen's market economy experiment and its innovation. Meanwhile, useful and constructive development experiences and resources accumulated in Shenzhen provide lessons and networks to cities and regions that have close ties with Shenzhen. Xi' an, for instance, an inland city in the Northwest of China, continues to utilize its local strength, well-known STEM research universities, while engaging with Shenzhen firms such as Huawei in developing Xi'an's vocational colleges as well as its automotive and manufacturing sectors. In *The*

Top 100 Science and Technology Clusters released by the World Intellectual Property Organization, eight Chinese cities rank in the top 50 global innovation clusters including Wuhan, Nanjing, Xi'an, which, once again, indicates the role of interconnection in national development and innovation. In addition, Xi'an ranks No. 40 in the global innovation cluster, ahead of Denver, Atlanta, Dallas, Cambridge, and Ann Arbor, the already established western technology centers or science cities. This indicates the significance of "Shenzhen—Inland collaboration model" in facilitating both Shenzhen and other cities' development and innovation.

A continuance of "Shenzhen—Inland collaboration model," as mentioned in Chapter 1, has been helping to reduce regional economic development disparity in China, in the form of "special economic zone + old revolutionary base area collaboration model", "*特区 + 老区模式.*" One of my interviewees, Zhi Hui Lin Network Technology headquartered in Shenzhen, is in the process of building their assembly factory in Quannan county in Ganzhou city, Jiangxi province since Ganzhou government has provided them with supportive policies under the umbrella of "special economic zone + old revolutionary base area collaboration model." According to my interviewee, it takes only roughly about two hours from Quannan in Ganzhou to Shenzhen by high-speed train, which is reasonable for them to transport core components to Quannan for assembly. In fact, since early 2023, Guangdong province has begun official collaboration with Jiangxi province to promote the revitalization and development of old revolutionary base areas. Two provincial governments (Guangdong and Jiangxi) jointly issued the "*Implementation Plan for Paired Cooperation between Shenzhen and Ganzhou (2023–2027)*[12]" (《*深圳市与赣州市对口合作实施方案(2023—2027年)*》) in 2023. Regional economic coordination is a key issue in China's Fifteenth Five-Year Plan. Though old revolutionary base area in China differs from the rust belt in the United States, Shenzhen's partnership with Ganzhou in Jiangxi indicates institutional capacity in balancing economic disparity in China. "Let some people get rich first," is not just a slogan to promote Shenzhen as China's modernization model; it was a reality that fits with China's historical circumstances. Therefore, it is critical for global south countries and even some developed countries to explore their development and innovation rooted in their own cultural and social contexts.

Figure 10.1 Author's summary on key nodes and their respective contributions to Shenzhen innovation model.

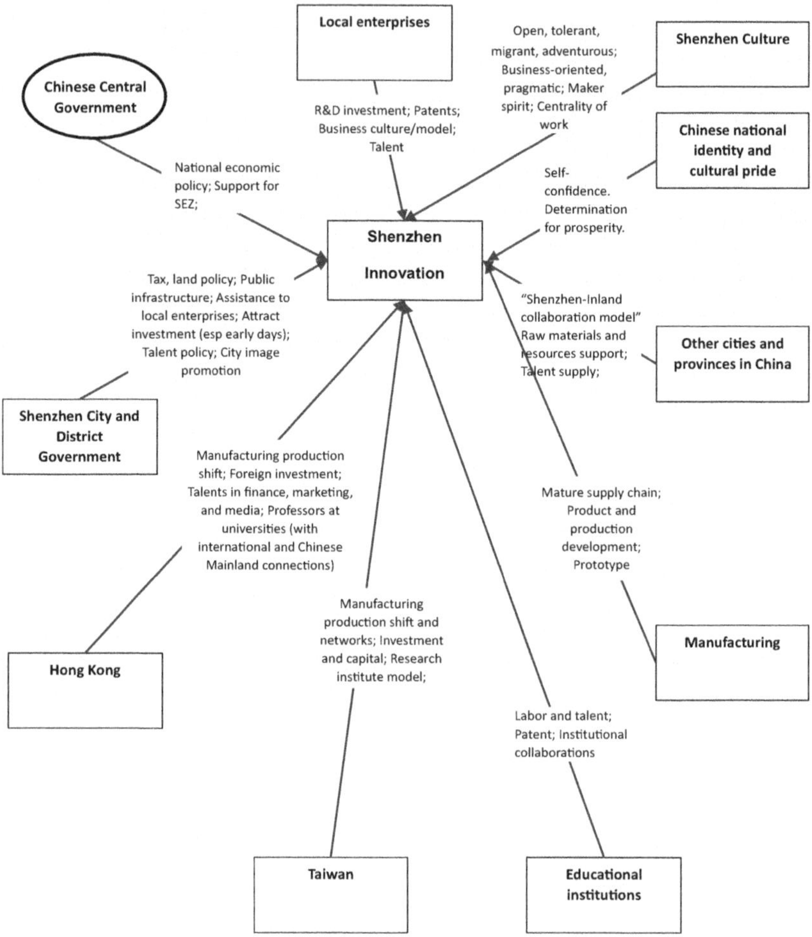

Fig. 10.1 Shenzhen innovation model

Lessons from Shenzhen Experience and Policy Implications

At the end of the conclusion section, I summarize key lessons from Shenzhen development and innovation success as well as the shortcomings that Shenzhen & China need to address, hoping to offer policy implications for other cities, regions and countries:

- Build convenient and accessible regional facilities. Airports, public transportation, affordable housing, will attract both human capital and investment.
- Develop and improve physical infrastructure such as electricity, water, telecommunications, internet connectivity and other digital infrastructure.
- Policy consistency matters. Innovation policy, economic policy, and talent policy should be consistent in the long run to achieve fruitful results.
- Local and national policy should play a constructive role in guiding domestic and international investment in certain industries and sectors.
- Enhance government officials (local, regional and national) comprehensive technical literacy to effectively engage with investors, entrepreneurs, academics and other stakeholders within a region or a sector.
- Fight regional and national corruption. Corruption and nepotism will discourage talented citizens from participating in building national innovation systems and prevent genuine innovators and entrepreneurs from competing in a fair environment and system.
- Ensure high-quality data collection, local demographics and economic statistics to guide decision-making.
- Develop and constantly upgrade local educational systems that can complement and benefit local economic development.
- Invest in training and attracting multi-disciplinary domestic talents. Synergy of human capital in certain cities or regions jointly advances local development and innovation. Technical talent, business executives, marketing and media practitioners with an international scope, lawyers, accountants, are all contributors to successful innovation clusters.

- Build sustainable international education and research programs within the global university network.
- Utilize interregional or inter-city collaboration within a country to maximize the utilization of resources, raw materials, and human capital.
- Upscale professors and scholars' (especially those in the global south) digital literacy and their understandings of the global economic and technological landscape, particularly in the aspect of AI.
- Set flexible visa categories. For instance, long time business and academic visa.
- Ensure the quality and diversity of cultural and entertainment facilities in a city that can target a wide range of populations of different ages.
- Foster a social culture of adventure and entrepreneurship that encourages risk-taking, experiments and innovation.
- Diversify funding and financial sources in private enterprises and local R&D.
- Establish regional social credibility in general. Enterprises are facing incredibly fierce market competition at the global stage nowadays. Product reputation is increasingly associated with regional and national image in addition to a country's cultural and social credibility.
- Develop multilevel educational institutions in a city or region. Comprehensive four-year universities, vocational schools, research-focused institutes, professional development colleges or schools provide distinct labor force that is needed in economic development and innovation.
- Strengthen education—industry partnership in the form of vocational education and training programs, research university labs and industry internships.

Notes

1. Information is retrieved from: https://www.bloomberg.com/news/newsletters/2025-02-13/deepseek-s-hometown-hangzhou-emerges-as-center-of-china-s-ai-universe.
2. Information is retrieved from: https://www.artificialintelligence-news.com/news/malaysia-huawei-ai-talent-training-program/

3. Interview quote retrieved from the report: *The Role of AI Innovation Clusters in Fostering Youth Employment in Africa*, p. 24.
4. News Article, from China Daily, *Top 10 Chinese cities by per capita GDP in 2019,* retrieved from: https://global.chinadaily.com.cn/a/202004/27/WS5ea60b68a310a8b241151c50.html
5. Information is retrieved from: https://www.worldatlas.com/articles/sick-man-of-europe.html
6. There were not many international research collaborations established at that time due to Shenzhen's lack of research institutes and universities.
7. The Dongjiang-Shenzhen Water Supply Project, in Mandarin Chinese, 东江深圳—香港供水工程, is a large-scale water diversion project that spans Dongguan and Shenzhen in Guangdong province. It draws its water from the Dongjiang River and is therefore commonly known as "Dongjiang Water". https://www.wsd.gov.hk/tc/core-businesses/water-resources/dongjiang-water/index.html
8. Causes and Lessons of the California Electricity Crisis, September 2001, released by Congress of the United States Congressional Budget Office. Retrieved from: https://www.cbo.gov/sites/default/files/107th-congress-2001-2002/reports/californiaenergy.pdf.
9. Tong Xiang, 同乡,refers to people from the same city or province.
10. Pony Ma Huateng's full speech in Mandarin Chinese can be found: http://tech.sina.com.cn/roll/2017-06-20/doc-ifyhfpat5484243.shtml.
11. News article in Chinese, is retrieved from: https://news.163.com/20/0824/18/FKQJE9JE00018M4D.html
12. Information is retrieved from: https://www.ndrc.gov.cn/fggz/dqzx/gglqzxfz/202302/t20230221_1349052.html

CHAPTER 11

Research Note: Emerging Sensitive Research: A Non-western Female Perspective

Research During Geopolitical Tensions

This research project started in late 2016, toward the end of the term in office of Barack Obama, who served as the United States President from January 2009 to January 2017. U.S.–China relations have been unprecedentedly complex, even during former President Obama's terms, with long-term unresolved issues such as U.S.–China economic competition, cyber-threats, the South China Sea and the Taiwan issue. Obama concluded his 2015 White House Speech in the Rose Garden by suggesting that the United States and China should take more steps to expand cooperation and connection between these two countries and their people by enhancing tourism and expanding Mandarin Chinese teaching programs among American students in the United States.

In 2016, when I started my informal research interviews with Chinese government officials from Shenzhen in an executive training program at an American university, local government officials were situated in a cultural and institutional environment that contrasts with the traditional Chinese government culture. Those officials received a one-month's training in the topics of artificial intelligence, technological innovation, public–private partnerships, and tech policy regulations on a U.S. university campus. All the courses were taught in English, with multiple student translators (I was the only one at the doctoral level at that time). All the government officials held bureaucratic positions above district level

G. Y. Wang, *Dragon Innovation: Shenzhen*, Governing China in the 21st Century, https://doi.org/10.1007/978-981-95-9637-9_11

in where they are from and their governmental positions are high in the municipal and provincial Chinese context. Quite different from the stereotypical view of Chinese government official as dull, rigid, and impersonal, the state officials in the executive training program were curious, engaging, and embodied critical thinking.

My role in the executive training program was lead interpreter. The program manager asked me to choose the course topics that matched with my research agenda, for instance, artificial intelligence and technology & innovation policy. The majority of program instructors were U.S. scholars and industry practitioners. Most of them lectured on U.S. technological and commercial innovations and examined case studies in the U.S. business and policy contexts. Comments such as "but this doesn't work in China…" and "we have completely different business environments…" arose quite often during the lectures, which required me to smoothly navigate the course materials and interpret between these two parties (i.e., American lecturers and Chinese government officials), relying on my own knowledge of U.S. and Chinese technological developments and commercial innovations under two regulatory and institutional systems. In such circumstances, I felt more like a moderator rather than an interpreter seeking to ensure that the two parties understand each other, even if they sometimes disagreed.

Interactions with Chinese government officials in the training program helped me establish professional relationships with some local government officials. The circumstances and contexts in which we initially met and interacted were, as mentioned above, an executive training program on an American university campus, making it possible to reduce or eliminate the power imbalance between me and them. As Harvey (2010) argues, "the type of respondent being interviewed as well as the predicated power relationship between the interviewer and respondent" (p. 202) alters depending on many factors, including the research context.

In my longitudinal research, I interviewed both elites and non-elites in diverse settings. Many of them hold leadership positions in either institutional or corporate entities, with elite status. Quite contrary to the conventional wisdom that corporate organizations must obey the government, some personnel at local startups displayed an unwilling attitude to accommodate visitors through local government introduction. At an artificial intelligence technology company, the head of government relations agreed to meet me. She was a middle-aged woman who had held a high position at a provincial newspaper before taking the job of handling government relations at that startup. It was obvious to me that she did not know much about my research agenda even after my brief explanation. She was one of the few people who suspected that I was an inspector sent by local government to monitor their corporate performances, or an investigative journalist. When asked about how local government officials facilitate or hinder local corporate development and innovation, instead of answering my question directly, she asked me in return to figure out the higher power official that I had been in touch with before this visit. Her words implied that she was a little displeased with the government for sending visitors and journalists to her company frequently, as doing so did not bring the company any commercial value but, instead, took up normal working time. In her words, "Our startup has grown very rapidly and successfully by far. The government regards us as a local flagship and always wants to brag about us." Her seemly unwilling attitude, reflected the relationship between Shenzhen local government officials and local enterprises, as documented and analyzed in this book. Local enterprises care more about generating profits and real values than spending time managing government relations.

Despite her impatience, in order to continue my interview with no interruption, I answered her honestly and emphasized once again that I am an independent researcher who was conducting fieldwork research for my doctoral study in the United States. Unexpectedly, my mention of the United States negatively intensified our conversations since the interview was conducted in early 2019, when the United States issued a new round of sanctions on Chinese technology companies. Sensitivity in conducting and continuing this research interview appeared at a critical space and time, when Chinese artificial intelligence technology was one of the United States' major targets. My interviewee immediately inquired about my private information.

That interviewee's caution in dealing with me and answering my interview questions indicated that sensitivity in research can emerge during the interview process due to the external political, social, and cultural environment. How participants view sensitivity can be subjective; hence, researchers are unable to predict it. She was finally soothed after I described how I had known about the city since I was a little child, which connected with her in a more personal way which convinced her of my authentic Chineseness. I consider this as my advantage in conducting this research, as a western-trained Chinese researcher who has life and educational experiences in China, which alleviates the tension of emerging sensitivity. It is not just the Chinese who are careful about handling interview questions during a critical time: Americans who study and work in China were facing sensitivity from both nations. My Chinese identity and American characteristics contribute to my ability to carry out successful interviews with Americans in China during my research since my "American attributes" make me relatable to them.

The same artificial intelligence startup held annual internship programs that welcome college students from all over the world. On the same day after my interview with the head of government relations, I was unexpectedly able to have conversations with a white male American intern in this company. Since internationalization, cultural affinity, and creative life are parts of my analysis, his satisfaction or discontent with Shenzhen, as well as his internship, added to my overall analysis. Nevertheless, he was as cautious as the head of government relations, my previous interviewee at this startup. However, after a few minutes' chat, my "English with a striking American accent"—as he put it exactly—persuaded him that I was not someone sent to monitor him by his university-industry internship program. As he started to open up, he tried to make our conversations mutually beneficial and asked for my advice on his career as an American tech geek with an international education and working experience in Asia.

The two examples outlined above—of how institutional power provides easy access for researchers but cannot guarantee interviewees' cooperation and trust during the interview process—stress the importance of interviewers' characteristics in navigating interviews, especially when interviewers cannot predict how sensitive a topic is or what a perspective means to the interviewee or their affiliated organization. My experience indicates that an interviewer's identity and characteristics play a crucial role in reducing tensions with interviewing participants and mitigating their concerns to enable the generation of firsthand, high-quality data.

As Harvey (2011) argues, "effective interviewers are those that are able to easily adjust their style and make the interviewee feel as comfortable as possible. This is important not only in generating high quality responses, but also in increasing the likelihood of elite members providing other interview opportunities such as additional contacts" (p. 434). Goldman and Swayze (2012) note that good interviewers are excellent conversationalists who make interviews seem like a good talk among good friends and never lose control of the conversation. It is not definite that interviewer effects have a significant influence on interview results. My research fieldwork and interviews suggest that the characteristics of researchers, such as age, gender, how long they have been studying, working, and residing in the United States, university affiliation and/or alma mater, and general political attitudes, have a tremendous impact on interviewees when sensitive research topics or topics that emerge as sensitive are addressed. In particular, those interviewer effects can either increase or decrease the extent to which participants assess the risk level of their interview participation.

Good interviews yield rich and meaningful data while making interviewees feel safe and at ease sharing personal information or sensitive experiences with interviewers (Knox & Burkard, 2009). Non-Chinese interviewees have different concerns than Chinese ones, which requires me to be empathic so that I do not offend them unconsciously. In my conversational interview with the white male American intern mentioned above, I was keen to know about working permit and business visas for non-Chinese passport holders to understand talent flow and international collaboration and mobility. Though I did not consider the question sensitive, he regarded it as such and attempted to avoid answering it. To make him feel comfortable and gain his trust, I told him that my Chinese and U.S. interviewees in the tech sector had expressed dissatisfaction over visa restrictions from both countries in recent years. I also rephrased my previous question in a personal way and asked how long he had been on the exchange program and the internship program as well as whether or not he had gone back to the United States during his stay in China.

My question about how long he had been on the study and internship program was designed to understand the type of visa he had applied for. Since it seemed more like a factual than a political question in his information process, he answered me with no hesitation and further shared with me that he wished the Chinese government could extend the length of business visas for foreigners. In his words, "I do not want a Chinese permanent residence, but I would like to work at a Chinese technology company longer than the visa allows." My conversation with him happened in 2019. In 2025, when I am completing this book in China, China has introduced the K-visa, a special type of visa for foreign young science and technology global talents in October, 2025. This means that my interviews and conversations with foreign students in Shenzhen had their own value, particularly for the policymaking communities, as foreign workers and students' concerns were revealed even before the implementation of K-visa.

One notable interviewer effect issue seen in my research fieldwork that is worth mentioning is the role of university affiliation and/or alma mater in research fields in China. Harvey (2010) argues that university affiliation may have both a positive and a negative impact on access to elite networks. For instance, his affiliation with the University of Cambridge and Harvard University provided him with access to elite members when undertaking his doctoral research in Boston since Boston is a city where the elite status of Cambridge and Harvard tends to be much appreciated (Harvey, 2010). In my case, university affiliations and alma mater play a more important role in my successes at securing interviews with technology entrepreneurs and investors who are overseas returnees. Chinese metropolitan cities accommodate many overseas returnees, and this particular group of people prefers to socialize more often with each other than with those who do not study overseas or obtain degrees abroad. Among the reasons for this preference may be that they have common ground or have experienced similar lifestyles overseas, although economic class division may also be one of the reasons, especially in entrepreneurship and venture capital investment industries. For self-sponsored young Chinese overseas returnees, to some extent, the same alma mater indicates an equivalent socio-economic class in China. People are more likely to raise investment funding or to go into business together. During my fieldwork, I gained access to interview several young technology entrepreneurs through personal alumni networks. It is hard to conclude that they granted me access to interviews because we had the same alma mater or university affiliations. However, sharing this kind of bond does facilitate conversations in the interview process. In one situation, my interviewee added me to a regional alumni WeChat group and told me that I could look for more technology entrepreneurs in that group. However, it is possible that not all links to universities generate potential respondents or welcoming interviewees. One of my interviewees was reluctant to share information with me at the beginning of our interview because I was affiliated with a university that he considered inferior to his alma mater.

Initially, I interpreted his reluctance as unwillingness to help me navigate a male-dominated group due to the gender effect. However, he started to share more information with me after I revealed my other study experience at a more prestigious institution by his standards. This experience speaks to Harvey's (2010) argument that institutional affiliations will be regarded differently, which will influence researchers' experiences of gaining interview access. Besides university affiliation and/or alma mater, interviewers' study subject or academic discipline can also influence whether they will gain access to interviews (i.e., elite interviewing) (Harvey, 2010) and if they will receive the truthful information they seek. In elite interviewing, especially with technical experts or seasoned industry practitioners in China, potential interviewees evaluate interviewer's level of understanding of China and the knowledge of the study topic before they agree to a final interview.

As documented in this book, I interviewed female migrant professionals who worked in Shenzhen. I consider them as "marginalized group of people" in the economy & technology dominant conversations. However, in some research contexts, they provided me with nuanced stories of Shenzhen, culture and technology through my conversations with them. Some of the topics they voluntarily brought up, for instance, a Huawei female employee's marriage wish written in Chapter Nine (see Chapter 9, Human Capital and National Competitiveness), indicated my advantage in conversing with marginalized female interviewees, which further revealed humane and emotional elements in research fieldworks. Her wish to getting married with an "elite of elite" at Huawei R&D center in Dongguang, implicitly indicates that "social order" and "family formation" might be desirable for Chinese scientific researchers since staying away from chaotic urban centers may help them focus on their work. This differs from the informal Silicon Valley innovation culture. For instance, grabbing a drink at a bar and exchanging work related information at "Homebrew Computer Club" were a routine for many scientists and tech professionals.

Emerging Sensitive Research Since Covid-19

Despite differing standpoints on phone interviews and in-person interviews prior to Covid-19, the global pandemic has affected qualitative fieldwork and research methodologies (Kim et al., 2021). In terms of emerging sensitive research, it is significant to note that I still have access to my interviewees, with whom I have built a rapport and established relatively good relationships in the past few years. Consequently, I was able to continue my conversations and follow-up informational research updates with them despite my absence from the research field during Covid. However, I have sensed increasing vigilance from several people, though not many. For instance, one of my interviewees enthusiastically replied to my congratulatory messages about his marriage and updated me with his job status. However, when I brought up my questions regarding technology and the global economy in our chats, he simply replied that he would not share any latest news unless I returned to my research field to have research-related conversations with him in person. When I asked if a phone call at his conveniences could work, he fell silent and never answered.

I interpret this attitudinal change as deriving from the increasing U.S.–China tensions and the global geopolitical uncertainties China has faced overseas. A Chinese-descent researcher who was absent from China during Covid-19 was likely to leave some participants an impression as an "outsider" which can decrease the level of trust previously built up. Therefore, even though technology is able to transcend geographical limitations to enable and maintain research relationships, the quality of research interviews and conversations may decline, in particular with regard to emerging sensitive research with future uncertainties. From 2023 to 2025, after my research in Africa, I have been working and staying in China while doing additional research for this book. My presence in China has two significant outcomes. First, I become immersed in China socially and culturally again. And I am able to obtain the most updated first-hand research information. Second, my China presence enables me to become a reliable "China voice" on the world stage as the outside (both western and non-western countries) world seeks China analysis and observations on the ground, in particular in a post-covid period when the world seeks to connect with China again. Additionally, I am able to participate in some tech startup demonstrations to keep track of the latest technology development trends in China.

Emerging sensitive research, is a concept that I coin in this section to summarize my longitudinal research on China's technology sector during uncertain and increasingly worsening U.S.–China relations in the past few years. I intend to use this research note to document some humane impact on both researcher (i.e. myself) and some Chinese and American citizens' cognition, which tries to identify the challenges to conducting emerging sensitive research in politically and economically uncertain international environments.

Researchers who conduct sensitive research have reported physical and emotional risks. Hence, proper training, preparation, and supervision are required to minimize researchers' risks and the potential threats to them (Dickson-Swift et al., 2008). Unlike social workers or counselors, social science researchers are not often trained in issues such as managing pressure, avoiding or terminating difficult research interview interactions, and successfully recognizing participants who can help them to further their research (Lee-Treweek & Linkogle, 2000). Despite the lack of training, either in class or fieldwork in conducting sensitive research, researchers still have somewhat expectation that they will encounter difficulties or taboo topics in the field.

Moreover, with increasing global research attention to the global south and the change of age demographics in some research subjects, it is necessary to include non-western young scholars' voices to advance methodological understanding in qualitative research. To some extent, my research interview journey has become a self-exploratory path. Improving researchers' interviewing skills, particularly with their "non-western, foreign" interviewees should be taught from aspects such as how to navigate power relations, build effective and genuine professional relationships, and maximize advantageous interviewer effects while minimizing disadvantageous ones to generate rewarding social science outcomes.

Bibliography

Agrawal, T. (2013). Vocational education and training programs (VET): An Asian perspective. *Asia-Pacific Journal of Cooperative Education, 14*(1), 15–26.

Amsden, A. H., & Chu, W. W. (2003). *Beyond late development: Taiwan's upgrading policies*. MIT Press.

Ansari, S., Munir, K., & Gregg, T. (2012). Impact at the 'bottom of the pyramid': The role of social capital in capability development and community empowerment. *Journal of Management Studies, 49*(4), 813–842.

Asian Development Bank. (2004). *Improving technical education and vocational training: Strategies for Asia*. Manila, Philippines: Asian Development Bank.

Beaverstock, J. V. (2002). Transnational elites in global cities: British expatriates in Singapore's financial district. *Geoforum, 33*(4), 525–538.

Berger, S., & Lester, R. K. (2015). *Global Taiwan: Building competitive strengths in a new international economy*. Routledge.

Block, F., & Keller, M. R. (2009). Where do innovations come from? Transformations in the US economy, 1970–2006. *Socio-Economic Review, 7*(3), 459–483.

Caillods, F. (1994). Converging trends amidst diversity in vocational training systems. *International Labor Review, 133*, 241.

Carnoy, M. (1994). The new global economy, information technology and restructuring education. *International Journal of Technology Management, 9*(3–4), 270–286.

Carsrud, A., & Brännback, M. (2011). Entrepreneurial motivations: What do we still need to know? *Journal of Small Business Management, 49*(1), 9–26.

G. Y. Wang, *Dragon Innovation: Shenzhen*, Governing China in the 21st Century, https://doi.org/10.1007/978-981-95-9637-9

Cartier, C., Castells, M., & Qiu, J. L. (2005). The information have-less: Inequality, mobility, and translocal networks in Chinese cities. *Studies in Comparative International Development, 40*(2), 9–34.

Castells, M. (1996). *The information age* (Vol. 1, No. s 81). Blackwell Publishers.

Castells, M. (1998). *End of millennium, the information age: Economy, society and culture* (Vol. III.). Blackwell Publishers.

Castells, M., & Hall, P. (1994). *Technopoles of the world: The making of 21st century industrial complexes*. Routledge.

Castells, M., & Himanen, P. (2002). *The information society and the welfare state: The Finnish model.* Oxford University Press.

Castells, M. (2010). *End of millennium.* Wiley-Blackwell.

Chang, L. (2009). *Factory girls: From village to city in a changing China.* Penguin Random House.

Cohen, S. S., & Zysman, J. (1987). *Manufacturing matters: The myth of the post-industrial economy.* Basic Books.

Cowhey, P. F., & Aronson, J. D. (2017). *Digital DNA: Disruption and the challenges for global governance.* Oxford University Press.

Currid-Halkett, E. (2007). *The Warhol economy: How fashion, art, and music drive New York City.* Princeton University Press.

Cyranoski, D. (2002). Plugging the brain drain. *Nature, 417*(6890), 683. https://www.nature.com/articles/417683a

Davis, D. (Ed.). (2000). *The consumer revolution in urban China.* University of California Press.

Dickson-Swift, V., James, E. L., Kippen, S., & Liamputtong, P. (2008). Risk to researchers in qualitative research on sensitive topics: Issues and strategies. *Qualitative Health Research, 18*(1), 133–144.

Du, J. (2020). *The Shenzhen experiment: The story of China's instant city.* Harvard University Press.

Ester, P., & Maas, A. (2016). *Silicon valley, planet startup: Disruptive innovation, passionate entrepreneurship and high-tech startups.* Amsterdam University Press. http://www.jstor.org/stable/j.ctt1zxxxjg

Ester, P. (2017). Accelerators in Silicon Valley. *Amsterdam University Press.* https://doi.org/10.2307/j.ctt1zrvhk7

Evans, R. (1993). *Deng Xiaoping and the making of modern China.* Hamish Hamilton.

Feldman, M. P., & Florida, R. (1994). The geographic sources of innovation: Technological infrastructure and product innovation in the United States. *Annals of the Association of American Geographers, 84*(2), 210–229.

Florida, R. (2000). *Competing in the age of talent: Environment, amenities, and the new economy* (p. 60). Report prepared for the RK Mellon Foundation, Heinz Endowments, and Sustainable Pittsburgh.

Florida, R. (2002). The economic geography of talent. *Annals of the Association of American Geographers, 92*(4), 743–755.

Florida, R. (2005). *Cities and the creative class*. Routledge.

Florida, R., & Ayres, I. (2008). Megaregions: The importance of place. *Harvard Business Review, 86*(3).

Forje, L. C. (2009). A historical development of entrepreneurship in the Cameroon economy from 1960–2007. *Journal of Asia Entrepreneurship and Sustainability, 5*(3), 1.

Fraser, S. E. (1967). Chapter V: International and comparative education. *Review of Educational Research, 37*(1), 57–73. https://doi.org/10.3102/00346543037001057

Froy, F., Giguère, S., & Hofer, A. R. (Eds.). (2009). *Designing local skills strategies*. Organization for Economic Co-operation and Development.

Fu, M. (2014). A cultural analysis of China's scientific brain drain: The case of Chinese immigrant scientists in Canadian academia. *Journal of International Migration and Integration, 15*(2), 197–215.

Geraldine, L. T., & Linkogle, S. (Eds.). (2000). *Danger in the field: Ethics and risk in social research*. Routledge.

Goldman, E. F., & Swayze, S. (2012). In-depth interviewing with healthcare corporate elites: Strategies for entry and engagement. *International Journal of Qualitative Methods, 11*(3), 230–243.

Goodman, J. L., Jr. (1979). Reasons for moves out of and into large cities. *Journal of the American Planning Association, 45*(4), 407–416.

Gupta, P., & Harris, J. (2010). How e-WOM recommendations influence product consideration and quality of choice: A motivation to process information perspective. *Journal of Business Research, 63*(9–10), 1041–1049.

Harvey, W. S. (2010). Methodological approaches for interviewing elites. *Geography Compass, 4*(3), 193–205.

Harvey, W. S. (2011). Strategies for conducting elite interviews. *Qualitative Research, 11*(4), 431–441.

Henderson, J. (2002). *Globalization of high technology production*. Routledge.

Hicks, D. (1995). Published papers, tacit competencies and corporate management of the public/private character of knowledge. *Industrial and Corporate Change, 4*(2), 401–424.

Himanen, P. (2001). *The hacker ethic*. Penguin Random House.

Hong, Y. (2017). *Networking China: The digital transformation of the Chinese economy. University* of Illinois Press.

Hsing, Y. T. (1998). *Making capitalism in China: The Taiwan connection*. Oxford University Press.

Jacobs, J. (1961). *The death and life of great American cities*. Vintage.

Jenkins, H. (1992). Textual poachers: Television fans and participatory culture. *Routledge*. https://doi.org/10.4324/9780203114339

Jenkins, H., Ito, M., & Boyd, D. (2015). *Participatory culture in a networked era: A conversation on youth, learning, commerce, and politics*. Polity.

Johnson, J. M. (1998). *Statistical profiles of foreign doctoral recipients in science and engineering: Plans to stay in the United States* (Vol. 99, No. 304). Division of Science Resources Studies, Directorate for Social, Behavioral and Economic Sciences, National Science Foundation.

Jones-Evans, D., Klofsten, M., Andersson, E., & Pandya, D. (1999). Creating a bridge between university and industry in small European countries: The role of the industrial liaison office. *R&D Management, 29*(1), 47–56.

Kafouros, W. (2009). Economic planning: Time to reconsider? *Panoeconomicus, 56*(4), 527–534. https://doi.org/10.2298/PAN0904527K

Keane, M., & Zhao, E. J. (2012). Renegades on the frontier of innovation: The Shanzhai grassroots communities of Shenzhen in China's creative economy. *Eurasian Geography and Economics, 53*(2), 216–230.

Keller, J. M. (1979). Motivation and instructional design: A theoretical perspective. *Journal of Instructional Development*, 26–34.

Kim, J. J., Williams, S., Eldridge, E. R., & Reinke, A. J. (2023). Digitally shaped ethnographic relationships during a global pandemic and beyond. *Qualitative Research, 23*(3), 809–824.

Knox, S., & Burkard, A. W. (2009). Qualitative research interviews. *Psychotherapy Research, 19*(4–5), 566–575.

Kwok, R. Y. W., & So, A. Y. (1995). *The Hong Kong-Guangdong link: Partnership in flux* (Vol. 6). Hong Kong University Press.

Lan, X. (2024). *How China works: An introduction to China's state-led economic development* (T. Gary Topp, Trans.). Palgrave Macmillan (Original work published 2021).

Lee, C. K. (1998). *Gender and the South China miracle: Two worlds of factory women*. University of California Press.

Lee, D. J., Pae, J. H., & Wong, Y. H. (2001). A model of close business relationships in China (Guanxi). *European Journal of Marketing, 35*(1/2), 51–69.

Lee, T. Y. (1998b). The development of ISO 9000 certification and the future of quality management: A survey of certified firms in Hong Kong. *International Journal of Quality & Reliability Management, 15*(2), 162–177.

Leloğlu, U. M. (2024). Establishing innovation systems in the global south: Challenges and the path forward through south-south cooperation. *BRIQ Belt & Road Initiative Quarterly, 6*(1), 20–35.

Lin, T. B. (1984). Foreign investment in the economy of Hong Kong. *Economic Bulletin*, 96.

Lindtner, S., Greenspan, A., & Li, D. (2015). Designed in Shenzhen: Shanzhai manufacturing and maker entrepreneurs. In *Proceedings of the fifth decennial Aarhus conference on critical alternatives* (pp. 85–96).

Liu, Y. (2017). Born global firms' growth and collaborative entry mode: The role of transnational entrepreneurs. *International Marketing Review, 34*(1), 46–67.

Lüthje, B., Hürtgen, S., Pawlicki, P., & Sproll, M. (2013). *From Silicon Valley to Shenzhen: Global production and work in the IT industry.* Rowman and Littlefield.

Lüthje, T. (2001). Intra industry trade in intermediate goods. *International Advances in Economic Research, 7*(4), 393–408.

Maclean, R., & Lai, A. (2011). The future of technical and vocational education and training: Global challenges and possibilities. *International Journal of Training Research, 9*(1–2), 2–15.

Mao, Z. (1965). *Selected works of Mao Tsetung* (Trans.). Foreign Language Press.

Mun, C. L. (2008). Polytechnic education. In L. S. Kong, G. C. Boon, B. Fredriksen, & T. J. Peng (Eds.), *Toward a better future: Education and training for economic development in Singapore since 1965* (pp. 135–148). The World Bank.

Ni, Z. (2005). Simple analysis of Haigui phenomenon. *Economic and Social Development, 6*, 78–80.

Nilsson, A. (2010). Vocational education and training—An engine for economic growth and a vehicle for social inclusion? *International Journal of Training and Development, 14*(4), 251–272.

Niu, X. (1996). Mao Zedong and Deng Xiaoping: A comparison of educational thought. *Comparative and International Education, 25*(1).

Oakey, R. P. (1985). Innovation and regional growth in small high technology firms: Evidence from Britain and the USA. In D. J. Storey (Ed.), *Small firms in regional economic development: Britain, Ireland and the United States* (pp. 135–165). Cambridge University Press.

O'Donnell, M. A., Wong, W., & Bach, J. (Eds.). (2017). *Learning from Shenzhen: China's post-Mao experiment from special zone to model city.* University of Chicago Press.

O'Mara, M. P. (2005). *Cities of knowledge: Cold War science and the search for the next Silicon Valley.* Princeton University Press. http://www.jstor.org/stable/j.ctt13x1fq5

Pansera, M., & Sarkar, S. (2016). Crafting sustainable development solutions: Frugal innovations of grassroots entrepreneurs. *Sustainability, 8*(1), 51.

Pohlmann, M., & Lim, H. C. (2014). A new spirit of capitalism?—Globalization and its impact on the diffusion of neoliberal management thinking in Germany and the East Asian economies. *Development and Society, 43*(1), 1–32.

Porter, M. E. (2000). Location, competition, and economic development: Local clusters in a global economy. *Economic Development Quarterly, 14*(1), 15–34.

Prahalad, C. K., & Hammond, A. (2002). Serving the world's poor. *Harvard Business Review, 80*(9), 48–57.

Prahalad, C. K., & Ramaswamy, V. (2004). Co-creating unique value with customers. *Strategy & Leadership, 32*(3), 4–9.

Prahalad, C. K. (2012). Bottom of the pyramid as a source of breakthrough innovations. *Journal of Product Innovation Management, 29*(1), 6–12.

Qiu, J. L. (2009). *Working-class network society: Communication technology and the information have-less in urban China*. MIT Press.

Radchenko, S. (2010). The Sino-Soviet split. In *Cambridge history of the cold war: Crises and Détente* (pp. 349–72). Cambridge University Press.

Rivoli, P. (2005). *The travels of a T-shirt in the global economy: An economist examines the markets, power, and politics of world trade*. Wiley.

Rosenberg, N. (2002). Knowledge and innovation for economic development: Should universities be economic institutions?. *Knowledge for inclusive development* (pp. 35–47).

Rotolo, D., Camerani, R., Grassano, N., & Martin, B. R. (2022). Why do firms publish? A systematic literature review and a conceptual framework. *Research Policy, 51*(10), Article 104606.

Sallaz, J. J. (2019). *Lives on the line: How the Philippines became the world's call center capital*. Oxford University Press.

Stark, D. (2009). *The sense of dissonance: Accounts of worth in economic life*. Princeton University Press.

Stark, O., Helmenstein, C., & Prskawetz, A. (1998). Human capital depletion, human capital formation, and migration: A blessing or a "curse"? *Economics Letters, 60*(3), 363–367.

Saxenian, A. (1983). The genesis of silicon valley. *Built environment (1978–)* (pp. 7–17).

Saxenian, A. (1996). *Regional advantage: Culture and competition in Silicon Valley and route 128*. Harvard University Press.

Saxenian, A. (2002). Silicon Valley's new immigrant high-growth entrepreneurs. *Economic Development Quarterly, 16*(1), 20–31.

Saxenian, A. (2005). From brain drain to brain circulation: Transnational communities and regional upgrading in India and China. *Studies in Comparative International Development, 40*(2), 35–61.

Schmookler, J. (1962). Economic sources of inventive activity. *The Journal of Economic History, 22*(1), 1–20. https://doi.org/10.1017/S0022050700102311

Schrank, A., & Whitford, J. (2011). The anatomy of network failure. *Sociological Theory, 29*(3), 151–177.

Shi, Y., & Rao, Y. (2010). China's research culture. *Science, 329*(5996), 1128–1128.

Simon, D. F., & Cao, C. (2009). *China's emerging technological edge: Assessing the role of high-end talent*. Cambridge University Press.

Spulber, N. (1969). The Soviet economy in the 1970's. *Current History, 57*(338), 214–219.

Sun, H. S. (1991). Urban development in Shenzhen SEZ. *Habitat International, 15*(3), 25–31. https://doi.org/10.1016/0197-3975(91)90025-G

Thompson, V. A. (1965). Bureaucracy and innovation. *Administrative science quarterly* (pp. 1–20).

Todaro M. P. (1985). *Economic development in the third world.* Longman Publishing Group.

Todd, M. D. (2000). *Open doors: Report on international educational exchange.* Institute of International Education. Retrieved July 29, 2020, from https://www.files.eric.ed.gov/fulltext/ED448658.Pdf

Tse, E., Ma, K., & Huang, Y. (2009). *Shan Zhai: A Chinese phenomenon.* Booz & Company.

Varshney, D. (2013). The return of the natives: Asian diaspora issues and dilemmas—The case of India. *African and Asian Studies, 12*(3), 290–321.

Vergara, B. (2009). *Pinoy capital: The Filipino nation in Daly city.* Temple University Press.

Vogel, E. F. (2011). Deng Xiaoping and the transformation of China. *Harvard University Press.* https://doi.org/10.2307/j.ctt2jbw2f

Wang, D. W. D. (2016). *Urban villages in the new China: Case of Shenzhen.* Palgrave Macmillan.

Wang, G. Y. (2022). Talent migration in knowledge economy: The case of China's Silicon Valley, Shenzhen. *Journal of International Migration and Integration, 23*(3), 1175–1196.

Wesser, C., & Sharma, S. (2025). *The architecture of AI leadership: Enforcement, innovation, and global trust.* Center for Strategic & International Studies.

Wu, Y., Du, H., Li, P., & Ouyang, H. (2024). Family structure of migrant workers and long-term local settlement intention in China. *Population, Space and Place, 30*(4), Article e2742.

Yan, Y. (1997). McDonald's in Beijing: The localization of Americana. In J. L. Watson (Ed.), *Golden arches east* (pp. 39–76). Stanford University Press.

Yeung, H. W. C., & Olds, K. (2000). *The globalization of Chinese business firms.* Palgrave Macmillan.

Zweig, D., Changgui, C., & Rosen, S. (2004). Globalization and transnational human capital: Overseas and returnee scholars to China. *The China Quarterly, 179*, 735–757.

Index

G. Y. Wang, *Dragon Innovation: Shenzhen*, Governing China in the 21st Century, https://doi.org/10.1007/978-981-95-9637-9

D

E

F

G

H

The manufacturer's authorised representative in the EU is Springer Nature Customer Service Centre GmbH, Europaplatz 3, 69115 Heidelberg, Germany. If you have any concerns regarding our products, please contact ProductSafety@springernature.com

Printed and bound by CPI Group (UK) Ltd, Croydon, CR0 4YY
21/09/2026
02220011-0007